HOW CITIES
ARE SAVED

HOW CITIES ARE SAVED

Herbert R. Lottman

UNIVERSE BOOKS
New York

Published in the United States of America in 1976
by Universe Books
381 Park Avenue South, New York, N.Y. 10016

© 1976 by Herbert R. Lottman

Library of Congress Catalog Card Number: 75-11142

ISBN 0-87663-260-6

Printed in the United States of America

To M.

Contents

List of Illustrations

Munich: Richard Strauss Fountain

Cologne: Pedestrian mall with benches and potted plants

Munich: Marienplatz before and after restoration

Stockholm: Letting light and air into the city center

Paris: The tallest building in Europe amid the intimacy of
Montparnasse

West Berlin: The new Hansa district on the outskirts

West Berlin: Gropius-Stadt

Bologna: Low-cost public housing along the periphery

Bologna: An arcaded street

Bologna: Block plans incorporating new houses in the old style

All photographs are reproduced by permission, and acknowledgment is made to the following: UNESCO (Venice); Gem. Bureau Monumentenzorg Amsterdam (Amsterdam restorations); Shalom Gardi (Jerusalem); Interphotothèque, Paris (La Grande Borne); Verkehrsamt der Stadt Stuttgart, Bildarchiv (Stuttgart vineyards); Stadsentwikkeling Dienst Publieke Werken Amsterdam (Bijlmermeer); Landesbildstelle Württemberg (Weissenhof); KLM Aerocarto, The Hague (aerial view of Amsterdam); Verkehrsamt der Stadt Köln (Hohe Strasse and Roman-German Museum); Landeshauptstadt München Fremdenverkehrsamt (Richard Strauss Fountain and Marienplatz today); Alfred Koch, Cologne (benches and plants); Landeshauptstadt München Baureferat (Marienplatz, before changes); Tour Maine Montparnasse (Paris skyscraper); Verkehrsamt Berlin (Hansa district and Gropius-Stadt); City of Bologna.

Introduction:
How They Ruin the Neighborhood

The purpose of this work is twofold. It intends to show, first of all, that the tendency to destroy the urban environment which earlier humans had constructed so lovingly (or at least so intelligently) is universal, and I shall call attention to gratuitous damage done to man's most intimate works, the large cities, so that by analogy any reader can identify potential danger in his own community. But in the very same breath I shall describe noble successes in saving, even bettering, the urban communities which after all are destined to shelter an increasingly large number of human beings.

It is estimated that the urban population represented 3% of the world total in 1800, 15% in 1900, and 30% in 1950, while today's figures for the major industrial nations are considerably higher: 85% in Japan, 82% in West Germany, 82% in Great Britain and Denmark, 75% in the United States and Canada (OECD figures). By 1985, 80% of the total population of Western Europe and North America will be urbanized. Another projection is that in the year 2000 over 90% of human beings will live in urban concentrations; certainly this will be true in the advanced nations. Here are some examples of density over a nation's total land mass (from the United Nations Demographic Yearbook): 319 inhabitants to the square kilometer in the Netherlands, 317 in Belgium, 240 in West Germany, 228 in the United Kingdom, 22 in the United States. Note that the Council of Europe's figures are considerably higher for the Netherlands: 360.

Once, a United Nations population study points out, a city of 100,000 inhabitants was rare. There were only six or seven such cities in Europe at the beginning of the 16th century; at the end of the 18th, there were still only 22; 42 by 1850; 120 by 1895. Today there are close to 1,600 cities in the world with over 100,000 population, while the number of cities with more than one million inhabitants has increased from 11 at the beginning of our century to about 162 today; the number containing two million or more increased from 3 in 1900 to an estimated 58 now.

Clearly we are witnessing the rise of "urbanized nations," with Europe leading the way. There are perhaps 50 agglomerations in Europe, excluding the Soviet Union, each with over one million inhabitants. The western Netherlands has a population density greater than that of the Northeastern Seaboard of the United States, that continuing strip of urban development which Jean Gottmann called Megalopolis: 296 inhabitants to the square kilometer along the American coast compared to 462 in the Rhine-Meuse-Scheldt Delta of northwestern Europe. Or, looking at Europe another way, the entire northwest of that continent including London and Paris can be taken as a single megalopolis, with a population of 133.3 million (against 107 million in northeastern America from Quebec and Boston to Norfolk, St. Louis, and Duluth), and a density of 283 inhabitants per square kilometer (73 per square kilometer in that portion of the Western Hemisphere megalopolis within the territory of the United States). Some also refer to a Tokaido megalopolis, consisting of the metropolitan area of Japan's three largest cities, Tokyo, Osaka, and Nagoya, with 50 million inhabitants in 1965, or 48% of Japan's population on only 19% of that country's land area.

In this urban world of ours, there are insufficient and inadequate housing, high land costs and rent, high risks of air, noise, and water pollution, traffic congestion. If there are also better facilities for living and working in the larger cities, it costs more per capita to run them.

Yet success can be contagious, for a solution workable in one city can often be applied elsewhere. This has been the case both for post-World War II highways-in-the-city and shopping-center urbanism, and for some positive innovations whose life-enhancing quality is less ambiguous: the conservation, often accompanied by rehabilitation, of old neighborhoods in city centers, pedestrian zones in busy downtown commercial districts, the occasional attempt to check suburban sprawl by curing the blight within the city, improved public transportation as a check on our automobile civilization. It may have seemed a publicity stunt, but there was sound reasoning behind the meeting of representatives of five metropolitan giants, New York, London, Moscow, Paris, and Tokyo, in the Japanese capital in 1972 to work out an exchange of experiences and technology in problem solving. At the Third World Conference of Mayors in Milan in 1974, a permanent body was set up to permit the exchange of information. Comparative urbanism may become a working tool before it is acknowledged as a science.

The cities of Europe are usually older than American cities (even the Industrial Revolution got there first). It is true that American cities caught up quickly, becoming blighted in record time. But American and European cities share many features; the urban crisis in the United States is different only in scale. And sometimes, as the statistics on density suggest, not even in scale. It is true that any threat to destroy vital urban tissue is more readily evident in an old and historic European town center: Somehow we all feel concern at the threat, and relief when, and if, it is overcome. This seemed another good reason to attack the general problems of cities through foreign examples. In a short span of time, say the adult life of a middle-aged man or woman, both Paris and Rome have changed, and no one would dare say for the better. Centuries-old Paris has lost its beauty gradually, as speculators defied its peculiarly human scale with a new skyline; few familiar sites or sights remain unscarred. At this writing, Paris continues to bow to the laws of motor-car civilization. So that many visitors in search of the familiar esthetic experience of the Place de la Concorde, and many native Parisians, have been killed trying to see that extraordinary urban prospect which runs from the courtyard to the Louvre, through the Tuileries and the Champs-Elysées, to the Arch of Triumph (itself now flanked by distant skyscrapers).

If Rome's physical beauty has not been violated, largely thanks to municipal poverty, the traffic congestion, the air and noise pollution on its streets and *piazze*, terrorize the private citizen in what is perhaps the worst-run city of its size in Europe. Neither Rome nor Paris will be used in this study as a good example (the exceptions being Paris's tardy but devoted attempt to save what is left of the Marais district, and Rome's several begruding efforts at pedestrian zoning).

Both in Paris and Rome, it is possible to see why these things are happening, and so to avoid them elsewhere. If Rome's municipal government has been partially paralyzed for most of this century, so that little planning is possible and few decisions ever get executed, Paris has one of the most sophisticated planning establishments of any city, but decisions are made in secret at a higher and political level. It happened that way under Napoleon III, too, but then Baron Haussmann had a method and imposed a scheme, whereas today's planners act by ad hoc "derogations" and "tolerances," destroying the city's fiber piecemeal and with less apparent motivation.

There are many examples of lost opportunities in the old world, of cities ruined by blind or selfish actions. Lawrence Halprin noted that when faced with contemporary problems, European results seem no better than American ones. Yet the best American thinking, such as the attempt to reverse migration from small communities, the subject of a Connecticut study I shall refer to again, is similar to programs under way in Europe—for example, the revitalization of medium-sized cities in France to permit them to serve as focal points for decentralization.

Negative examples can also serve. Some of the latter come from history. Private interests are blamed for having blocked the ideal urban projects of Brunelleschi, Alberti, even of Leonardo da Vinci, in Florence and Rome. Haussmann's otherwise efficient urbanism destroyed much of that intimate tissue of medieval Paris which we are now ready to accept as healthy, even vital to the social organism as well as to individual human beings. Often mistakes are made in a good cause: Bernini really believed that he was right in seeking to transform Paris according to his baroque lights. In our own time, we employ bulldozers to level entire central districts, repeating the destruction accomplished in wartime by equally righteous bombing crews in the name of good causes. It's usually much later on that we have second thoughts. Australia is a comparatively young country, and yet after a rush into urbanization (85% of its population lives in cities), it is already suffering from congestion and blight, despite all those open spaces (two inhabitants per square kilometer). Is there no halfway house between a concentrated skyscraper way of life and equally tiresome suburban sprawl?

The future, in any case (Paul Valéry is credited with saying this), isn't what it used to be. Suddenly in the autumn of 1973, the ordinary citizen woke up to headlines about an energy crisis which had been predicted by the long-range planners (and the shorter-range political scientists). It became apparent that a major cause of profligate expenditure of our resources was the low-density suburb, whose inhabitants require twice as much energy as city dwellers, just as the priority given to highway construction at the expense of public transportation systems put the United States at the mercy of anybody's turning off the oil faucet. Urban renewal, as Anthony Lewis pointed out in *The New York Times*, led to destruction of solid old buildings in favor of uneconomic high-rise construction, advantageous from the point of view of tax depreciation but enormously wasteful of resources. So that what might have seemed slightly quaint, even anachronistic wisdom before October 1973—I am speaking of saving city centers from the bulldozers—suddenly becomes a matter of intelligent use of available resources.

Some warnings. This book should not be dismissed as a reactionary tract. Skyscrapers do have a place in our world, just as new towns and new districts are necessary to house our expanding urban populations. Obviously an historic and picturesque city center of limited dimensions cannot provide shelter, office and shopping facilities for everyone. While garden cities have often been dreary reproductions of the original dream, and our greatest architects have occasionally endorsed housing little better than prisons, isolated and besieged by a labyrinth of highways, high and concentrated building is often the only way to save green space and reduce the time it takes to get to work and home again.

Visiting Pompeii, the historian Taine reflected that "A city used to be a real home, and not an administrative collection of furnished apartments as it is today. . . . What is Paris, but a heap of bedrooms whose life comes from offices with file cabinets and white-collar workers?" I do not believe with Taine that a city must be a holiday resort or a tourist attraction; the most liveable cities are often the dense and busy ones. An Italian authority was more discerning when he distinguished three kinds of problem cities: those like Venice, once prosperous, which now live on their tourist-drawing monuments; those which are as alive as they were generations or centuries ago, and which need protection against destruction in the form of urban renewal; and those with a shorter history but possessing landmarks worth saving, the works of Sullivan and Wright in Chicago for example. I believe that cities can be both commercially viable and satisfying places to live in. I know a good many such cities, as the chapters which follow will indicate. Nor is there anything inevitable about urban blight, destruction of the reason for being of city life, the neighborhood mix allowing marginal but desirable activities to survive in an atmosphere of health and safety.

Another danger is in the possible exoticism of these case-book studies from far-off lands. One may prefer the armchair journey through these often remarkable places to the more serious job of seeking to match up these observations to situations closer to the reader. While I may be talking, and presumably thinking, about Bologna or Rotterdam, the reader would do well to be thinking of his own Bologna or Rotterdam in the making, or manqué. It might have been prudent to disguise the cities described in this study through the use of initials or neutral names such as Middle-town, but the user might not have appreciated that any more than the author would.

For there is nothing neutral about this subject. Objectivity, yes. Dispassionate examination of the facts, yes. If I consider Rome the most beautiful of all cities, for instance, I must nevertheless refrain from discussing it in a work concentrating on good examples. I have already mentioned it sufficiently in my Introduction.

Each section is designed to take the full measure of a situation, putting on stage the contending forces that are usually present in any urban situation where a decision is made to do or not to do something. The examples have been collected for their possible use to town planners and the leaders of public opinion on whom they must lean, so that an effort has been made to provide a certain amount of technical information. Yet I admit to a preoccupation with human as opposed to economic or political concerns, human input, human product, quality of life, social rather than economic indicators. It is obvious that financial considerations have much to do with city-wrecking and city-saving; some would say that they have everything to do with them. And the intelligent planners of Stockholm and of Amsterdam began with a program of land purchases over a period of decades, even generations, which is beginning to pay off today. It will surely be clear that profitability is a paramount concern in urban renewal, which is why I invoke anti-economic considerations, or at least try to highlight examples of profit-making which protected human values. It is so very clear that economic considerations are at the bottom of most planning decisions, in fact, that one can afford the luxury of taking the time to examine other considerations.

Thus the very harsh report on Paris commissioned but not appreciated by the French government, and released with great reluctance in 1973, described how Paris had all but lost its soul because its planners had ignored history and culture in the interests of economic expansion, "profitability being necessarily destructive of amenity." And if business interests did not wish to hear why Paris needed to reconcile quality of life and technological and financial efficacy, the writers of the contested report nudged them ever so gently: Living conditions, a human urban environment, were responsible for the city's attractiveness to skilled managers and workers, not to speak of talented foreigners who have contributed so much to making Paris what it was.

Indeed, certain preoccupations, certain themes run through these chapters: the primordial role of the street and public place, an historical consideration which is confirmed in the contemporary city, sometimes by what happens when the planners overlook its importance. A persistent return to the vital center of the city, doubtless an atavism shared by many Americans with distant origins in an old world teeming with city folk, kindled by the romantic fantasy of Elliot Paul's *The Last Time I Saw Paris* or the romantic practicality of Jane Jacobs' *The Death and Life of Great American Cities.* (It was when Paris abandoned romanticism that it began to pollute its landscape.) Actually, of course, there is nothing romantic about city centers. A study of their dynamics makes it apparent that they are usually the ideal site for social transformations. "When a group bearing a new vision of the world wants to manifest itself," wrote Roger Klaine, "it chooses the center to do it."

I will perhaps be criticized for taking many examples from smaller cities, when our problems today and tomorrow will be in the context of the metropolis, conurbation, archipelago, megalopolis. Yet one alternative to dull new districts and new towns may well be the renewed emphasis on conserving, and then centering new development around, the life-giving cores of our old cities, even towns and villages. In one example of planning for the year 2000, France's Mediterranean industrial and harbor development at Fos-sur-Mer, new settlements will cluster around charming fishing villages, which become the centers of animation for a population many times the size of the original communities. The example of saving a city center for the vital mix of population which gives it an identity comes from Bologna, a city of well under one million inhabitants, yet it could have immediate application in the very largest metropolitan areas of the industrial nations. I take full responsibility for my attempt to construct a moral out of what I have observed.

But I am indebted to those who have thought about similar things, even if they share none of the blame for the construction of this book, and have not read it in manuscript. First to Jean Gottmann, head of the School of Geography at the University of Oxford, who allowed me to test my theses on him at the very inception of my work. Professor Gottmann would tend to emphasize the need for modern adaptations while I lean to conservation, but he preceded most of us in concern for the greatness of the great cities.

To Marc Emery, founder of France's first urban affairs monthly,

a no-nonsense planner who helps me avoid excessive sentimentality, a weakness to which I confess, and which might have prevented
acceptance of my models (it still might).

To Suzanne Berger, of MIT, who contributed lucidity at times
when I was bogged down in detail.

And to the Ford Foundation, which helped me get to the places
I write about, and to acquire the material essential to closer study
of them.

Sections of this book have appeared in earlier versions in *Colum-
bia Forum* (and *Empire State Architect—AIA*), *Cultural Affairs,
Intellectual Digest, The New York Times, Metropolis* (Paris), and
Present Tense, to whom I am grateful for encouragement and
support.

I. SAVING THE CITY'S HEART

1. Rebuilding City Centers

Historically there have been two chief reasons for inner-city rebuilding. One is war damage. The massive air raids that burned out wooden Tokyo inevitably brought about major postwar transformation; fire bombs and rockets flattened London; blockbusters left Germany with no choice but to build new cities over the old. Architect Martin Pawley compares this wartime destruction requiring complete urban renewal to Nero's "slum clearance" of Rome by fire, and to the Great Fire of London of 1666. In Hamburg alone, half of the 600,000 prewar dwelling units were destroyed in World War II; another 200,000 were damaged. The damaged were repaired and 400,000 new units were built, which still left a housing shortage in expanding postwar Hamburg, and a land shortage as well.

The other stimulus has been the will of the planning authority, and/or the promoter, to renew. To remove urban blight, to allow more efficient transportation, to offer better housing. To make more money.

As it happens, neither motivation guarantees a successful reconstruction or renovation. After a war one must rebuild quickly and usually cheaply; even a prestigious architect produced grim post-liberation Le Havre. Most of the continental European towns and villages battered by aerial bombs or artillery have been rebuilt sadly, their barrackslike buildings of cheap materials already, thirty years after the war, ripe for demolition. One doesn't blame the victims of bombing. Not every city can marshal the energy of postwar Warsaw, lovingly reconstructing an entire old town, even following the precise detail of Canaletto's views of the city to guarantee authenticity, or of Budapest's similar reconstructions; both Poland and Hungary had harsh state-centered economies when they did it. Later, France attempted to give soul to its war-ravaged towns—as in Tours, where classic houses along the avenue leading from the Loire River bridge, largely destroyed in June 1940, were duplicated in a somewhat stereotyped manner after World War II. With prosperity, West Germany gave thought to its vestiges; postwar Cologne, still an exciting place for admirers of ancient cityscapes, is one result. These are exceptions. Sad postwar London is more like the rule.

Emergencies aside, even a peacetime reconstruction undertaken in cold blood can be a disaster. Baron Haussmann had the mind of an engineer and all the power of Emperor Napoleon III behind him when he performed his 19th-century renovation of Paris which, he made it clear, he was prepared to slice into as many pieces as necessary. And so he did, drawing straight lines and diagonals on his map and proceeding to demolish whatever was keeping the lines crooked on the ground. When he had finished the job, it was said that his real surprise was to find that narrow winding streets and old landmarks continued to exist behind the broad new boulevards he had carved through the city.

Napoleon III had appointed Haussmann *préfet* of the Seine—that is, governor of the Paris district—and explained what he expected of his man: to clear up the areas around the centers of command, the Louvre palace, city hall, Notre Dame Cathedral, to build wide avenues connecting the railroad stations to each other and to the center. In his reign of 17 years, during most of which he was "more powerful than a Minister," Haussmann wiped out whole neighborhoods, and any old palace or monument preventing his projected avenues from following their straight lines. He planned east-west, north-south roads through Paris, ignoring what stood in their way. It is easier, he was quoted as saying, to attack the inside of the *pâté* than the crust. He gave the coup de grâce to medieval Paris, while Parisians have inherited those uniform boulevards along which trucks can rumble 24 hours a day: They are the highways of Paris. Of course, the city now sought out by visitors is largely what escaped Haussmann—for example, the Rue Bonaparte from St. Germain des Prés to the Seine River, which (apparently thanks to the protests of a left-bank citizens' committee, the ancestor of all such neighborhood action organizations in that part of the world) never got widened into an extension of the new Rue de Rennes. Increasingly, if rehabilitation and the prices of real estate in the 1970s are taken as criteria, the non-Haussmann Paris (of the 4th, 5th, 6th, and 7th *arrondissements*, or wards) is the Paris preferred by its native inhabitants as well.

Haussmann called these vestigial areas "ignoble quarters, sordid houses, horrible cesspools." His tastes ran to such things as the new Tribunal de Commerce building on the north bank of the Ile de la Cité. All this was beautification to Napoleon III, too. He, like Joseph Stalin later, could impose an architecture on his capital.

Haussmann's Paris, which was to influence the renewers in other leading cities at the time, was conceived with Napoleon III's bourgeois constituency in mind. There were inevitable spillover benefits for other citizens as well, and traffic did flow more smoothly afterward. The good versus the bad in Haussmannism will be debated forever. A recent French critic blames him for having ignored the suburbs, no small indictment considering the situation of present-day Paris *banlieues*. At worst, Napoleon III's *préfet* did not (did not succeed although he tried to?) destroy the old neighborhoods behind his wide avenues with their uniform façades, and they have continued to provide sustenance to the city even until today.

We seldom have to cope with extreme situations like these in day-to-day city life. Yet without any doubt, the city gutted by bombs or dictatorial planners bears a certain resemblance to the American inner city touched by urban blight. Here, too, the decision is made to call in the wreckers, and often everything goes. The temptation is great, when a city's downtown deterioration has reached the point of despair, when nobody wants to try to freshen up the paint on his shop sign or clean in front of his stoop, when the central business district as presently laid out represents a traffic bottleneck no police commissioner can resolve, to tear everything down and start over. It is going on somewhere, in some American city, at this very moment; the process is repeated again and again, as soon as the capital can be gotten together. Almost always it seems like a good idea on paper.

"It is inconceivable to me that the center of a European city could decay like so many of your cities in the United States," French political scientist Raymond Aron remarked to an interviewer in 1970. "The difference is, I am sure, that Americans think of their cities as way stations, to which they owe no real obligation. Our cities are rooted in our history, our culture and our lives." In fact, and in history, most American cities grew out from their centers; there was also a downtown exercising a force of attraction, for business, shopping, entertainment. Going downtown was a way of relieving boredom. Certain sections of the city were easily identifiable, frequented by all, often universally known (they became trademarks of the city). Many Americans grew up in them, and surely some Americans loved them. But they are what the bulldozers are razing.

And few of the wholly rebuilt centers succeed. The soul has gone out of them. They become dead, even deadly, after business hours, deserted by everyone who can afford to get out to suburbs, that other spiritual wasteland. All costs, in transportation, commuting time, public services, go up. Meanwhile, a city has disappeared.

The hard way is to restore, to rebuild in and around the old streets, to keep buildings of varying sizes and shapes and especially conditions, allowing a choice of rent levels, maintaining a neighborhood mix. Or, when urban blight has destroyed this mix, selective renewal of presently standing buildings can bring people back, as in restored London, Amsterdam, Paris.

It is almost never too late. Rotterdam was largely destroyed in vast air raids. It couldn't be restored; it had to be rebuilt. The downtown was done on a small scale, even now strange to see in the directional center of the world's largest ocean port. The pedestrian mall, the Lijnbaan, became a prototype of humane inner-city living. Nor is it a matter of public versus private initiative, for the two are not necessarily antagonistic. "It cannot be too often remarked," Christopher Tunnard wrote in *The City of Man,* "that the majority of the world's most beautiful squares, crescents and circuses were conceived and executed by the business mind, with architects assisting in the designs and sometimes in the financing. It was the architect Hardouin-Mansart and his associates in real estate who persuaded Louis XIV in 1685 to buy the land occupied by the Place Vendôme . . . Wealth, fashion and gambling also combined to produce one of the world's most admired cities—18th century Bath."

Some of Europe's oldest cities have been preserving their historic, life-enhancing centers, placing new construction in new districts, on unused land or land abandoned by industry, especially when the present use of the land has a lower social priority. Such planning is not without its flaws, the drawbacks including the proximity of the old city. Should the new district be farther away, should tall buildings be allowed so close to the historic city center, and be visible from it?

On the one hand, the demographic call to find housing for increasing numbers of persons in or close to the city, the economy's need for more office space, manufacturing and selling space—

problems of every dynamic city. In some, the value of downtown property has been rising at astronomical rates.

On the other, the inevitable truth that cities which have thrived have thrived when they were concentrated, when they represented a promiscuous mixture of classes and occupations. At their worst, those who have bulldozed still-workable buildings out of old neighborhoods can be likened to mindless vandals. In a recent study of vandalism published by The Architectural Press in London, the contributors don't hesitate to include bulldozing, private or official, as of a piece with the petty vandals who damage property maliciously. Chapters of the study deal with "Planners as Vandals" and "Developers as Vandals." "All these crimes," writes editor Colin Ward, "are the consequence of economic necessity."

Some cities are proud of their crimes, and renew them. After Haussmann, planners in Paris have been destroying old quarters methodically, putting in their place some of the world's most lugubrious constructions, such as the Maine-Montparnasse buildings sitting atop a railroad station, part of an urban renewal scheme which as its most conspicuous manifestation produced the tallest building in Paris (at the present writing, still the tallest in Europe), within walking distance of some of that city's most beautiful old neighborhoods. Such renewal calls for more renewal, and much of Montparnasse of small streets lined with artists' studios has disappeared in recent years. The same fate is in store for the old central market district, the Halles. The French Senate's Committee on Cultural Affairs noted in 1972: "Paris is no longer a beautiful city and it took only four years to deface it." The blame was placed on "the system of point of no return" which prevents any effective control over a project once launched, together with a system of "exceptions" to every building regulation. "Haussmann the ripper was a child compared to the 20th-century promoters," a 20th-century Frenchman wrote.

It isn't that they ignore the consequences, for today neighborhood and environmental defense groups are calling public attention to what is being planned, and have suggested more humane alternatives. Nor is it necessary to call a halt to needed rehabilitation of old neighborhoods. Even in West Germany, with its massive rebuilding after World War II destruction, it has been estimated that nearly half of the 22 million dwelling units are prewar; 13 million lack central heating, 5 million have no bathroom, or they are too small, badly ventilated. Some 2 million are in poor condition. No one should suggest that rehabilitation should be postponed or abandoned. It is the choice of methods that concerns us.

Once a city center is gutted, the complex interrelationships of people and things built up over generations are lost; often they cannot be replaced to the satisfaction of the new inhabitants. Modern slums develop at an accelerating rate; is it any wonder?

And yet: It sometimes requires no more than one familiar landmark, a single old street saved in its entirety, to keep an old center alive; often from this nucleus the rest can follow. It can be something new, like a pocket park as an alternative use of space to one more parking lot or eventually one more building. It can be something old: a 17th-century farmhouse left standing in the heart of the new neighborhood built on New York's Roosevelt Island. These human touches in a machine age are by no means caviar or (to switch metaphors) window dressing. They can stimulate the secretion of the vital juices which keep cities alive. Demolition of an old theater in Times Square or on Paris's *grands boulevards,* of an old pub in London or in Dublin, is more than symbolic loss. It affects the way city dwellers look at and act toward their cities from that point on. It affects their decision to stay and rehabilitate or to move out. This, in turn, affects the promoter's decision to invest or not, more importantly to bulldoze or to conserve. The known process by which a vandal attacks street furniture or a building already in dilapidated condition more readily than he would something in good repair, applies to public vandalism as well. If you can save the respected and revered old structures, you may save the inner city. Introduction of the concept of neighborhood "mini-plans" in New York City in 1974 would seem to have been undertaken in this spirit of city-saving.

From this it might follow that piecemeal, random development, however inefficient it may seem to doctrinaire planners and developers, is better for business, for the prosperity of the city, than large-scale development. In *The Necessary Monument,* Theo Crosby attributes such a magnetic function to London's Tower Bridge:

> still a place to walk on; it invites a crossing. . . . a participation in the working life of the river . . . the sensations of participating in history . . . This multitude of experiences, intricately and subconsciously overlaid, is the very stuff of cities, the product of a rich mix of uses and associations . . . It is the rewarding end product of complexity (and it has also a very real cash value).

Very real cash value: nothing sentimental here. The city savers are wrongly but repeatedly accused of unreal, archaic, sentimental views. In fact, as I have shown, the city environment and particularly the environment of large metropolitan areas will have to provide shelter for an increasing percentage of the world's population, and more in absolute numbers, in the years around the next bend. It is therefore the environment of most active people that we are talking about. Destroying the life and the spirit of their city centers while planning for increased use of these centers would seem to be a particularly inhumane activity, and ultimately an uneconomical one as well. "Saving old city centers is no longer a cultural caprice," noted a French cultural affairs official, "but the point of departure for urban renewal."

Planners know that people will soon be living as far from the cities they work in as is possible for them to travel to in a morning or evening rush hour; they will have to start coming back. What kind of city are we building for them, leaving to them? Many of the most significant improvements in the cities, however efficient they may seem, provoke in the user the desire to get out of them, after the day's work is done, as fast and as far as he is able. Once a pole of attraction, Montparnasse in Paris was the victim of such a development scheme. The visitor to the Maine-Montparnasse zone gets out of it to a suburb, or to a more livable Paris neighborhood which has somehow been saved from development, as soon as he has completed his business there.

We have the universal phenomenon of Sunday promenaders not able or not desiring to go to the country descending en masse on their city's "undeveloped" neighborhoods. It has reached such a point, this pressure on old towns and neighborhoods, that there have been complaints of "tourist colonialism," manifesting itself in the invasion of souvenir and postcard vendors, real and fake antique and crafts shops, which drive out local shopkeepers in rehabilitated districts. A meeting sponsored by Civitas Nostra, an international city-saving organization, examined this dilemma: "When the tourists arrive, degeneration sets in. But we have no choice; if they don't come, others come to tear everything down."

The first answer is: *Keep the centers vital.* It is also the answer to depopulation of the inner city which has overloaded the suburban infrastructure. In his inaugural lecture at Oxford's School of Geography, Jean Gottmann proposed a remedy for old city centers: Remove the industrial plants and warehouses from them, allowing the cities to retain the permanent functions of the ancient agora, acropolis, and forum, to which would be added the large complexes of offices and laboratories necessary to quaternary (trans-actional) economic activities.

This need not mean tearing down and rebuilding. As will be shown in another chapter, one of the most exciting elements of contemporary city saving in Europe has been the rehabilitation of old buildings for new uses: old town houses as company head-quarters or as private dwellings. "Conventional wisdom," noted Arthur Cotton Moore in an article in *Progressive Architecture*, "has always held that complete demolition and all-new construc-tion is not only cleaner and neater but also cheaper; the preserva-tionist must show that conventional wisdom is wrong."

It is an urgent problem, for urban decay spreads rapidly. Even in densely populated Amsterdam, population in the last decade was declining each year as a result of slum clearance and renova-tion, and with this decline small businesses, shops, even schools and churches were being deprived of means of sustenance. Then the city's planners moved in, calling for a concentration of func-tions in the center, all the while maintaining the city's residential function, shopping facilities, even the in-town university. It was understood that such a decision required public acknowledgment of the desirability of the center, which meant keeping it on a scale with which people could identify. A Dutch author pointed out that "a city heart does not start to beat and does not exist in that sense until the center has become so attractive that large numbers of the population go there more often than is functionally strictly necessary."

The Dutch planners (of the Ministry of Housing and Physical Planning) hope that the free play of social forces will insure the development of the city center as an economic focal point. What no planner in a free economy can cope with, however, is the kind of city wrecking called for in such projects as the original schemes for face-lifting London's downtown Piccadilly Circus or Covent Garden central market (and entertainment) district. Here the common sense answer is: *Scale down developers' projects* until they stand no higher than human beings can reach.

Indeed, there is a growing tendency of municipal authorities and public defense groups to oppose the easy way out represented by the early 20th-century renewal philosophy of "tear everything down and start over." In London, the original Covent Garden scheme met strong resistance, leading to the government's promise to avoid creating a new concrete jungle; under the latest revision of the project, some 250 historic buildings are to be preserved on a 34-acre site. In Paris, the controversy over the renovation of Les

Halles, the central markets whose wholesalers were moved beyond city limits after the government decided to remove all such activity from the central business district, is not yet over, although many of the original projects for the cleared area, including the most voluminous, have been suspended on orders of the French president himself. Even industrial Frankfurt, a businessman's city par excellence, has a building code limiting the height of new buildings. One promoter who violated it was told to remove the top three floors of a building.

But where planners and promoters can do most to keep a city center viable is in making sure that new buildings and large-scale developments do not obliterate the recognizable tissue of the city. This can be done only by saving and rehabilitating wherever possible, building anew only when necessary, and then by *integrating new and old*. It is what had been planned for even in the most outrageous schemes for redeveloping Les Halles: Every successive plan showed familiar old façades rigorously conserved, lovingly restored, the interiors rehabilitated or rebuilt, as a backdrop to the new construction above and below ground. The Beaubourg cultural center at the east end of the Halles district is Paris's most daring building in decades, also one of its largest; yet it was artfully planted among the characteristic façades of past centuries, the intention being to build new or virtually new buildings behind the façades, as has already been carried out in such cities as Brussels (Rue de la Montagne) or in Cologne (the concert hall Gürzenich, whose restored 15th-century Gothic façade introduces a contemporary interior, designed by the man who rebuilt much of bombed-out Cologne, Rudolf Schwarz). No one doubts that Parisians and other Frenchmen, notably those condemned to live in some of the modern world's most depressing suburbs, will take more comfort from the new Halles district because of the preservation of vestiges of the old one.

Hence the fight for every square foot of old façade in London, the preservation of many gracious squares of Georgian, even of Victorian London, for contemporary living and working. The protest against Covent Garden renewal was based on the obvious fact that Covent Garden is very much alive now, whereas the scale of the planned redevelopment makes it likely that the result will be as lifeless as all the other large-scale projects carried out since World War II in that city.

What can be done even in a city largely destroyed, a city which even its admirers have never in our time called beautiful, is seen in Frankfurt on Main, surely the prototype of the soulless business city, the no-nonsense financial capital of the nation, with 700,000 inhabitants, and the economic support of two million in its region. Of all German cities, Frankfurt has to cope with the greatest number of daily migrations; motor vehicle and public transportation is a major factor in planning.

Although it is easy to ridicule Frankfurt's efforts at beautification, and that easy way has been taken often enough, Frankfurt has gone to extraordinary lengths to save what could be saved. The city itself represents only a small fraction of the total area of the metropolitan region; the downtown, especially the core of the ancient city, is smaller than in many cities of similar size and importance. Yet great care has been given to keeping downtown Frankfurt on a human scale. What was left of old landmarks after World War II destructions was saved, what could be restored or reconstituted was brought back to life. Soon after the war, the city rebuilt Goethe's house stone by stone, refurnished it room by room. It has restored the city hall (Römer) and its square—certainly not for tourists, who represent a negligible element in the city's economy. In a later phase of the restoration, the Römer square was turned into a pedestrian zone, a parking garage beneath it. Narrow streets were kept, or perhaps redesigned, such as the Neue Kräme and Liebfrauenberg leading from the Römer to the Hauptwache. An old church here, a baroque-style palace (now a bank) there, a predominance of postwar construction: the whole seems almost intimate.

The Hauptwache is certainly the masterpiece of this reconstruction. On the ground level, low buildings on an acceptable scale, most of them new. Beneath the square, a shopping gallery; below that, on descending levels, a major railroad station and a transfer point of two subway lines. Yet the outdoor cafés on the surface do not seem out of place. When the renewal of Frankfurt is completed, it will be possible to follow pedestrians-only streets through the entire old city; the Zeil, the principal commercial artery, is earmarked to become a pedestrian promenade as well, with small shops covering the surface of what is now the roadway. As a first step, all motor traffic except trams has been banned; the trams, too, will eventually be rerouted.

So that the universal problem of the automobile is solved in the simplest, most absolute way. And yet the Frankfurters surely have as many automobiles per capita as any Germans (perhaps more of them and bigger ones, or so it sometimes seems). Frankfurt began to build a subway in 1965, designed, of course, to reduce the need for automobiles. A certain amount of underground and surface parking, dissuasively expensive if used for a whole day, is available near the car-free center. The planners have also resorted to more traditional ways of removing pressure from the central business district, with giant shopping centers and satellite towns (Main-Taunus Zentrum and Nordweststadt with its own Zentrum).

Those who are familiar with it do not find Frankfurt an attractive city. That it has nevertheless made this effort to be pleasant, despite all the economic pressures working against such a result, is remarkable.

Elsewhere, similar sentiment for conservation of the old in the face of the requirements of growth has kept many cities alive for their inhabitants. The old nuclei of Dutch cities, Delft or Haarlem or even remote Maastricht, far from any tourist itinerary, remain magnets. Geneva, like Frankfurt a banking capital not known for the sentimentality of its burghers, was one of the first cities to preserve its ancient center; if that center seems like an outdoor museum to the visitor, it is also the administrative core of French Switzerland's largest city, the site of its city hall and law courts.

But none of these city-saving rules helps very much if unaccompanied by means of *keeping people where they live and work,* avoiding expulsions and exile to suburbs, inhuman for the inhabitants, uneconomic for the collectivity.

Mass deportations are one of the most frequent accompaniments of urban renewal, one of the most easily accepted. In the United States, when the older structures are removed from desirable neighborhoods, the original occupants are removed along with them. Rents in the new housing put up to replace them are higher than they can afford. In Europe, even in cities with otherwise enlightened urban planning, when the old structures are rehabilitated (for usually they are not removed anymore), the result is a similar exodus of the original inhabitants, destroying the mix, social and economic, and thus the relationship between the attacked neighborhood and adjacent neighborhoods. The consequences of such deportations are described so well in Jane Jacobs's *Death and Life of Great American Cities* as not to require repetition here.

Seldom, except when they are shamed into it, do cities act to prevent the exodus. The result is not only homogenized upper-rental housing in the new neighborhoods, but homogenized, uniformly low-rent distant suburbs to house the emigrés, when they are lucky enough to find suburbs they can afford; otherwise they slip into slum neighborhoods waiting renovation. A novel way to combine city-saving with people-saving is being carried out on a small scale in a few American cities; the pioneer is Wilmington, Delaware, where the city government offered old houses to its citizens free of charge provided that they repair them to city standards within 18 months and reside in them for three years. Early reports from Wilmington (and from Philadelphia, Baltimore, and Newark) suggest that initial enthusiasm has been dampened by the hard realities of high interest rates and rising costs. Because Bologna in Italy refuses to tolerate the renovation-expulsion syndrome, I have devoted a chapter of this book to the Bologna experiment.

Meanwhile in Paris, half-hearted attempts to keep some of the city's original population within city limits have gone on, or have been talked about, for years, in the face of massive destruction and rebuilding in peripheral neighborhoods. But with the growing realization of Parisians that they possess a priceless heritage even in deteriorated residential areas in the heart of the city, the last decade has seen an extraordinary invasion of these once-abandoned old neighborhoods, particularly in the Latin Quarter and vicinity, close to the geographical heart of the city (5th and 6th *arrondissements*). Buildings taken over by promoters, often by piecemeal purchase of apartments from a number of different proprietors— occupancy in Paris being based on ownership of individual apartments by the occupant or his landlord—are renovated, often with great attention to economy of means and the accouterments of antiquity (for example, exposed ceiling beams), for resale or rental at prices far beyond the means of the original inhabitants, who are already living far enough away not to be in competition with the new occupants in any case.

In 1970, a government agency for housing improvement (Agence Nationale pour l'Amélioration de l'Habitat) was set up in France to facilitate renovation of rented apartments, with emphasis on group action by owners and tenants. The agency's subsidies, drawn from a fund based on a tax on rentals, are concentrated on interior rehabilitation. Estimating the average cost of putting an old apartment into shape at 15,000 francs (somewhat over $3,000), the Agence provides lump-sum grants rather than basing them on actual cost of the work, to avoid excessive charges and unnecessary frills. Once the job is done the rents go up, but a separate system of rent subsidies is supposed to help occupants stay in their original dwellings. The new system has yet to prove itself, and no one has suggested that the resources of the governmental agency will allow it to solve all of the problems of Paris's tenants. Indeed, large numbers of Parisians continue at this writing to lose their old apartments to the promoters and the speculators.

In order to counter this, a second step was taken: the decision to authorize the French public housing authorities (known collectively as HLM, for *habitations à loyer modéré*—medium-rent housing) to buy up old downtown houses and to renovate them for moderate-income tenants. Heretofore, the HLM companies were concerned exclusively with the construction and rental of *new* dwelling units on the *periphery* of the cities. Still, the proposed modification of the HLM charter is likely to be a negligible factor in improving the situation, in view of the limited resources of the societies, which cannot even meet the demand for new construction. Again, in one small Paris neighborhood, the city is engaged in a pilot program of renovation of slum housing with the intention of keeping the rents low so that the present inhabitants can stay put, although the means of keeping them in the neighborhood during the renovation, or to bring them back from suburban exile when it is completed, have not been spelled out. See Bologna again. Finally, a French proposal (approved for submission to the parliament by a cabinet meeting in April 1974) would seem to go in the right direction: Promoters or landlords will have to inform present occupants of their rights, giving them time to reflect even if they have agreed to move out, the complaint of course being that occupants are usually bluffed or tricked into abandoning their homes. New housing, according to the proposed law, must be close to the evicted tenant's old home. We shall see what happens.

A final measure—one offers it timidly in view of the demonstrable helplessness of most city residents to exercise control over their destinies—is *consultation with the inhabitants* on urban renovation. It is of course being attempted in a number of places, sometimes very formally, by vote, more often by polls or evaluating the comments of visitors to a public display of plans and models— obviously a very small and special fraction of the public at large. Most often, we know what people think through their reactions to the lack of consultation: neighborhood defense groups, environmental associations, aided by the press and other media, attack what has already been done or is in the planning stage. In few places in the world, the United States included, do public or private planners voluntarily share decision-making with the end-users, the people who will live and work in the renovated neighborhood.

2. Recreating Neighborhoods

Le Marais

For years, wise Parisians and knowing foreigners had been exploring a vast district of eastern Paris whose dilapidated streets and deteriorated façades occasionally revealed a marvel: a palatial old manor house boarded up, or with broken windows betraying its abandon, or, if used, then occupied by storerooms, artisans' workshops, the smudged façades defaced with advertising or shop awnings, the interiors partitioned into office cubicles. The cognoscenti would venture into a courtyard, discover an elaborate wrought-iron stairway, ceremonial marble steps, niches holding statuettes but more often lacking them, richly carved beams, a bit of fresco or painted ceiling. Probably some of the city's worst slums were concentrated here; the decline was steep enough to allow use of an entire palace to store shoeboxes or lampshades. Here and there a marvel stood out. The Place des Vosges, its deteriorated façades scarcely recognizable as the stately homes of Henri IV's court, had been the center of the Paris that mattered in the 17th century; Madame de Sévigné had been born in one of them. The Hôtel de Sens was one of only two remaining medieval mansions in the city. Many of the district's priceless landmarks had disappeared; in a number of cases known to national cultural authorities, woodwork and panels, ceilings, and whole rooms had been dismantled and shipped as far away as Antwerp and Vienna to decorate newer mansions.

Incredibly, the neighborhood was only a few hundred feet, a five-minute walk, from Paris's city hall and adjacent city administrative buildings. It was served by the major east-west subway line and city buses, bordered on the Seine River at one of its most scenic points, facing that jewel of a city island, the Ile St. Louis. In a city short of downtown living and working space, whose citizens were moving farther and farther beyond its boundaries in search of comfort, the proximity of this ghetto of palatial buildings in an advanced state of blight was remarkable.

Some 82,000 persons lived, mostly badly, in this ghetto, in a density often twice as high as the city average. About 7,000 small businesses employing 40,000 persons were counted. When a survey was undertaken at the inception of the restoration effort, 56 buildings were judged to be of great historical value, another 121 were considered worthy of landmark status, 526 were candidates for the same classification, and nearly 1,000 others joined the list as pleasing adjuncts to the ensemble. Together, they represented a storehouse of national treasures capable of filling as many leaflets as a nation's tourist industry might publish. It would be worth a trip to Paris just to see them, a trip during which the visitor might skip the Eiffel Tower, the Arch of Triumph, the Champs-Elysées, the Louvre, and the Opéra.

In the history of Paris urbanism, the Marais represented the desire of the rulers of France in the last half of the 16th and most of the 17th century to leave their mark on an area of the city where it was still possible to lay out large squares (such as the Place Royale, to become the Place des Vosges), to build town houses with gardens, and new churches in the spirit and style of the times. The name of the district, Le Marais, means "marshy ground," which was its condition prior to the Middle Ages, as alternate riverbed of the Seine. Much of it lay outside the fortified walls of Paris prior to Henri IV, who carried out a veritable real estate development here. He saw the Place Royale as the centerpiece of the new neighborhood, reserving the south side of the square for himself and his court, turning over the three remaining sides to promoters who agreed to respect the overall plan and style. It is said that the king visited the square every day during the construction, though he died before it was completed. It was not only good urbanism, but a money-making proposition for the king and his heirs.

In recent decades, the visitor who strayed into this old quarter might have been delighted, then increasingly alarmed, as he pursued his explorations. He could learn, if he tried, that the district had more substandard housing than any other in Paris; 30% of the dwelling units were without running water, 68% without private toilets (in one sector, the figures were 36% and 74%). In part of the district, 10% of the dwelling units lacked electricity in 1959.

On the main avenue, the Hôtel de Sully was impossible to miss. And yet the visitor might walk right by it without knowing that it was there. Onetime residence of the finance minister of Henri IV, it served prior to restoration as working and storage area for a vendor of umbrellas, a barber, a mattress maker, a clinic, a dealer in straw hats, a coal merchant. A small tenement had actually been built above the street entrance, joining the two wings of the façade. Signs painted directly on the façade or placed over it, and the awnings of three shops and a café, made it difficult to make out any of the telltale signs of early 17th-century architecture. One was not likely to enter the front yard *cour d'honneur* to attempt to recognize the ornate sculptures beneath the grime; one could certainly not guess that the partitions of work and storage rooms inside concealed some of the original painted ceilings and wood paneling.

The modern history of the Marais began in the early 1960s, with the activity of a small group of private citizens enamored of the district and despairing that anything would be done to protect or restore it. This was a time when official efforts in this area were still timid, and limited to universally recognized landmarks. Private initiatives were even rarer. The group first took on an old mansion known as the Hôtel de Vigny (hôtel, in this context, signifying town house). A petition was drawn up to oppose the demolition of another old building, the Hôtel de Guillaume Barbès. In 1962, the volunteers, with Michel Raude as founder-president, declared themselves an Association pour la Sauvegarde et la Mise en Valeur du Paris Historique (Association for the Protection and Restoration of Historic Paris), and began to compile photographic and archeological data on all the notable constructions of the Marais, which was to be the basis for a widely acclaimed map-inventory published in 1965.

To raise money, the Association sponsored the first of its summer festivals, outdoors in the courtyards of ancient palaces undergoing restoration, indoors in neighborhood churches and other halls. In its heyday, for there were good years and bad (a rainy summer, a student revolution), the festival presented 84 performances in a single season, drawing 110,000 spectators. There were elegant souvenir programs filled with advertising; by 1969, the program was able to acknowledge the support of the minister of state for cultural affairs, André Malraux; the prefect of Paris; the prefect of police; the chairman of the city council, Paris's "mayor." The honorary sponsoring committee then included the Duchess de la Rouchefoucauld, patron of the arts; Prince Jean de Broglie, member of the French Academy; curators of the National Archives, the Historical Library of the City of Paris, and the Museum of the History of Paris (Carnavalet). Other members included Baroness Elie de Rothschild, the Banque de France, Banque de Paris et du Pays-Bas, Banque Nationale de Paris, and other leading banking institutions and manufacturing companies, advertising agencies and film producers, makers of alcoholic beverages, the Cannes Casino.

But a visitor to the Association's headquarters on the Rue François Miron, numbers 44 and 46, which happened to be one of the buildings it was engaged in bringing back to life, a 17th-century construction built over 13th-century Gothic cellars, would find young men and women preparing for a weekend of roof-climbing to remove tiles, eliminate and replace the broken ones; there might be a bulletin board notice referring to an unfortunate volunteer who had fallen into a pit while helping in the renovation of the vaulted cellars of an historic mansion: The François Miron building had been given to the Association by the city of Paris; tickets to the summer festivals were available here.

During the early years, and apart from the festival, the Marais was still the end of the world for many Parisians, and believers in its salvation seemed to be pioneers. As late as 1968, the Association's annual report spoke of the disastrous financial situation caused by cancellation of its festival that year because of the student and worker agitation in May. Heavy debts caused a reduction in staff to one administrative secretary. The Association almost disappeared that year, saved in extremis by voluntary efforts and contributions; festival ticket holders waived reimbursement of canceled performances; the city came forth with a supplementary grant.

All over France, it was a time of waking consciousness. André Malraux's Cultural Ministry was talking about saving the national heritage, and many ordinary people as well as municipal officials were looking around them to see what required saving. As the Marais Association won more supporters, the city gave it more landmarks to restore. Some of the score of buildings it had been asked to take responsibility for would become dwelling units. The Association's volunteers did the hard labor, removing later additions to find the original structure of a building, probing for hidden ceilings, cellars, stripping roofs, simple demolition, cleaning wooden beams, recovering and cleaning tiles, after which the specialized labor of restoration and preparing new living or working quarters was turned over to professionals. Volunteers, whose mini-

mum age was 18, were not expected to have any particular archeological or architectural competence, but it was hoped that they
would have a technical skill. They were asked to pledge two days'
work a month, weekends or Tuesday evenings. Volunteers were
given the opportunity to attend the Association's guided visits to
local landmarks, as well as illustrated lectures on protecting old
neighborhoods, architecture and urbanism. Of the Association's
300 active members, 10% are students and 60% are in the liberal
professions.

The map-guide published by the Association—remarkable for its
clear perspective drawings of every building of note, and the use
of a color key to distinguish sites of great value or of secondary
interest, but also of mediocre quality, even those requiring demolition or transformation—was accompanied by a description, street
by street, of 1,893 separate structures distributed through the
Marais. The programs and other publications prepared for the
summer festivals also contained descriptions and histories of buildings in the process of restoration—or requiring it—and ample illustrations. In its first ten years of cataloging, some 30,000 photographs
had been collected of Marais streets and landmarks.

But the greatest achievement of the small band of volunteers
and true believers was certainly that it focused public attention
on the district. By the end of the 1960s, the Marais was of national
interest. In 1965, the French government placed the area under
its protection as a *secteur sauvegardé* in accordance with the 1962
law concerning protection and restoration of historic neighborhoods. True, the government's boundaries, about 310 acres, were
somewhat less generous than those of the volunteers. But in principle, the listing not only authorized the drawing up of a comprehensive plan for restoration but banned any transformations within
the protected zone which might alter its character. The national
press, even the world press, began to talk about the Marais.
Seekers of apartments in the city's perenially tight real estate market began to rent or purchase space for restoration, and from that
point on, the promoters moved in; the number of antique shops
and art galleries, fashion boutiques and trendy restaurants increased geometrically.

The biggest breakthrough may have been the renewed recognition, applied to this district, that a restored landmark could
serve as a public building or a company's headquarters, thereby
contributing to the collective heritage, solving a space problem,
benefiting from a subsidy or a tax rebate, all at once. The Caisse

Nationale des Mounments Historiques et des Sites, whose job it is to "animate" landmarks for their protection and thus to help pay for their upkeep—see the following chapter—became a sponsor of the Festival du Marais. A good example of making use of a landmark was the city's takeover of the restoration of the magnificent Hôtel de Lamoignon on the Rue Pavée, built in 1585-90 for Diane de France, daughter of Henri II and a young Italian woman. This veritable palace, with its curious streetcorner watchtower, was acquired by the city in 1928 for an extension of the Carnavalet (history of Paris) museum across the way, but it was only after World War II that the architects attacked the job of removing the commercial signs and shop and storeroom partitions; the courtyard had become the wild garden of a vacant lot with temporary shacks, rusted cans. Sculpted wooden panels, polychrome ceilings, other signs of grandeur were uncovered bit by bit over years of restoration. The Hôtel has now become the historical library of the city of Paris. A modern wing was added in the "style." Purists might object, but perhaps they would accept the assurance of an observer who knew the Hôtel de Lamoignon before its restoration that it is well worth paying for its eternal preservation with this annex.

As time went on, more and more institutions acquired and proceeded to restore Marais buildings. The Swedish Cultural Institute is housed in a particularly delightful, relatively modest example— modest in contrast to the huge Hôtel Carnavalet (built in 1548, once the home of Madame de Sévigné), just across the narrow Rue Payenne. The Hôtel de Sully (formal title: Hôtel de Béthune-Sully) is now the headquarters of the Caisse Nationale des Monuments Historiques et des Sites, with an information office and library and temporary exhibitions. The Hôtel de Savoury contains fifteen apartments (including four in the high-rent category). The Hôtel des Parlementaires de la Fronde also contains apartments, and other rehabilitated dwellings were becoming available in restored town houses and humbler adjacent structures. The Hôtel des Ambassadeurs de Hollande, in which Beaumarchais wrote *The Marriage of Figaro*, shelters a foundation for elderly actors, some of whom reside in it (but this extraordinary ensemble had already been restored prior to World War II). The Hôtel Guénegaud was transformed by a philanthropist into a hunting museum; the Hôtel Liberal Bruant would become a locksmith museum. At 75 Rue du Temple, the Hôtel St. Aignan, an extraordinary Romanesque palace designed by one of the architects of Paris's Val

de Grace church, provides headquarters for the International
Council of Monuments and Sites and the archives of the city of
Paris.

Old buildings in the Marais that had never been quite lost, such
as the Palais Soubise housing the National Archives, were refur-
bished. The neighborhoods gradually came back to life; what
happened there began to be of news value. Façades of the principle monuments and landmarks were illuminated in the evening.
On at least one occasion, the entire quarter held "open house,"
with building façades heretofore unknown and unnoticed even by
local residents illuminated for their edification and delight.

And at any point in the 1960s and early 1970s, even up to the
time of writing, the visitor could share this experience of discovery.
Many buildings were only then beginning to be restored, such as
the Hôtel Jeanne d'Albret at 31 Rue des Francs Bourgeois, with
broken windows, its dilapidated interior housing a craftsman's
workshop and storerooms; perhaps by the time this is read, it will
be the magnificent 16th-century palace it had once been. It is to
be utilized as a journalists' center, with a basement garage for
members and 4,700 square meters of floor space for two restaurants, a bar, lounge, sauna, room for press conferences, radio and
television studios, photo laboratory, telex facilities, a library, a
working area for journalists, as well as offices for professional
associations desiring to use it as their headquarters. Such buildings
are placed at the disposal of recognized organizations, with restoration largely paid for by government and city funds. In the case
of the journalists' foundation, the new tenants were asked to pay
only 5% of the cost of restoration, furnishing, and other equipment.

To see a building not yet restored within eyesight of the Hôtel
Jeanne d'Albret, see number 30 of the same street, a jewel of an
Henri IV manor, now a wholesale materials concern.

Fortunately, an area as large as the Marais can well afford the
commercial exploitation that often accompanies otherwise disinterested attempts at faithful and useful restoration. Concurrently
with the restorations, of course, commercial and touristic exploitation was to take place. Yet in this district running from the Seine
River to the south, as far north as the Boulevard St. Martin, west
(at least on the Association's map) to the Boulevard Sébastopol,
east to the Boulevards des Filles du Calvaire and du Temple, no
protection of a practical nature could be enforced against the
vendors of picturesque. And perhaps there should be none, for
they are in part responsible for arousing interest in the Marais
among rank-and-file taxpayers who eventually pay for restoration.

The Marais became good for you. A folder containing small photographs of the principal landmarks with brief descriptions was distributed by a Société des Amis du Marais, the Jeune Chambre Economique de Paris (Junior Chamber of Commerce), and the concessioners of Coca-Cola. What this conservation effort could mean for local business is suggested by some of the trade names listed in the 1969 program of the Marais festival: restaurants called La Grille du Marais and Les Routiers du Marais, a club-bar called Le Marais, a supper club for "candlelit dinners" called Le Marais Cage, La Boutique du Marais (antiques and decoration), Le Marais Galant (gifts), Les Editions Décoratives du Marais (wallpaper), Les Soldes du Marais (ready-to-wear).

Establishment of the district as a landmark led to official designation of a smaller zone, 41 acres of the 310, as a ZAD (*zone d'aménagement différé*), which served to freeze real estate speculation. The plan drawn up by the city in 1969, which initiated an investigatory and ratifying process to last for years (from inception to approval the process would go into its second decade and at this writing is still pending), calls for creation of gardens in vacant lots between and within structures (some of this space to be created by removal of "unesthetic" houses of comparatively recent date), rehabilitation of buildings, and provision of new uses for these buildings. Light industry would be shifted to the periphery of the district, while commercial activity would be maintained in the heart of the area wherever it was feasible. Traffic problems were to be resolved through underground garages and pedestrian zones. A major restoration was undertaken on the Place des Vosges, which remains the masterwork of the Marais, by a semipublic corporation, Sorema (for Société d'Economie Mixte de Restauration du Marais), sister organization to Serma (Société d'Etudes pour la Restauration du Marais). In the city's own history of the restoration, of course, the municipality takes credit for rediscovery and protection of the area starting in 1953—although the first study by Serma was commissioned only in July 1962. Then an "operational sector" of 8.6 acres was earmarked in 1969 to serve as a prototype operation, with a deadline of five years for expropriation of its buildings by Sorema Meanwhile, the chief architect of Bâtiments de France, installed in the Hôtel de Béthune-Sully, would henceforth control and authorize all transformations, constructions, and demolitions in the protected 310-acre district. It happens that the chief architect's staff is quite small; it must deal with 150 cases each month but cannot provide on-the-spot inspections; in any district as

large as this one, all kinds of pressures are being applied at any
moment in time.

Nor are all the official plans ideal from the point of view of
city saving. In this area of great residential density, the city
expected some 20,000 of the original inhabitants—or nearly a
quarter of the total—to move out. Obviously, it would not be the
wealthy or the near-wealthy who would do the moving out to
suburbs, which are as bleak as the old tenements to be torn down.
Restoration and rehabilitation benefited those who could somehow find the means to hang on, but above all the new inhabitants
attracted to the neighborhood by its restored chic and comfortable lodgings. And the official and well-publicized restorations
were soon outflanked by slipshod rehabilitation of ordinary buildings in the protected zone, for sale or rental at scalpers' prices
(one-room "studio" apartments starting at $200 a month). The
authorities, by concentrating their efforts on costly restorations
of monuments of prestige at the expense of desperately needed
housing, did little to relieve the pressures which encouraged these
speculative operations. For the present, then, these public interventions are a drop in the bucket compared to the private ones.
"The Marais becomes attractive, thus expensive," a journalist
noted in Le Monde, "because of the efforts of the authorities to
save it. It would be shocking if private speculators are the only
ones to profit from it." "Thanks to the magic wand of the promoters," began a tract sponsored by a Christian protest group
called Commission Justice et Paix du Marais, "the Marais district,
poor, unhealthy, its woodwork grimy, is becoming the home of
millionaires, of landmark zoning, and exposed ceiling beams. The
old inhabitants of the neighborhood, artisans, migrant workers
. . . don't belong in the new decor designed by big money and
official culture. They are bad for business; they frighten away
young management and the hoity-toity. They get deported to the
periphery." The tract was distributed during the 1974 Festival
du Marais, to the accompaniment of a song:

> The elderly have gone in a legal way
> With kicks in the rear to the cemetery,
> They aren't good enough for the Marais
> So the bulldozers sweep their memory away;
> If only they paid taxes. . . .

But no one was claiming that the millennium had arrived. In
an area as large and as depressed as this one, no Utopian solution could be expected; how many cities, regardless of their

political system or wealth, had ever managed to salvage a neighborhood for its original inhabitants? One could hope that the
vastly improved quality of the surroundings, and of the individual
structures for living or for business, would somehow compensate
for the deportations and for the increased incidence of souvenir
shoppes. Public opinion now counts for something in these matters, and voluntary organizations can ignite the sparks that lead
to major city-saving projects.

Rue Mouffetard

The scale here is different, but in any case the stakes in the
Mouffetard neighborhood of Paris's Latin Quarter are not as
high. In the 660-yard length of the narrow street itself there are
few buildings of more than passing interest: a small fountain
here, a stone well, a couple of sculptured façades. To the north,
a charming square with old trees, Place de la Contrescarpe, which
succeeding generations of students and other funlovers have
frequented, the styles of cafés and restaurants changing to suit
their changing tastes. Still farther north, beyond the Rue Des-
cartes, runs the ever-popular Montagne Sainte Geneviève restaurant district. Ernest Hemingway had lived above the shop with
the sign "Le Nègre Joyeux" on the Place de la Contrescarpe;
Rabelais is supposed to have favored a cabaret on the square;
Pascal died in a house on the Rue du Cardinal Lemoine just off
the square.

The Rue Mouffetard is bounded on the south by the Jansenist
church of St. Medard. Tourists from outside France seldom
visited the Mouffetard quarter because it led nowhere; none of
the monuments here would be mentioned in a three- or five-day
itinerary. Public transportation facilities are not helpful in this
district of narrow lanes and relatively steep gradings.

But this is the Paris Edith Piaf sang about, where until recently the cafés and the bistros were patently authentic, evoca-
tive of Paris between the wars (because they did indeed date
from that time, and in the present decor). One cannot help liking
the Place de la Contrescarpe and the street popularly known as
"La Mouffe," once one finds them. It was ever a neighborhood
for improvisation, and in the latest generation this has meant an
invasion of café-theaters, restaurants offering exotic foods, inexpensive but modish shops in the Carnaby Street tradition. The
lower part of the street is a food market serving a largely lower-

income group neighborhood of long-time residents. On a Sunday morning, the street vendors and the shoppers contribute to an atmosphere which could not be duplicated in post-World War II Paris.

One might have thought that this lost corner of Paris, lost to all but its modest residents and a few sentimental outsiders, would remain lost. But at a time (in the 1960s) when priority in Paris was being given to fast movement of motor traffic, a plan first prepared in prewar days was revived which would cut a wide avenue across the lower half of the Rue Mouffetard, connecting two existing broader streets, the Rues Jean Calvin and Mirbel. One immediate consequence was the eviction notice served on a makeshift theater (Epée du Bois) which had a small but national reputation for its sponsorship of experimental plays. As it happened, the threat to the theater—the cultural barbarity represented by the threat—served the protest campaign that was to come.

In a city with a weak tradition of voluntary organizational work (although I have noted several remarkable exceptions in this book), in a neighborhood which perhaps had fewer potential leaders than others in more bourgeois sections of the city, a campaign was organized to fight the new road, and not incidentally to call attention to the urgency of protecting the neighborhood in its entirety. Two young psychologists, Pierre and Nicole Boyer, who lived in a building facing Place de la Contrescarpe, resolved to make the city listen to them. In November 1969, they founded an Association for the Protection of the Fifth Arrondissement. (Paris is divided into 20 wards, called *arrondissements;* the 5th includes the Latin Quarter.)

Their first activity, undertaken in collaboration with the Association for the Rights of the Pedestrian, to which I have devoted a separate section of this book, took the form of a campaign against the inconvenience and noise brought to the neighborhood by a rash of new nightclubs which had moved in to exploit the area's inherent charm. The police agreed to close off two nearby streets to evening automobile traffic. And if voluntary action is rare in Paris, success is rarer still. Their victory over nighttime noise allowed the Boyers to recruit 400 members in a further effort to save the neighborhood from destruction by the road builders.

Another veteran campaigner for La Mouffe had been Raph Feigelson, owner of an avant-garde fashion boutique on the street. As president of the Montagne Saint Geneviève Merchants

Association and of a liaison committee of neighborhood defense associations, he lent his impressive public relations skills and his mimeograph to the campaign against the new road. The neighborhood began to get attention in the daily and weekly press. A special issue of a magazine was devoted to Rue Mouffetard. The official *Paris Projet* reported the decision to save and salvage the street.

For La Mouffe was saved, or mainly. A question put to the prefect of Paris by a city councilman brought a formal promise and (six months later) a revised plan which protected the essential. The widening of the roads that would have joined on the street was abandoned. Yet new buildings would go up at either side of the street at the intersection, spelling the definitive closing and eviction of the Théâtre de l'Epée du Bois. The new buildings would respect the alignment and presumably the eclectic style, more picturesque than worthy of mention in histories of architecture, as I have already noted. In addition, a number of pedestrians-only walks would be written into the scheme, adding to the charming interior streets (badly in need of touching up), Passage des Postes and Passage des Patriarches. Yet neither in the drawing up of this plan nor after its release was there any consultation with the defense associations or with inhabitants of the neighborhood, as the former complained in a statement issued by Feigelson's liaison committee in the name of a dozen of them, including l'Association Mouffetard, Mouffetard Mon Quartier, the committee to save the Epée du Bois theater, and several neighborhood tenants' groups.

Without the protests of the Boyers and Feigelson, no one can affirm that the Rue Mouffetard would not have been cut to pieces by automobile progress. "An exceptional urban site was threatened," admitted *Paris Projet*, "if not with disappearance, at least with the loss of its unity, to be regrouped in small enclaves and thus to deteroriate considerably."

The Rue Mouffetard will not become a paradise for its inhabitants. As public improvements are carried out, the site will inevitably attract speculators. The present tenants of virtual slums will be replaced by those who can afford the high-rent studios the promoters will be preparing for them. The defense associations have called attention to this. All we can say now is that the physical site will be preserved, and with that assured, in theory everything else is possible.

3. Protecting Landmarks

There is no longer any need to offer justification for preserving landmarks, whether they be ancient Greek or Roman ruins, a 17th-century mansion, a skyscraper. Human beings identify with their physical surroundings. They seem to live and work better in the proximity of reminders of their heritage, which means that monuments may also be good for productivity. Pride in a landmark helps keep the surrounding area from deteriorating; a monument, in our time at least, can be an antidote to urban blight. The decline of American city centers coincided with their refusal to assimilate the heritage of every earlier generation. While it would be simplistic to blame urban blight on the wanton destruction of downtown landmarks, the two combined have made American cities ever less liveable, places of which we may stand in awe perhaps, but not respect or love. Yet there are people in many parts of the world who love their cities. The result is better care of them, much of it voluntary. So that love of cities should also mean less expenditure of public moneys for their upkeep, fewer taxes.

Still, love of one's past has never sufficed to guarantee protection of these tangible manifestations of it. The traditional British respect for the nation's history did not prevent destruction of priceless monuments from the moment that the Industrial Revolution began to demand such destruction. Even today, newly discovered landmarks, such as archaeological vestiges uncovered during clearing of a renewal site, are covered up again, or dispersed in the name of getting on with progress. Nor does there seem to be a correspondence between the abundance or scarcity of physical evidence of the past and a nation's respect for it. Both Italy, burdened with the palpable remains of well over twenty centuries, and the United States are equally haphazard and pragmatic about protection. We are told by the National Trust for Historic Preservation that in the United States over a quarter of the nation's registered landmarks have been destroyed in the space of forty years, largely due to the financial pressures on owners of these properties, especially in urban areas. Sometimes the possessors of a landmark themselves resist its designation as such, as happened in New York City when the owners of the Woolworth Building opposed the "onerous restrictions" on use of their property brought on by designation under the city's landmark law.

One rule seems to be that nations with traditionally liberal economic policies follow similar laissez-faire attitudes with respect to what has been left to them of the past. Countries with traditionally centralized systems or authoritarian rule are better armed to protect, eventually to restore and preserve, their landmarks. It then often becomes, in the latter group of countries, a matter of the will to use the many instrumentalities at the disposal of the central government, or the availability of funds to subsidize the work.

Often, as noted just above, the British give the impression of being of two minds about their heritage. Monuments are set up only to be knocked down again. To protect themselves against themselves (against their worst nature), the British enact laws to prevent landmark destruction and the blockbusting of old neighborhoods. Much of old London is now under this protection. In fact, the existence of a legal instrument is only a first step: The determining factor is public policy with respect to the salvaging of a particular monument, an ensemble, a city.

To demonstrate that there is nothing automatic about British safeguards, one turns to the case of the city of Bath. Everyone seems to agree that the town center must be saved, but how does one define the limits between old and less old, historic and less historic? A bitter account of the threat to Bath—despite the legislation, despite the widespread demands for preserving the heritage —was published in Britain's *Architectural Review*, which estimated that over 2,000 structures had been torn down since 1950 in what had been a perfect Georgian city. Recognizable monuments, the Circus and the Royal Crescent, were saved, while the surrounding streets which gave the town a setting and an atmosphere, above all a unity, were allowed to disappear. Thus there had been that excellent—and expensive—report to the Ministry of

Housing and Local Government by Colin Buchanan and Associates, *Bath: A Study in Conservation* (1968), which made the revealing point: "We have worked on a sampling basis in the sense that we have restricted our study (as required by our terms of reference, in fact) to a small area of the city, not by any means covering all the facts of historic and archaeological value in Bath." In the same way, as I shall show in a later chapter, have Jerusalem's city authorities concentrated on saving the very oldest parts of the city, but not the environment in which these oldest parts were placed.

By the early 1970s, Bath had become a major issue in the British press, with charges of official vandalism. A writer for *The Times* of London produced an illustrated book on *The Sack of Bath: A Record and an Indictment*.

What the British have, as I have said, is the technique for saving, and the infrastructure through which to carry it out. The Environment Ministry, or whatever it may be called when this is read, is responsible for "the preservation of amenity, the protection of the coast and countryside, the preservation of historic towns and monuments, and the control of air, water and noise pollution." Under the 1967 Civic Amenities Act, local authorities designate sectors of architectural or historical interest as conservation areas, where alterations and new construction are subject to approval. Loans can be made to help owners carry out preservation measures; indeed, they can be obliged to make necessary repairs, under threat of expropriation. Ada Louise Huxtable has pointed out that the key word here is "amenities," involving as it does total environmental excellence, the complete effect of a neighborhood, and not merely an isolated landmark.

Earlier legislation in the United Kingdom included the Ancient Monuments Act of 1913 and the Historic Buildings and Ancient Monuments Act of 1953. A National Trust takes over old buildings for conservation, usually allowing the former owners to continue to reside in them. In 1962, the Local Authorities Historic Buildings Act authorized towns to contribute to landmark maintenance through low- or no-interest loans and grants. Both this legislation and the National Trust Acts provide for visits to the landmarks by the public.

Armed with this battery of laws, a British government or local authority can do much, or nothing. Ruins of an ancient castle found during digging on a building site may be saved, or buried again. Not only ancient castles are involved. In 1973, the Ministry for the Environment earmarked a number of characteristic pub façades in the Covent Garden renewal zone; none can henceforth be altered or destroyed without authorization. Here the determination of the public was clear enough: The old pubs had to be saved, and Britain possessed the appropriate legal instruments to do it.

Belgium is another nation of laissez faire, experimenting with protective legislation, often succeeding nobly in the salvage of a venerable neighborhood, while many others of equally great environmental value are allowed to deteriorate until their turns come for urban renewal. Brussels, like New York City, has been in continual upheaval in our generation. Perhaps more new building has been done, proportionately, in the Belgian capital since the end of World War II. A few areas of obvious architectural interest have been allowed to stand, including one of the most beautiful public places in the world, the Grand'Place encompassing Brussels' city hall. The Grand'Place and the surrounding streets have been officially designated a "sacred island," *îlot sacré,* where building height is severely controlled and existing architecture must be conserved. There is even a city subsidy of 25% of the cost of restoration of façades, which has led to the curious renovation of the Rue de la Montagne: old Flemish gabled exteriors, the houses behind them completely rebuilt; sometimes the façades themselves must be reconstructed in typical 17th- and 18th-century style. The result will not please everyone, but the alternative, applied almost everywhere else in that city, would have been destruction of whatever charm remained.

The improvised character of neighborhood saving in Belgium has stimulated the growth of private conservation groups. They are not made up of elderly citizens of historic bent, as has been the case in some other countries, but of politically oriented architects and concerned citizens. When all the promoters are on one side and the socially inclined forces are on the other, city saving of course takes on the trappings of class struggle. One active movement, the Workshop for Urban Research and Action (ARAU for its French initials), has produced a brief map-guide to "Alternative Brussels" in the hope of arousing opinion to "the steady deterioration of the Brussels conurbation as a place to live in." The guide lists some 65 sites or neighborhoods worthy of saving, which are threatened, deteriorating, or already lost. (Of the Place des Barricades, for example, it notes: "A circular square, the only one of its kind in Brussels; soon to be spoiled by a high-rise building towering over it.") "The impression you will get of Brussels from the trips we propose is probably not very cheerful," ARAU warns in *Alternative Brussels* (which comes with an English-language text). "What you see happening in Brussels could happen to your own city too, unless people get organized to resist the pressures on the city that result from land and property speculation under the capitalist system." ARAU conducts seminars in urbanism and has issued a belligerent urban charter demanding, among other things, the introduction of democracy into city planning. Forty such associations and neighborhood committees are now working together in a movement called Inter-environment, with a charter of its own, the chief demand of which is that the long-awaited city plan for Brussels be drafted in consultation with the people who live in the city. Actually, in a way, democracy of a sort represented by the give and take of interests is what prevails now.

A Belgian law of 1931 calls for conservation of designated monuments and sites; with the growing consciousness of what this has come to mean in other places, the provisions of this act are probably being invoked more often today than they ever were before. Thus a typical royal decree will cite a castle, a town hall, a church, a palace interior, roofs and façades on a square, an ensemble of monuments, or even a farm building, a linden tree, or a rock formation. Differences of opinion are aired in public. A group called "Free the Grand'Place" lobbies for a total ban of automobile traffic on this cobblestone square completely sur-rounded by baroque buildings—an outdoor museum if ever there was one. So far, the city has preferred to listen to local business-men who believe that a ban on traffic, or even on use of the square as a parking lot, would be their ruin.

What is new in Belgium is the official commitment to protect monuments and sites of obvious historical or architectural inter-est, while saving and bringing new life to old neighborhoods with no distinctive landmark. Although lacking appropriate legis-lation or experience in this area, the national government and local authorities have launched a pilot project in the Walloon city of Namur, where a street which had deteriorated was selected for rehabilitation and animation, both to keep the old city alive and to contribute to solving the housing problem. In Brussels itself, residents of several neighborhoods have formed their own preservation groups. One such, in a district of blue collar workers, blocked an expansion of the imposing Palais de Justice which would have wiped out their streets; after the victory the local committee drew up a plan to rehabilitate the neighborhood for its present inhabitants.

West Germany is also a land where vigilantes have taken to the streets to save their landmarks. It happens that the Federal Republic has no law for the protection of historical monuments as such. Where they are saved, it has been the wise decision of city fathers, or the product of give and take between developers and local conservationists. German cities lost both ancient and modern monuments in the massive air raids of World War II. The very wreckage has sometimes served as a dramatic site— purposely, as in Berlin, where the fragments of the old and the new Kaiser Wilhelm Memorial Church towers standing on the main avenue in the city center have become a symbol of the reconstruction of Berlin of significance to Germans and non-Germans alike; accidentally, as during the years before its restoration when the gutted opera house of Frankfurt, a wounded giant, dominated a major traffic intersection of that busy city. In the absence of national legislation, German cities do have the power to preserve what they desire to, to restore, to encompass their most pleasing cityscapes in pedestrian malls.

In Stuttgart, strict observance of a 1971 land use plan has not only permitted preservation and restoration of a large monumental district within the downtown business center, maintaining green areas and even vineyards among the office buildings, but it calls for still more green areas in the future, and these regulations are strictly enforced to make sure that land set aside for parks doesn't evaporate. The vineyards only 200 yards from the railroad terminal are rightly claimed by Stuttgarters to be the most expensive in the world.

But cities also have the power to destroy, so that a town such as Bamberg, with hundreds of recognized landmarks and above all an extraordinary harmony, has generated a citizens committee to save the old city from what many townspeople feel is dangerous renovation.

In Italy, preservation of the townscapes and individual monuments of hundreds of cities and towns, representing what is perhaps the largest collection of noteworthy vestiges existing in a single country, has resulted largely from inertia and poverty.

Protective legislation in Italy never amounted to much; at any rate, modern Italy has a history of violation of city plans and building regulations, so that more laws would not have helped.

Inertia and poverty: Town centers were generally not the objects of speculation prior to the 1960s, for the money to be made in real estate was in the new quarters of major cities, in the central business districts of metropolitan areas whose character had long since been transformed, above all in the peripheral districts where land was cheap to buy and development uncomplicated.

Importantly, in the central city, new uses were found for old buildings out of economic necessity. (This matter of new uses will be treated separately at the close of this chapter.) Or the old uses, especially for religious edifices, city and provincial administrative buildings, were maintained. Italians use the word *palazzi* to refer to large buildings new or old. They were quite willing to make do with the old. Certainly the centuries of successive holders of a family title and the town palace that went with it have much to do with the present look of the better neighborhoods of Italy's old cities.

In recent years, a new concept of historical center, *centro storico,* has crystallized what was prevailing practice. In theory, if not yet in law, the townscapes which have come down to us will not disappear. If they continue to be used as they have been until now, they need not.

Switzerland is another example of a nation with a loose system of preservation laws reminiscent of the situation in the United States. When city fathers wish to save a significant part of their heritage, they can do so. Geneva, the city of banks and time-pieces, cordoned off the heart of the city, site of its town hall, to rehabilitate it for future use, years before it was considered fashionable or wise to do so. By 1915, plans were being made to save the old city. Since 1940, the city building law specifically protects old Geneva from the best intentions of promoters and speculators. In the land of free capital, par excellence, care and cash have been expended not only to conserve the old town but when necessary to renovate it, respecting the character of the site. Building permits are issued only on approval of architectural and landmark commissions; city and government provide grants for restoring building fronts. Street lamps and pavements have been preserved or restored.

Elsewhere in Switzerland, the town of Fribourg possesses one of the largest surviving medieval quarters. To protect it from itself—that is, from its more enterprising citizens—the town council enacted restrictive legislation but also proceeded to bring new life to the area. Fribourg has a citizens organization called Pro Fribourg, with a magazine of its own (6,000 circulation), dedicated to active conservation of the town. The organization takes responsibility for instructing private citizens on how they should —or should not—carry out renovations. Saving Fribourg, its citizens believe, can't be accomplished by city regulations alone; it is everybody's business.

The national traditions of some nations demand a great deal from individual citizens. Joint effort and voluntary restraint created the Netherlands, out of or in spite of the sea, and the people have never forgotten how to submit individual wills (though they are known for their stubbornness) to the common need.

When the priorities were different—protection from the sea, reclamation of land, rebuilding after wartime destruction and enemy occupation—such matters as caring for monuments and conserving old city centers may not have been considered paramount. For a considerable period of contemporary history, however, saving their heritage has been on the minds of Dutchmen. Already in 1918, a governmental Committee for Historic Preservation had been set up to supervise a decade-long census of monuments. A provisional Monuments Act in 1950 was followed by permanent legislation in 1961, providing for grants to private owners to help cover restoration costs. In Amsterdam alone, where some 6,800 of the national total of 40,000 inventoried monuments are found, a separate Preservation Bureau advises on restorations and negotiates the subsidies which the city offers (national government and city each provide some 20% of restoration costs). Through 1971, a total of 1,600 buildings was restored in the city thanks to a combination of city, province, national, and private funds. The oldest preservation group, the Hendrick de Keyser Society (1918), owns 185 landmarks in the Netherlands, 66 of which are in Amsterdam.

Clearly, the most efficient regulation can be expected from countries in which state control is the predominant feature of the system of government and economic life. The world press was prompt to report the unexpected closing of Moscow's Red Square in 1974, and the apparent thoroughness of a restoration for which all of that city's energies seemed to have been marshaled. The project had been kept secret up to the day the boardings went up. Actually, republics throughout the Soviet Union are now engaged in systematic resurrection and restoration of their monumental heritage. As these actions are unlikely to be a result of public interest or debate, it is presumed that authorities on the highest level have decided that tradition is good for the people, or for tourism. The restorations affect cathedrals, convents, and churches, landmarks which had been played down during decades of deliberate antireligious propaganda. Within the walls of the Convent of the Intercession in the old town of Suzdal in the Moscow region, old wooden houses are being built as tourist accommodations; outside the town, a modern tourist complex is to include a new hotel with swimming pool.

Some very successful restorations have been carried out in Eastern Europe. Budapest has recreated an old town which is one of the most attractive and certainly one of the most liveable districts of the Hungarian capital.

The area surrounding Buda Castle was a forest of landmarks. Nearly every house was constructed during the baroque period, in the characteristic elegance of that time. The entire quarter had been destroyed during the recapture of Buda from the Turks by Christian troops in 1686, so that when it was rebuilt during the 18th century it had an extraordinary unity.

Once more, during the winter siege of 1944-45, when German SS troops held the area against the Red Army which by then had surrounded the city, Castle Hill was destroyed; only four buildings remained standing. In the castle itself, ravaged by fire, only a chair leg remained of all its rich furnishings. In 1946, the ruins were subjected to archaeological examination. The baroque palace was rebuilt, starting in 1948, with the help of a commission of art historians and architects brought together by the national and city authorities. In 1947, the reconstruction of the residential buildings in the neighborhood began; it was to continue until the 1950s. In the course of clearing the debris, vestiges of earlier periods were discovered: walls dating back to the Middle Ages, characteristic Gothic stone window frames. In contrast to the reconstruction done in the 18th century, this time the restorers saved the earlier vestiges and used them in the external decor when possible. Indeed, some wholly salvaged Gothic façades were maintained, so that post-World War II Castle Hill looked older than the prewar site.

The visitor who walks these streets now finds it difficult to believe that these are restored and rebuilt houses. Indeed, some are entirely new, though in an appropriate style, for they were put up on vacant lots. The sacrifices demanded by this reconstruction are apparent: Reconstruction after bombing, involving as it does working from fragments, from photographs and drawings, is always more time-consuming and costly than building anew. War-torn Hungary, desperate for housing, nevertheless felt that the re-creation of the city's prewar appearance was necessary, perhaps a matter of survival.

The same story can be told of another country in which state control of the economy allows the concentration of energies and public finances, even for a labor of love. Following the uprising of Warsaw's population in 1944, German troops acting at Hitler's orders systematically razed the city, having divided it into liquidation zones; a team of specialists, including scientific advisers, had produced detailed instructions on the techniques of demolition. The emphasis was apparently placed on destruction of Poland's historical and cultural heritage. Certainly the results on the ground would suggest this, even in the absence of historical proof. Of the 957 landmarks in the city, 782 were demolished, 141 partially destroyed, 34 damaged; there wasn't time to do worse.

When the Nazi troops had gone, the Poles made an early decision to rebuild Warsaw as their capital. At the time (January 1945), not a single building was intact; there was no water, electricity, transportation, or telephone service. Most of the population was gone—dead or refugees. An early priority, despite the immense needs in every sector of building and indeed of economic life as a whole, was reconstruction of the old town, Stare Miasto, stone by stone, façade by façade, beginning in 1949, continuing for four years. Walking through Warsaw's old town now, or along the city's most popular avenue, Nowy Swiat, entirely destroyed in 1944 and reconstructed building by building, after the war, one needs to be told that these buildings are copies.

Clearly, the opportunity to be able to live among its landmarks was of the highest social importance to postwar Poland. How many more housing developments and factories could have been constructed, when they were so desperately needed, by the men and money concentrated on the Stare Miasto project? Landmarks can be a nation's highest priority, political as well as social. Hitler's desire to destroy Poland took the form of demolition of old houses on an old street. Polish determination to show (themselves first of all) that their land was eternal took the form of rebuilding the landmarks. It was a matter at least as urgent as building factories.

France is a nation with a more than average recognition of the role of history, one's art and architectural heritage, in daily life. It is also a nation with a relatively free (though highly centralized) economy. Sometimes the preservation of landmarks comes naturally here; no one would dream of tearing down Notre Dame de Paris or of putting a skyscraper next to the cathedral. (The latter was recently done alongside St. Patrick's in New York City, dwarfing that edifice even more monstrously than before, but it is a frequent practice even in the old cities of Europe, where cathedrals happen to stand in central business districts, and so must abide shapeless modern office buildings as near neighbors.)

The French way is characterized by extraordinary sophistication in the mechanics of monument saving, an incredibly large but overworked bureaucracy. Some of the world's best-produced reports come out of French organizations on territorial planning and regional development. Whole departments deal with the planning of major cities. Only adequate funding lacks for realization of these ideal projects.

It is also a nation where decisions are made at the top and forced downward and onward. The French president began his seven-year term in 1974 with a series of decisions affecting the life of the capital city, whose highest and most powerful officer is appointed by the government (an elected city council having largely advisory functions). Specifically, in a series of breathtaking decisions which earned front-page headlines in the French press, President Valéry Giscard d'Estaing (1) saved a tiny (one-acre) garden and 29 contiguous artists' studios, La Cité Fleurie, from demolition by a promoter desiring to put up a ten-story building, after a three-year fight by its inhabitants and environmentalists to conserve it, and after court decisions going against the conservationists; (2) withdrew national financial help from, hence effectively vetoing, a previously approved expressway which would have run along the left bank of the Seine through Paris's most admired cityscape; (3) ordered that a large plot of ground being prepared in the old Halles central market district for construction of an international trade center be transformed instead into a park. It was not the first time that a chief of state had intervened on environmental and urban matters in Paris, for I have already mentioned two earlier examples, Henri IV and Napoleon III, but President Giscard d'Estaing's predecessors had usually intervened in another direction.

Apart from such spectacular and ad hoc interventions, however, the French make use of an arsenal of protective measures. Some

30,000 landmarks in that country are protected by listing in the Inventaire Supplémentaire des Monuments Historiques, which prevents the owner of the designated property from altering it without approval of the authorities. Of these 30,000, 12,000 benefit from the higher degree of protection represented by classification (*monuments classés*), whose upkeep and restoration may be carried out with governmental financial help. If the owner of a landmark so classified refuses to make urgent and essential repairs, the government, under a 1966 amendment to the original legislation of 1913, can take it over temporarily, have the work done and bill the owner for half. It rarely happens, but sometimes does.

The list of landmarks classified during the year is published in France's *Journal officiel*. It might include the work of a contemporary architect—Le Corbusier's apartment, designed by himself —as well as works of the past and the distant past. Indeed, in 1974 a new state secretary for culture announced that in future an attempt would be made to protect outstanding industrial architecture of the 19th and 20th centuries, such as the work of Tony Garnier, commonly considered too industrial to be of landmark rank, just as the metal-frame Baltard pavilions of Paris's central market were demolished in our own decade despite strong minority sentiment for their preservation.

In a recent year (1973), 90 structures were listed in the *Journal officiel* as landmarks, while another 353 were enrolled in the inventory. Listings in either category are always a matter of necessity rather than a joy, since state funds available for their upkeep are so limited. In 1974, for instance, 32 million francs, some $6.5 million, was available for all 30,000 landmarks. This means that only the most urgent repairs can be carried out, such as roofing and protective fences. It has been estimated that to save the *monuments classés* alone would require 600 million francs a year for five years.

A parallel activity of the government, in the Fine Arts Department until 1957, later in the Ministry of Cultural Affairs, which at the present writing has been replaced by a lower-ranking state secretariat, is a documentation program which, thanks to the utilization of computer technology, will eventually list all of the "artistic wealth" of France: paintings, stained glass, objects of art, as well as architectural landmarks. It is a work for the long haul, though it is hoped that the preliminary work of identification, description, and photographing of each work will be of immediate use to landmark protection agencies. The estimate is that the pre-inventory alone will take about fifteen years (it was launched in 1966), the final Inventaire Général des Monuments et des Richesses Artistiques de la France many decades. To do the work the government has appealed to all its specialized functionaries, to members of learned societies, and to amateur specialists in a geographical region or a field of art.

Still another aspect of the French way is the work of the Caisse Nationale des Monuments Historiques et des Sites, or National Fund for Historic Monuments and Sites, whose main efforts are to go into furnishing and then "animating" landmarks, with sound and light spectacles, temporary exhibitions, the availability of well-informed guides, even tea rooms on the premises, Traveling festivals have been organized, as well as theatrical performances touring the major monuments of the French provinces. The Fund was a co-sponsor of the Festival du Marais, as noted in the previous chapter.

Another achievement of the Fund, fulfilling its "animating" function, is to rent out restored palaces and other appropriate sites for public or private receptions. This has been done at the Château de Maisons in the Paris suburb of Maisons-Lafitte, a building designed by Mansart. A project to come will transform the Orangerie of the Hôtel de Béthune-Sully in the Marais district of Paris into a public hall. The French press has carried advertisements for the Fund's restored Salle St. Louis in the medieval Conciergerie on Paris's Ile de la Cité:

> For your receptions,
> exceptional surroundings
>   Businessmen today have at their disposal,
>   for the success of their receptions,
>   for the satisfaction of their customers,
>   and for the prestige of their companies,
>   the backdrop of several great French historical monuments.
>   Certain examples of our architectural heritage
>   are thus available for the holding of receptions
>   on which they confer a particular excitement.
>   One such is the Salle St. Louis of
>   the Conciergerie in Paris, others are the Château
>   de Maisons at Maisons-Lafitte. . . .
>   the Abbaye de Fontevrault,
>   Mont St. Michel, the château of Pierrefonds
>   and the walled city of Carcassonne.
>   This initiative
> is due to the National
> Fund for Historic Monuments and Sites,
> a public institution under the
> minister of cultural affairs whose essential mission
> is to assure the presentation

of French historic monuments,
their animation, their best integration
into contemporary society.

The guest invited to a reception in the Salle St. Louis might be received by pages in livery holding candles; inside, candlelit tables are set between the vaulted columns. It is indeed a way to keep ancient landmarks in use.

France has also developed the concept of the "protected sector," *secteur sauvegardé,* codified in 1962 legislation. This is the so-called Malraux Law, named for the minister of culture under Charles de Gaulle. The law is designed to conserve entire neighborhoods, such as the medieval district of an old town, but it has also been applied to a considerable area of Paris, including the largest *secteur sauvegardé* to the time of writing, the entire 7th ward (*arrondissement*) of Paris, as well as several areas of Versailles representing a fifth of that township. Once listed under the law, the sector becomes the object of a plan for preservation and rehabilitation (*plan de sauvegarde et de mise en valeur*). To build, to demolish, to transform, or to restore structures within the sector, owners must conform to this plan, while they in turn are eligible for special loans for the work.

It is not as easy as it sounds, or as automatic. In the case of Versailles, it took seven years to reach a decision. The mayor and his council opposed it tenaciously, every step of the way. The result was a negotiated compromise. (In the mayor's opinion, the law contained too many easements for owners of private property.)

By the end of 1974, there were 46 protected sectors in France in Chartres, Avignon, and Arles, but also in major industrial centers such as Lyons and Lille. Either a city or the national government can initiate a classification procedure, while the dimensions of the zone are a matter of negotiation. If, as in the case of Versailles, resistance has come from the possessors of private property, there has also been criticism of national governmental stalling in creating new sectors because of the eventual costs of work undertaken in them. Classification has the effect of annulling all previous urban plans. Restorations, when they take place, are accompanied by subsidized rehabilitation of dwelling units in the protected sector under provisions of a 1970 law setting up an agency for housing improvement, Agence Nationale pour l'Amélioration de l'Habitat (ANAH). At this writing, few of the protected sectors have become operational; the paperwork required before actual work begins is formidable. But the instrument is also impressive.

Even without the new legislation, the French protective arsenal had a number of weapons of earlier vintage with similar aims. A law of 1930 protects sites, which can mean parks, patches of urban greenery, a famous avenue (the Champs-Elysées in Paris), prospects (the tip of the Ile de la Cité in the Seine), a stretch of coast, even an olive grove. The protection of such sites is entrusted to a governmental agency, Bâtiments de France, with delegations in every French *département* (state). Thus, in far off Finistère department, for example—the westernmost point of Brittany and therefore of France—characteristic towns and their centuries-old architecture are protected as ensembles together with outstanding churches and other landmarks. The Bâtiments de France representative for Finistère, headquartered in the oldest part of the town of Quimper, keeps as close a watch as means allow on what kind of construction and destruction goes on in his sector. Any renovation or new building must be approved by the agency's chief architect (the city itself is not involved in the chain of command). The Quimper agency, for example, gives prospective renovators a list of "Principal Errors to Avoid" in building new houses in traditional Breton style. Among the "don'ts": "Any color not adapted to the environment (pure white is often aggressive in a context of greenery or of houses in granite)."

Are Frenchmen, then, natural conservationists? No one who has lived or traveled widely in that country would claim it. The ravages of promoters along the French Riviera have led to the classification of a number of natural sites along that coast, in which sectors there can be no construction without authorization. In fact, the entire Côte d'Azur from Nice to the Italian border has been placed on an *inventaire supplémentaire des sites*, obliging would-be builders to notify the state five months prior to beginning construction. West of Nice, huge building projects for high-rent housing and yachting basins led to a celebrated court case, when promoters of an outsized "marina" on the seacoast near Cannes sued the authors of an angry denunciation in book form, *La Côte d'Azur Assassinée*, and local environmental groups for having led a campaign which "impressed public authorities and influenced the public," leading to suspension of their building permit. The court ruled for the environmentalists. The authors of the tract, said the decision, had helped the state "resist the promoters" and so to ban "skyscrapers which would have destroyed the landscape." "The authors of a book, in employing a polemical style to state a thing essentially true in defense of the nation's biological and esthetic heritage," the decision continued, "while public authorities and elected leaders who are natural defenders of the population kept silent or seemed content with platonic statements, acted in good faith and with the useful purpose of informing the public and the momentarily misled administration."

French people are like everybody else. They try to get around the law, to avoid its restrictions, when they can. Real estate speculation is a major problem in France, an acute one in zones of architectural and historical value. Promoters were not slow to realize the value of a central city site sure to improve steadily. Here, too, the public powers dispose of a number of legal instruments, one being the designation of *zones d'aménagement différé* (ZAD), zones of deferred development, which have the effect of freezing prices. In such sectors, the state reserves the right to prempt land that would otherwise be sold above a given price, to prevent construction on designated property, and to authorize the building up of a property reserve. There are voluminous city plans, land use plans, regulations on building heights, although speculators have made much money from these plans by buying ostensibly restricted land cheap and then obtaining special exemptions, *dérogations,* to the regulations. Great old squares in the cities are spoiled by being dug up for underground parking garages, then permanently scarred with round-the-clock illuminated entrance and exit ramps for the automobiles.

When workers clearing a construction site for Marseilles's new downtown administrative center uncovered a Greek harbor 2,300 years old, many townspeople seemed sorry to hear about it. Archeologists with their finicky precautions were delaying a major urban renewal scheme designed to kindle new prosperity in a long-abandoned district. Founded six centuries before Christ, Marseilles had been a major Greek colony. The rediscovered old harbor had been constructed long before the present "old harbor" (Vieux Port) some hundreds of yards away. Apparently the city hoped to clear away the cumbersome archeological ruins and go on with the digging. A tug of war began, developers and municipal authorities on one side, national cultural officials and archeologists on the other, for every square meter of ground. The result was compromise: The new project for Marseilles's *centre directionnel* would be pursued around the excavation site, although the city managed to slice away 3,000 square meters of it for the garage (and when it discovered still further vestiges on the site of the future garage it got permission to move them). There will still be space for 2,000 automobiles contiguous to the site, 13,000 in the downtown renovation area as a whole. When one has watched

Marseillais fighting for available parking space, one realizes why they regret that the Greeks left any trace at all in their city.

Why should it have been different in Marseilles than anywhere else? Paris had a chance to show the world a segment of its Gallo-Roman heritage when digging for an underground garage directly in front of Notre Dame Cathedral unearthed a city-blockful of ancient ruins, but preferred to pursue the parking project, with partial preservation of the archeological finds in a crypt. Saving the heritage is always an uphill fight, a compromise between private interests and apparent public interest. It often comes to the surface in France, not only because of that country's enormous monumental wealth, but also because of the very abundance of legal instruments available to protect them. Elsewhere, there may be less conflict, but also less protection; it's assumed that owners of private property will win the right to dispose of it against the collectivity.

And although the French traditionally are less effective in voluntary associations, protection of the natural and artistic environment has proved to be an exception to this rule. One of France's largest cities, prosperous and growing, kingpin of industrial development in south-central France, Lyons has saved a strategic center of old neighborhoods extending over 50 acres of the heart of the city. The area was the first to be decreed a protected sector, *secteur sauvegardé*, under the 1962 Malraux Law. But a dozen years earlier, local residents and craftsmen, businessmen in the Chamber of Commerce and Junior Chamber of Commerce, were already working together in an association which can be considered a model of its kind, Renaissance du Vieux Lyon. While the local architectural representative of the national government was carrying out a study of the old district, the volunteers were bringing this city treasure to public notice. The private initiative included an inventory of the entire area, the putting up of signs to indicate landmarks of note, a program of guided visits, even the creation of a revolving fund to make loans available to shopkeepers and artisans wishing to remove unsightly and (now that they realized what they were sitting on) inappropriate storefronts. The committee set up a youth section to do voluntary restorations while contributing to "animation" of the restored neighborhood. It published a booklet containing elementary advice on what to do and not to do in rehabilitating an old house or shop. It opposed the national government's plan for the conservation of the old quarters of Lyons on the grounds that this plan considered them as an isolated entity and not as part of the living city. And the Lyonnais asked why it is always the architects of Paris who draw up the plans, resulting in a leveling and a sameness.

A company was created with a mix of public and private funds, Semirely (Société d'Économie Mixte pour la Restauration du Vieux Lyon), which began to restore a two-acre tract inhabited by 1,200 persons in the center of the landmark district, and at a price considerably lower than comparable new housing put up in the same city by private promoters. Begun with the intention of conserving only one building in three and making public park area out of the rest, the final plan was to save a great deal more, the modest with the elegant. Rents and purchase prices of apartments went up, nevertheless (three to four times, sometimes as much as five or six). This forced the older inhabitants and young or marginal artisans to move. Some of them could have come back, but they preferred to avoid the process of moving into temporary quarters while waiting to return to permanent ones; in any case, the restored tract contained 150 fewer dwelling units. "The operations were considerably slowed by these problems of rehousing," confessed the director of Semirely. "Families always refuse new low-rental housing because of the higher rents and charges, as well as the cost of transport and loss of time due to the greater distances to travel."

But, as I say elsewhere in this book, keeping people in their salvaged neighborhoods almost never happens. It seems to be a logical priority that the neighborhood be saved first and foremost.

Here and there, similar voluntary work has led to the preservation, then the rehabilitation, of other old neighborhoods. I have discussed the Paris Marais experience in the previous chapter. Sometimes it is not a whole neighborhood, but a particular building. The Association of Friends of Rouen's Monuments raised money to purchase an ancient town house slated for demolition in that Norman city, to rehabilitate it as living quarters. Other groups have gone to court to prevent demolitions and destructions, in the name of site protection. It has become a good habit in France of the 1970s. Court action of this kind even blocked the renovation of Paris's Halles district, allowing time for the new French president to go into action, as I indicated earlier in this chapter. There are now about one hundred such defense groups in Paris alone, often ad hoc committees set up to prevent a specific desecration, such as the digging of an underground garage beneath the park alongside Notre Dame Cathedral (it was actually an official project, in addition to the project I described earlier which was carried out, covering up the archeological site directly in front of the cathedral).

If these organizations have seldom succeeded in blocking a major project definitively, such as the destruction of the Baltard pavilions of Les Halles or the planting of a high-rise skyscraper close to the center of old Paris (Tour Maine-Montparnasse), they are doing better every day. They have learned that France's centralized administration, known for its resistance to change from within or from without, is beginning to pay attention to the petitions of organized groups. The latter are asking for protection of sites, but also for guarantees that the sites will continue to live. Naturally, the conservationists also include less imaginative elements. In some instances, they have even opposed the implementation of pedestrian zones, fearing an invasion of night life and of hippies and street vagabonds. But these protection groups are usually found to be controlled by local storekeepers who have not understood the principles of pedestrian zones any more than the traffic administrators do (that is, that they be planned for active downtown districts and not for dead-end streets which had little traffic to begin with).

At their best, French associations have learned to make their voices heard at the top. Sixty of them, grouped in a Committee for a Nature Charter, posed questions to the presidential candidates in France's 1974 elections. During the campaign, they heard representatives of the candidates explain their positions on protection of the natural and man-made environment. The representative of the man who was to become president had to defend his candidate on problems such as Les Halles and the left-bank expressway, for the candidate's allies in the Paris council had voted badly on these issues in the past. I have already said that this encounter was not a wasted effort, for only a short time after his election President Giscard saved what was left of Les Halles, and blocked the expressway.

City-savers public and private are beginning to exploit new opportunities for international cooperation. The role of the international and regional organizations is outlined in the final chapter of this book. In the specific area of protection of landmarks, UNESCO has published a whole library of descriptive and how-to books, notably *The Conservation of Cultural Property* and *Preserving and Restoring Monuments and Historic Buildings,* both containing practical and even technical advice. The Council of Europe has taken a leading role in "the active maintenance of monuments, groups and areas of buildings of historical or artistic interest within the context of regional planning" (title of a resolution adopted by member countries in 1968, following the holding of a series of symposia dealing with practical aspects of landmark protection). While member governments are not legally obligated to follow Council of Europe recommendations, they are now confronted by a formal request that they do what they can, which in the world of bureaucracy means that someone in each national government must be in a position to report to the international community on progress in this area.

The Council of Europe proclaimed 1975 European Architectural Heritage Year, and offered its seventeen member states the help of specialists to study preservation of landmarks as well as the maintenance of the social and economic equilibrium of an old neighborhood (the technical advice to be paid for by the Council).

Among notable private-public efforts is the work of the International Council of Monuments and Sites (ICOMOS), now housed, as I have already noted, in a restored Marais building in Paris. This organization was set up in Venice in 1964 with UNESCO encouragement to promote international cooperation in the preservation of landmarks. It brings together institutions, even public bodies, and concerned individuals, although active members must be qualified specialists in conservation or personnel of national conservation bodies. There is an associate member category for other interested individuals and organizations and for private donors. ICOMOS publishes a semiannual book-length journal containing technical articles and reports in its field, in addition to a series of publications, principally reports of conferences and seminars. A UNESCO-ICOMOS Documentation Center on the Conservation of Monuments and Sites will attempt to assemble and make available the world output of technical material on the subject. The fourth General Assembly of the Council was held in May 1975 in Rotherburg, Germany, on the theme "The Protection of Small Historic Towns."

Civitas Nostra, an international federation of old neighborhood preservation groups, held its tenth anniversary congress in Lyons in 1974 under the aegis of Renaissance du Vieux Lyon. Indeed, the Lyons group has been a major force in Civitas Nostra, which includes eight local organizations, most of which themselves sprang up out of a sudden consciousness of threats to their old neighborhoods. An allied organization with similar goals, Europa Nostra was founded in 1963 and elected as its first president the head of Italia Nostra. It acts by exchanges of information on safeguarding and rehabilitation efforts in member countries, and by making the general public more aware of what the stakes are.

Yet none of these efforts to preserve and refurbish is likely to do as much for the protection of the heritage as the implementation of ways and means to keep a neighborhood, a street, a building, in active use. Such neighborhoods and buildings are not likely to die; they are also less likely to be earmarked for replacement. Rehabilitation should include a plan for occupancy of the building, whether by private tenants and businesses or public, governmental or voluntary institutions. The most effective restorations have been for a purpose. Notable American achievements cited by James Biddle, president of the National Trust for Historic Preservation, are the widely praised Ghiradelli Square in San Francisco, Larimer Square in Denver, and Canal Square on the Georgetown waterfront of Washington, D.C.

In the United Kingdom, the Department of the Environment has published a booklet containing twenty-two case histories of adaptation of historic buildings to legitimate contemporary needs. "The long-term use of a building," it says, "particularly in a commercial area, has to be related to the existing and future economic planning of the area as a whole. If this economic background is sound, it will help to ensure that the costs of immediate repair and future maintenance can be met to an appropriate standard" (*New Life for Old Buildings,* 1971, with "before and after" illustrations).

In some instances, official, voluntary, and other private agencies have undertaken restorations, for residential use, student housing, an office, even a hotel. Or a barn is converted to a private house, a branch library is installed in an ancient corn exchange, an old merchant's house becomes an old people's day center, terraced houses become offices. There is no restriction on the kind of capital or motive that will be applied to conservation and continued use. If a bank or a tradesman is willing to rehabilitate an old building, chances are that the building, and the surrounding buildings, the neighborhood as a whole, will remain vital. In a publication of the Historic Buildings Board of the Greater London Council, *Do You Care About Historic Buildings?,* the general public is informed in direct language and with generous illustrated evidence that their familiar and often deteriorated landmarks may still have a 20th-century use: "Warehouses converted into riverside flats; mansions which are now offices; and countless small houses of another era which are up-to-date homes."

There need be no danger that commercial greed will deface or transform an ancient building requiring remodeling: It is simple enough to enforce restrictions on rehabilitating both exteriors and interiors. In our day, a library of international experience and technical advice is available. And the traveler abroad can see examples of this in a random walk. Having a landmark as company headquarters is now an element of prestige in many places, and it may bring tax deductions and subsidies in the bargain.

4. Planning New Districts

How our cities prepare for inevitable expansion of national population, most of which, as we see, goes to urban areas now, is perhaps the crucial social problem of our time. Every possibility is being tried out: new towns at varying distances from present metropolitan centers to draw off, or head off, population; expansion of existing smaller towns to receive these migrants; satellite towns at the edge of existing cities, or (when major demolition is possible) right smack in their centers.

To determine what to do, how to do it, the advanced industrial nations and their major regional or municipal subdivisions have developed extraordinarily sophisticated planning groups. Perhaps the most notable product of this effort is the *Schema directeur d'aménagement et d'urbanisme de la Région de Paris*, published in 1965 to provide a framework for coping with the problems and future expansion of the entire Paris district. A highly specialized organization, the Institut d'Aménagement et d'Urbanisme de la Région Parisienne (IAURP) continues to produce and publish what must be the most conscientious technical reports and surveys of which any nation disposes, including continuing investigation of the best experiences of other nations' cities. National studies on the same level of competence are the responsibility of DATAR, Délégation à l'Aménagement du Territoire et à l'Action Régionale.

In the United Kingdom, the Greater London Council's continuing survey of the progress of that city and the mountain of literature produced for the Great London Development Plan are remarkable examples of how a civilized people can monitor its day-to-day life while controlling the orientation of its future.

In some areas, planning for the long term has been going on for half a century or more. While these cities are not always among the world's largest, so that there is a tendency to dismiss their efforts as not applicable to the rest of us, in fact their experience is often quite appropriate to the needs of our largest metropolitan areas. In the Netherlands, for example, the practice of compulsory purchase by cities of all available land in surrounding areas, which has made possible orderly expansion without speculation (the land is given to industries or to housing developers in leasehold, with all the restrictions such an arrangement implies), has been dismissed as of only local significance. The Netherlands, after all, is a special case. The land in question came into existence only because of collective efforts at reclamation. Yet Sweden provides another notable example of regular purchase of available land surrounding cities. Here leasehold has been a significant means of controlling land use. Public ownership of land in the Stockholm area allowed the city's planners to proceed with decentralization through satellite towns, designed and built on rational lines precisely when and where the city needed and wanted them (on planned transportation routes, particularly on new subway lines). In Sweden, a town wishing to buy land in advance for future development can obtain government loans for the purpose. When ripe for improvement, the ground is leased or sold to developers.

A city with a plan, and the legislative power to back up that plan, particularly when combined with such a policy as public ownership of land and leasehold, need not fear the future. Density need not explode and then blight the city center; there are incentives for living and working in a new district allowing continuing (and convenient) relations with that center. Sweden's 1947 plan ning law divests private landowners of the right to make sub-divisions for building development. Construction can be carried out only when it is considered to be of public interest, conforming to economic and social as well as sanitary criteria.

None of these tools—a sophisticated planning department, the use of compulsory or voluntary public purchase of land—has proved to be perfect. Whole volumes could be written, and they have been, on the urban problems of Stockholm and of the Dutch cities, for example. The remarkable planning apparatus at the disposal of Paris doesn't prevent enormous and frequent errors. The explanation may be that cities are not very pliable, not very convenient to handle. They represent increments of properties, clashing interests, rising and declining neighborhoods reflected by their values—above all, the conflicting needs and wishes of the majority of a nation's population. London has a highly civilized and disinterested group of planners with a mandate to look at not only the city itself but a vast region of England, but they have to work with the London they find.

Even in those societies believed to be most closely regulated, urban planning reveals many a slip. Thus we learn that in the Soviet Union, where internal movement of citizens is severely controlled by passport, people interfere with the plan. Moscow has attempted to limit its growth, but new inhabitants manage to get there all the same—one million of them over the goal for the 1960s, for example. Those who have the right to be there, but who fear to leave because they won't be allowed to return, stay on after retirement, resulting in an increasingly older population. More recently, the government's decision to please consumers has permitted expansion of the automobile population beyond the planners' desires or the city's population. Moscow has its suburban sprawl.

On the other hand, in a region with little respect for or enforcement of the law, the combination of speculative development and a bankrupt city can threaten catastrophe on a national scale. In a widely publicized report in early 1974, the citizens group Italia Nostra published the findings of a committee of planners, architects, sociologists, and doctors to the effect that living conditions in Rome are worse now than they were in ancient Roman times. Today, the city receives only half the fresh water it had in the time of the Emperor Augustus; there is more typhoid in this one city than in all the United States, insufficient schools and parks, continual violations of zoning by developers and city officials alike. The new districts of Rome are usually unauthorized, let alone unplanned, benefit from few public services. They are virtually designed as new slums.

I must resist the temptation to compile an encyclopedia of desirable urbanism, for this would make one more shelf of volumes for the libraries of specialists and so defeat my original purpose. All I can do in the space of a chapter is to point to notable examples. In a sense, the chapter, then, becomes a table of contents not to existing literature but to the sites themselves, which must be experienced. This is not to say that a collection of relevant documents does not exist for preliminary study and to serve as a guide; one can fill a library with them. Many nations with experiences worth repeating, such as Sweden and the Netherlands, have published technical material in English. If my efforts result in calling attention to a heretofore unknown or insufficiently explained project or to one feature of it, I will feel that I have not wasted my time or the reader's.

The major changes in our cityscape, those that come suddenly, are the result of a deliberate decision of a public or private authority to remake a downtown or peripheral district, replacing what was there before (for seldom was the land vacant). I have elsewhere described the destruction of a city's soul caused by the bulldozing of a neighborhood whose existing buildings might have been remodeled for new uses, given new life. But for one reason or another, such areas do become available. We have any number of theories about garden cities deriving from Ebenezer Howard but not necessarily as logically consistent. Out of them grew the new towns. Following World War II, the British planned a network of fourteen entirely new urban areas as "planned overspill" of the populations of blighted areas of London and Glasgow. A second wave of new towns was launched in the 1960s, and there are now thirty-two in all. The principle of a new town, as opposed to a suburb or a satellite town, is its (hoped-for) autonomy, with new commercial and cultural centers designed to make it unnecessary to turn to the old metropolis, plus a number of utopian features: pedestrian-only central areas so that children walk to school unaccompanied and without danger, or prototype transportation systems, for example. Yet in what is called a third-generation new town, Milton Keynes, being completed 50 miles north of London for 250,000 inhabitants, the original new town pattern which is said to have underestimated the automotive urge of its inhabitants has been overcompensated for, in what one observer called a miniature, planned Los Angeles of a city.

In practice, the new towns are not as desirable or autonomous as the planners hoped they would be. The populations drained toward them are all too homogeneous, of social and economic classes not traditionally involved in many of the cultural activities that made the old city live. The dullness of these new settlements keeps the most dynamic elements away. France is repeating the same experience, but the extent to which it succeeds will depend on how far the new inhabitants will be able to go in thwarting the original intentions of autonomy and isolation. In fact, the French new towns are not as isolated as the planners expected that they would be; unlike the inhabitants of Britain's prototypes, the French population will possess the means—that is, small fast automobiles—to bridge the gap between old Paris and new Evry, Cergy, St. Quentin en Yvelines, Melun-Sénart, Marne la Vallée, in no time.

Indeed, the most successful examples—I speak from the point of view of civilized living, and therefore of making economic and social improvement of the new settlers more likely—do not pretend to autonomy. New districts of German cities are attached to the old ones, which perhaps allows for greater creative freedom and even experimentation. In Hansa, the celebrated in-town district of Berlin, some of the world's great architects were invited to design individual buildings, just as the famous Weissenhof colony in Stuttgart, zoned by Ludwig Mies van der Rohe in 1925, contains houses by Mies himself, as well as by Le Corbusier, Gropius, and other outstanding designers of prewar Germany, the Netherlands, Belgium, and Austria. These prototypes should have set standards for architectural excellence, but unfortunately they had few offspring, in addition to which, many post-World War II garden cities such as the Hamburg suburb of Hohnerkamp were built at a time of great need for housing and inadequate time or funds to allow excessive concern for esthetic considerations.

When a new district is developed by separate architects or promoters, the results can vary greatly as to quality. Paris is committing artistic murder on the banks of the Seine within a few hundred yards of the Eiffel Tower, with a grim office and housing development covering 65 acres called Front de Seine, which might be taken for a particularly horrid product of the early Industrial Revolution were it not for the prevalence of high-rise buildings—sixteen of them built or planned to 1977. The famous and controversial business district just west of Paris called La Défense was better conceived, with access by road and a new express subway line, but somewhere along the way the planning went wild, and unexpected heights were authorized. Certainly the Défense district will be included in all future textbooks on urbanism until the end of the century, but at this writing the results, from the point of view of viability or of architectural excellence, are still very much in dispute.

We know that a good plan, by a good planner, carried out faithfully, may still miss the boat. One of the world's outstanding architects and urban planners, Oscar Niemeyer, designed the new Brazilian capital of Brasilia, a cerebral triumph which in practice became an urban wilderness, a collection of brilliantly designed administrative and commercial buildings without life, actually (in the lack of attention given to ordinary people without motor vehicles) denying the possibility of life. As Rome's EUR district was in its early years, it is a beautiful site to drive through.

The problem must therefore not be looked for in terms of architectural excellence, but in the way a collection of buildings is brought to life. The most futuristic new town of all, Le Vaudreuil between Paris and Rouen, is so perfect in theory that it seems unable to materialize on the ground. Its site was determined scientifically; its transportation systems will be ideal. Experimental in every way, innovating in the introduction of citizens' participation in planning, already the subject of a highly technical and theoretical literature, Le Vaudreuil has been a dream since 1965. The intention is to make of this bare ground a lively city of 100,000 to 150,000 inhabitants by the year 2000. There are still skeptics among those familiar with Le Vaudreuil's plan and progress.

The safest rule is: If you want to design a new district, make sure that you have the support of a traditional urban nucleus, and a need. A new district in a busy metropolitan downtown can hardly go wrong—see the postwar reconstruction of Rotterdam: It is pleasant and inviting, but people would have wanted to go there anyway, would almost have had to. Put it in touch with transportation, so that people are not penalized for using it. Tokyo's new Shinjuku district, centered on a railroad station and the subway network, literally swarms with activity, with several levels beneath the street devoted to transportation and shopping. Purposefully planned nearly 5 miles from the city's business center, it helps to decentralize a city whose population pressures are notorious, brings commercial activity closer to residential areas served by the four railway lines which stop here.

There are, on the other hand, new developments in the heart of our cities which are so ill-conceived, so lacking in communications and human scale, that they seem to their inhabitants leagues away from the living center of things. These developments sometimes claim to derive from Le Corbusier, who advocated concentrations and open areas between the concentrations. Followed without art, even Le Corbusier's principles have led to fearsome wasteland, windswept and crime-ridden.

One of the most interesting of the large-scale experiments is the French effort to create an industrial and harbor complex out of nothing, at Fos-sur-Mer. The scheme has already made Marseilles, whose port authority supervises the Fos complex, Europe's second largest port. Marseilles had been badly hit by the ending of France's colonial era, by the closing of the Suez Canal; its population had been inflated by the influx of repatriated Frenchmen from the North African territories. Fos was built to accommodate the new generation of supertankers of 400,000 tons right up to wharfside. The industrial zone along the strip of coast be-

tween the Rhone Delta and Marseilles covers 18,000 acres, prepared for industries based on oil, natural gas, and steel. Before
pollution could become a problem, Fos invented solutions; anti-
pollution measures were built into the project.

But the Fos development also had to determine means to house
the new population: 12,000 new jobs created up to 1975, an
estimated growth of population for the long term of 500,000 to
600,000. The solution chosen was to utilize urban communities
already existing in this region of about 200 square miles and to
build around them; communities would grow to 50,000 and up to
200,000 persons, separated by distances of 5 to 10 miles and by
natural green belts and existing recreational areas. Five main zones
were mapped out, their future populations set.

What the visitor sees at once at Fos is that a serious attempt is
being made to carry out the plan. The little town of Fos-sur-Mer
exists, with remains of its citadel and 14th-century castle dominat-
ing the Mediterranean coast; it had 2,800 inhabitants in 1972. But
now, all around it, new housing has been integrated into the small
township without destroying its character, although from the top
of the old walls one now sees the oil tankers in the sea, refineries
in the plain. Fos is listed in old books as a small beach resort; on
the other hand, its name comes from a canal built here by the
ancient Romans—Fossae Marianae—between the Rhone and the
Mediterranean.

Nearby, Port de Bouc has ramparts built by Louis XIV's military
architect, Vauban. Miramas has its old walled town, ruins of a
13th-century castle. The old fishing village of Martigues is still
worth an illustration in the Michelin guidebook to Provence
("From the bridge, fine view of the boats with their lively colors . . . A favorite corner for painters"). Corot painted here; many
writers worked here. Martigues is one of the population centers
of the Fos project. With nearby Port de Bouc and St. Mitre, it
had 45,000 inhabitants in 1973 and is being prepared to receive
150,000 (Martigues alone grew from 15,000 inhabitants, according
to a 1958 guidebook, to 28,000 in 1971). Some of the new housing,
in attractive developments or in Levittown-like individual family
units, can already be visited, such as the Paradis St. Roch quarter
whose 1,500 dwelling units form a little village, but with a clear
advantage over the older Mediterranean villages: Motor vehicles
are herded into a corral in the center; the apartment houses and
shopping center surrounding it have their principal entrances on
pedestrians-only walks.

Of course, one sees immediately what is being attempted at Fos: No worker need feel that he has been exiled to an impersonal new town. He is close, usually within walking distance, of a center which has had hundreds of years of life, which has the familiar old look some people seek and need. His family has access to the facilities and amenities which made the town attractive to its original inhabitants for generations, usually over a period of centuries.

Meanwhile, in closer proximity to the industrial zones, "centers of life" have been created with essential administrative and health services, shopping and leisure-time activities, or a hotel with dining facilities for visiting and resident businessmen. Here everything the visitor sees (in 1974) is new. Early in the process of development, construction workers were housed in temporary sites, with dormitories for single men, some accommodations for couples, or in trailer cities. The typical phenomenon of industrial zone shantytowns has not prevailed here, while the planners have had the time to see what the industrial zone is going to turn out to be before pursuing the implantation of permanent housing.

If the Fos development keeps its promise, the new people who will spend their lives here will be able to draw on the resources of several major, and still more ancient population centers. Marseilles itself, directional center of the new zone, is only 25 miles away via express road, the Marseilles airport is closer, and there are plans for still faster communication via a new monorail aerotrain system. Arles, with 46,000 inhabitants, is a well-known tourist attraction of Provence, its residential function enhanced by attractive old streets and famous Roman vestiges. Between Arles and the Fos industrial and harbor complex there is a buffer zone, La Crau, which thanks to this planned growth is to be maintained as breathing space. An earlier type of industrialization would have seen oil-stain urbanization throughout the Crau plain. Hard by, across the Rhone River, the Camargue is France's Wild West.

The urban program of Fos was initiated by a Mission d'Aménagement de l'Etang de Berre (Aménagement=territorial planning; Etang de Berre=the inner lake behind Martigues, separated from the Mediterranean Sea by a strip of land containing the Estaque chain of hills) which had the responsibility for developing the seven townships covered by the scheme. The regional prefect, directly responsible to the central government in Paris, was the supervising officer. Today two separate bodies share responsibility, l'Etablissement Public d'Aménagement des Rives de l'Etang de

Berre, and a Mission Interministérielle pour l'Aménagement de la Région Fos-Etang de Berre, which coordinates national governmental action in the Fos and Arles regions (also under the authority of the prefect). Some fifteen towns between Marseilles and the Rhone also participate in a working committee. Public and private developers coordinate their programs with local townships through a Union des Constructeurs des Rives de l'Etang de Berre which oversees land purchases to prevent speculation, pools land for development, plans short- and long-term housing programs. Independent polls undertaken in 1973 showed that 56% of those questioned in the Fos region felt that the project is a success (28% felt it was not). The affirmatives were even higher within the industrial and port zones. Those who have taken the time to study the dossiers know that all is not perfect at Fos. One report tells of inadequate coordination by the aforementioned planning organisms, of too much authority vested in Paris, of the slow start on housing, of highways planned too close to populated centers; even of use of the Crau plain as a garbage dump by the city, of barracks-like conditions in the temporary workers' housing. There is disappointment that the industrial complex has not absorbed all of the region's unemployed. What you do have in Fos is a first attempt on such a scale at planning and then proceeding to develop a region, with its factories, housing, communications, and all the infrastructure required for each. If it only begins to work in a decade it will still be a notable event.

Planning on a smaller scale is involved in Grenoble, whose essential features are described in a later chapter on culture in that city. The dynamism of Grenoble, its predilection for advanced industry, electronics, and electricity, the presence of a strong university, a nuclear energy plant, and an engineering school, have placed it in the group of ten or fifteen cities which will play the major role in France of the year 2000, a nation which if we credit the futurologists will have the strongest economy in Europe at that time. Grenoble needs to grow and will grow. But its geographical position, in a valley lined with mountains, with two-thirds of its region consisting of slopes preventing the implantation of industry or mechanized agriculture or the construction of housing, makes planning for this growth almost a matter of acrobatics. Grenoble is a Y-shaped basin, which can expand only toward the arms of the Y. Its city plan calls for close coordination with the nearest metropolitan areas, Lyons and St. Etienne. Indeed, they are being considered for planning purposes as a single metropolis of 2.3 million inhabitants, with 4.4 million predicted by the end of the century; a single *schéma d'aménagement* (territorial plan) has been established for the three cities (distance from Grenoble to Lyons, 65 miles; from Grenoble to St. Etienne, 84 miles).

Expansion until the year 2000 will require increased urbanization of Grenoble. The hope is to channel growth, and so to avoid uncontrolled development, the wiping out of farmland, degradation of the natural environment. The present population of Grenoble and the twenty-seven other townships in its agglomeration is 320,000; whatever the regional requirements might become, Grenoble intends to prevent it from exceeding 500,000 in 1985 or 600,000 in the year 2000.

The Grenoble planners have been trying to impose qualitative growth on this inevitable quantitative expansion. One notable example of this has been its creation of a secondary pole of urbanization at Villeneuve de Grenoble-Echirolles, at the southern edge of the older city. Villeneuve was conceived—its name says so—as a city of the future. On its 785 acres, housing is being constructed for 50,000 inhabitants (the goal for 1977). Everything about the new district, or satellite town, has been conceived to allow people to identify with it rather than with the old city of Grenoble: Industrial and office employment are to be available on the site, along with attractive shops. The ground floor of all buildings leads to a pedestrians-only mall, which of course has become almost a sine qua non of cities of the year 2000.

Still, the first group of apartment buildings, in a neighborhood called L'Arlequin, will disappoint advocates of the New City. To save space in this linear city, buildings are high-rise. The land made available thanks to this option includes a 30-acre park, fields for sports, games, small ponds. Despite varying heights and polychrome façades, the buildings themselves, built to the specifications of subsidized low-rent housing, tend to be depressing.

But in this first test, Grenoble wishes to be judged by accessory equipment. A kindergarten and a primary school, a high school doubling as neighborhood community center, welfare and medical offices, gymnasium, all stand on the pedestrian mall. Schools are integrated with street; parents are never far from the classrooms. The next projects are to be a clinic and a swimming pool. A vast shopping center separating Grenoble from the new district will allow access by pedestrian overpasses, and car-less strolling within the shopping area. A widely publicized feature-to-come, so far unknown in France, is a cable television network. Meanwhile, an audiovisual center open to all allows immediate access to television cameras producing neighborhood scenarios on video tape. Parents in an early experiment produced a twenty-minute film which carried their protest against the lack of a nursery; adolescents, a film on the problems created by living in a neighborhood with on-going construction. Villeneuve employs four technicians in its fully-equipped studio located in the high school. Eventually, all residents of Villeneuve will be able to receive studio broadcasts on their sets, a revolution in itself in a country with a national television monopoly.

There is a centralized heating system to serve the entire district, and a pneumatic garbage disposal system.

Undoubtedly, a good deal of breaking in will have to be done before Villeneuve becomes a home for its occupants. Grenoble is close, and not all that big. Halfway between them stands the futuristic Maison de la Culture described in a later chapter, which now uses only part of its potential. In downtown Grenoble itself, city authorities have continued to experiment with recipes for better living, such as the pedestrian area in the town center.

I have already mentioned the Scandinavian experience in this chapter, but I do not intend to explore it in detail, an abundant literature being available in English. It should be clear that the Scandinavian contribution, in my view, is above all in the creation of wholly planned communities on virgin ground. The prototypes, of course, are Farsta and Vällingby on the Stockholm subway line (in opposite directions), with their small-scale pedestrian shopping malls and generous spaces, and the famous Tapiola garden city outside Helsinki, one of the few wholly planned environments whose amenities have made it a place its inhabitants chose to live in. A skeptical reader may object that the abundant land available, the open spaces and the clean air, have made it easy for the Scandinavians, to which I would reply that housing is a problem in Scandinavia as it is everywhere else. Finland suffered extensive damage during its war with the Soviet Union; Tapiola was built in response to a severe housing shortage. Rapid urbanization has kept the Finns on the run; the province containing Helsinki is expecting 90% urbanization by 1990.

Sweden's housing crisis is a long-standing one. That nation has one of the world's highest rates of urbanization. In 1904, Stockholm initiated a policy of systematic purchase of development land at its periphery, so that the city now owns about three-quarters of the land within its territory; as the city spread out, it spread out on its own property. Meanwhile, these cities—even in their downtown business districts—have focused on making urban existence a joy—Copenhagen with its ancient pedestrian streets, Stockholm with its newly designed pedestrian mall, and a carefully restored old town.

5. Suburbs vs. Cities

The decision to escape to the suburbs, leaving urban blight behind us, contributes to the spread of urban blight. As the dream of house-and-garden living develops within us, our concern for the city center, our interest in improving it for ourselves or for other people, grows weaker. Which came first, the desire to get away to our dream home, or the deterioration of city life making suburban life ever more desirable? (Formerly, one moved from country to town and then to suburb. Now in the United States, the route has a shortcut: One moves from country directly to suburb.)

I wrote in the Introduction of the universal trend toward urbanization, with larger and larger percentages of national population nearly everywhere concentrating in cities. Accompanying this trend is inevitably increasing density; but often now this is not so much in the cities themselves as in the districts surrounding them. In regions of almost contiguous metropolitan areas, so that they can be taken as a single entity which Jean Gottmann called Megalopolis—the northeastern seaboard of the United States, the Rhine-Meuse-Scheldt Delta of Europe which includes parts of Belgium, the Netherlands, France, and Germany—we find a pattern for development increasingly spreading to other parts of the world as global population rises. Every country that has made such projections foresees notable rises in the percentage of urbanization in years to come (the popular dates are 1985 and 2000).

In some areas, the pressure of rapid growth, due to mass migration from rural areas (Turin in northern Italy is now known as "Capital of the South"), has been a subject of nationwide alarm—in Spain and Italy, but in tiny Switzerland as well. Americans may not always feel the shift as intensely because, as I have observed, in most American cities urbanization is accompanied by movements from inner cities to suburbs and outward expansion of these suburbs. The most recent gains have apparently been due to movements toward the suburbs from outside the area rather than from the metropolis on which the suburb depends. And despite the phenomenon peculiar to the United States of replacement of inner city population by black immigration, large metropolitan areas have lost population to suburbs. The entire state of New Jersey is now being considered an "urbanized" area, containing 958 persons per square mile, highest density of any American state. In 1970, 58% of Americans lived on 10% of the national territory.

The story is the same in many leading European cities. Paris is losing population thanks to the renovation and replacement of rundown residential districts, the substitution of offices for dwelling units. Statistics show that the city's downtown districts have lost more population than the peripheral ones still within city limits. The same pattern of loss of population in the center and growth in the immediate periphery was noted in Marseilles, France's second city, in the 1960s. City growth has slowed in the United Kingdom, either because of the deliberate governmental policy or spontaneously, and in West Germany and in Switzerland.

What do people want? Deep down inside, they seem to want to get out of their cities now. The Potomac Associates survey *State of the Nation* in 1972 found that more than half of Americans polled would prefer to live in a town, village, or rural area, although only one in three now lives in such regions. Some 70% of black Americans living in cities wish to leave them. According to Herman Kahn, three-quarters of all Americans wish to live in a house with a lot or a farm. One would be able to repeat this kind of popularity contest in most places. In Europe, the French vote with their feet. The major cities empty on weekends, and everyone who can do so has a secondary residence or a room in the family's rural home. By contrast, in an area where city living is particularly new and attractive, Stockholm, a survey made of householders expressing a desire to move found that 60% were looking for an apartment, only 30% wanted a detached or a town house, the remaining 10% preferring an attached house.

The desire to get out of the city coupled with the need to remain close to it has produced our suburbs. When there are enough people needing to be close to the city but unwilling to live in it, or unable to afford to live in it the way they'd like to or need to, the suburbs begin to spread, usually in a manner that catches local authorities unready. Before they or the regional planners can do anything about it, suburban sprawl has begun to take its

toll: incalculable financial burdens on the host community, inadequate public works, a lack of sewers, water, and electricity,
above all chaotic, overcrowded public transport, choked roads;
eventually, the wiping out of the green areas surrounding towns,
for often the suburbs of one city grow out to meet the suburbs
of a neighboring city. In many places, it is good or necessary
politics to give people what they say they want, and both France
and the United States have long encouraged spreading out, single-
family homes, the commuting solution. Paris, like New York, has
moved to the country, with mushrooming of all nearby villages,
unchecked expansion of towns, disappearance of wooded and agricultural land. A photograph in a French daily newspaper advertisement is worth a thousand words here, showing a leafy meadow
in L'Etang la Ville, until very recently a charming rural village
less than an hour from Paris by train or automobile: "On this
spot," the promoter's advertisement proclaims, "we are building a
village." Shopping centers have sprouted all over the European
countryside.

The result, of course, has been that the very qualities sought by
those who move out of the big cities no longer prevail, except in
certain luxury-class suburbs where the very rich are protected by
abundant land and the high cost of settling there, accompanied
by zoning which freezes the present desirable state of affairs.
Everywhere else, suburbs are increasingly disappointing to suburbanites. They are hell on trees and meadows. They spell the end
of agriculture in a wide area surrounding every metropolitan district, complicating and increasing the cost of growing and distribution. Most New Yorkers no longer expect to be able to buy fresh
food, and the same is true for suburban areas of New York or a
growing number of other metropolitan areas coupled with suburbs,
no matter how many fruitless trees and vegetable-less gardens
surround one's home.

In Europe, the phenomenon of secondary residences has led to
the rapid destruction of scenic areas such as the Mediterranean
coasts of France and Spain or the Austrian Alps near popular
resorts. The phenomenon has its parallel in "the ordeal of Martha's
Vineyard" described in Anne Simon's book *No Island is an Island*.
A Belgian planner expressed the fear that if the rural instinct
caught on among his countrymen, all of Belgium would become
a single city, which of course is happening to New Jersey. Moving
the city to the country has, by every report, proved a disaster to
both. Scientists are reminding us that a few green leaves do precious little to absorb surrounding pollution. At the same time, there

is a growing feeling among planners that it does little good to infiltrate country decor into the city. Cities would function more efficiently, and perhaps more attention would be given to their improvement, if we accepted evidence that they are cities, and not countryside. Neither Venice nor Bologna is a garden city; nor are there many gardens in either city. Each accepts its role as urban center, and they are no less liveable or lovable because of that.

In hearing the word suburb an American might think of a middle- to upper-income district of lawns, reasonably well designed and well-kept single family homes, trees in the street. The suburbs on the immediate periphery of major European cities are quite different: They were built for the poor, while the prosperous were able to remain in the better neighborhoods of the inner city or (with increasing frequency) in rehabilitated houses whose value has risen as a consequence. The suburb, in Le Corbusier's *Charter of Athens* as today, does not have the same connotation in Europe or Japan as it does in the United States; the better-off class in Europe is more likely to be found in what we now call an exurb.

That being said, many of the problems are the same, especially when the European or Japanese or American suburbanite must travel to and from the city to work. To meet at least some of these problems, British planners since World War II have experimented with ways to check unplanned expansion and the havoc it creates around metropolitan centers. The green belt concept attempts to draw a line around the city, protecting land between the last suburb and the next authorized building sites. Applied by itself, such a policy leads to greater density within permissible building zones in the city. The new town policy, which gave another direction to expansion, was the next step. (I have discussed it briefly in the previous chapter.)

Many European cities have initiated policies of decentralization in an attempt to encourage desirable activities while moving all the others out to their hinterland. Many of these efforts remain in the experimental stage. Hamburg has been trying to redistribute population and activities to the neighboring provinces; the pressure on Stockholm is to be relieved by transferring governmental employees to the smaller cities while enhancing the attractiveness of these places to the new settlers. Obviously the scale of London's effort is something else again.

What the British have not been able to do is to provide poles of attraction for the people whom the planners wish to remove or to keep out of London, equivalent to those existing in the original metropolitan area. The attempt to lure populations from cities was the subject of a study undertaken in the United States by Peter Goldmark (the inventor of long-playing records, a color television process, and a video recording system). If communications can be improved between large metropolitan areas on one hand and small towns and villages on the other, the belief is that businesses and residents would be tempted to stay in the small towns and villages, thereby taking advantage of the best features of both worlds. A similar experiment is being tried, without its planners being conscious of it, in Grenoble's Villeneuve district (see the previous chapter).

An extensive program to reduce the congestion of big cities and head off further suburban sprawl is taking place in France, where the major demographic and economic fact for nearly two hundred years has been the centralization of political, administrative, and business activities in Paris, so that manufacturers in far-off provinces feel that they must have their head offices in the capital, and the only prestige address for professionals is Paris. It goes without saying that in the arts and letters Paris is the only city in France. Napoleon encouraged centralization in every field—the economy, the arts and sciences, transportation and communications. All of France's railroad networks and major highways converge on Paris like the spokes of a wheel. A famous attack on this system was published in 1947: *Paris et le désert français (Paris and the French Desert)*, by Jean-François Gravier.

In order to break Paris's hold on its hinterland, to irrigate the French "desert," various solutions have been put forth over the years. The one that has finally been adopted involves a system of weights and balances: Smaller cities all over France, called *métropoles d'équilibre*, are to be made more attractive culturally, economically, socially, so as to dissuade inhabitants from running off to Paris, even to lure new people—Parisians included—to these smaller cities; the demographers call them growth poles. France expects its urban population to double by the year 2000. To ensure that other regions and their capitals can become magnets for this new population, they will be assisted in their attempts to offer comparable advantages in research, governmental facilities, education, and culture, but also good and efficient transportation (not only between these growth poles and Paris, but among constituent units of the region itself). When necessary, new residential districts will be developed. Areas already earmarked for the task, grouped into metropolitan clusters, are Lille–Roubaix–Tourcoing in the northeast; Nancy–Metz–Thionville and (separately) Strasbourg, in the east; Lyons–St. Etienne (to which Grenoble has since been added) in the southeast interior; the Marseilles–Aix–Rhône Delta for the Mediterranean; Toulouse for the Pyrenees; Bordeaux and its southwest region; Nantes–St. Nazaire for the west.

Working on each of the *métropoles d'equilibre* is an OREAM—Organisation d'Etudes d'Aménagement de l'Aire Metropolitaine. In a brightly illustrated promotional leaflet, OREAM–Lorraine (for Nancy and Metz and the highly industrial surrounding zone including Thionville, Toul, and Luneville) explained the program:

> Paris weighs a third of France
> For centuries France has made Paris the unique center of all activities. Result: Paris is choking and hampers the development of other regions.
> Will Paris become a monster? Will the other French regions become deserts? To confront this situation we have created
> Eight *métropoles d'equilibre* to serve as a counterweight to Paris. What is a *métropole d'equilibre?*
> The creation of a powerful center of activities, grouping a population sufficiently important to represent a force, offers everyone
> • many and varied jobs
> • the advantages of a big city (wide choice of stores, entertainment, etc.) and everything that makes life easy and agreeable. This will be possible because companies will find everything necessary to their functioning in a modern economy—means of communication, transportation, telephone, telex, etc., and will decide to settle here.
> We don't want to build new Parises in the provinces or to copy Paris's defects and excesses. A metropolis should not monopolize regional life for its own profit and develop to the detriment of other cities.

As idealistic as this plan may sound, it is not a pipe dream. But Paris has always resisted decentralization. Its prefect, although in principle only the mouthpiece and the operating arm of the national government, has in the past blocked efforts to limit growth, arguing that this would condemn 80,000 Parisians to migrate to the provinces each year (which of course is a key objective of the program). The opinion he represents has been appeased by promising Paris a greater international role even as its national role is diminished. Since 1948, in any case, French law has banned conversion of dwelling units into commercial premises in cities of more than 10,000 inhabitants, although of course any visitor to Paris can see the exemptions for himself, so that the housing shortage worsens while office space gluts the market. The rules were tightened in 1972.

Local officials fear that Paris will continue to colonize its provinces (for example, by subsidizing fares on the national railroads in the suburbs of Paris but not in the suburbs of the far-off *métro-*

poles d'equilibre). "Who decides which expenses are of national interest and which are only to satisfy local needs of Paris?" wondered aloud the mayor of Lyons.

One very practical measure has been to move companies out of Paris, by putting a quota on the building of new office buildings, and by negotiating with individual companies to reserve a certain amount of their activity for the provincial capitals. Major national companies such as Crédit Lyonnais (bank), Union des Assurances de Paris, Renault, and C.G.E. (electricity) are involved. According to Jerôme Monod, author of the program as head of the Délégation à l'Aménagement du Territore et à l'Action Régionale, in the period 1955-71 the activation of 2,700 operations of decentralization contributed to the creation of 400,000 jobs outside of Paris.

A complementary program of planned growth poles launched in 1972 affects what the French call *villes moyennes*, medium-sized cities, what we might also call towns. Their populations are in five digits (with one exception); some have as few as 12,000 inhabitants. Forty-seven of them have been earmarked under this scheme. They include Auxerre (population 38,000), Annecy (54,-000), Carcassonne (43,000), Dieppe (29,000), Fécamp (21,000), Nevers (42,000), Orange (17,000), Saumur (31,000), to choose as examples those most likely to be known by non-Frenchmen. In each case, the national government as part of its decentralization policy will negotiate a contract with the city, engaging each party to contribute to financing elements of an infrastructure to make the town more attractive to present and future inhabitants, more viable, more likely to become a magnet. Among the first contracts to be completed were those with Auxerre, to conserve the city centers with parks and pedestrian streets, while increasing the viability of a peripheral boulevard and building facilities for sports; Chambéry (50,000 population), to support a public transport system, create green space, set up an architectural advisory service to help property owners restore houses in the *secteurs sauvegardés;* Rochefort (28,000), to rehabilitate neighborhoods in the town center; Rodez (23,000), for pedestrian streets, café-theaters, art galleries, and cinema houses, restoration of an old neighborhood for crafts, student and tourist lodgings, beautification of the area around the cathedral, street lighting.

By the end of 1974, fifteen contracts were completed between the government and the medium-sized towns. The program has also had its critics, who believe that the pronouncements of the government were made for electoral reasons, the choice of towns is arbitrary, there is an apparent contradiction between the programs of *métropoles d'equilibre* and *villes moyennes*. Yet the announcement of the first completed contracts and the setting up of an operational group to work on the scene with local authorities made the project seem responsible enough. It was pointed out by urbanists that showy solutions weren't enough; to matter, they would have to be accompanied by a reform of local finances, measures against real estate speculation, decentralization of decision-making. Meanwhile the government proceeds to decentralize on other fronts, in areas not necessarily connected with one of the two aforementioned programs: spending of public scientific research funds in cities far from Paris, sending parts of the social security administration out of Paris, drawing up territorial plans for still other regions.

A variation of growth-pole theory is being applied in Britain's East Midlands, where five towns, the largest containing 56,000 inhabitants, are joined in an urban renewal scheme to become a center of attraction, a loosely formed metropolitan area, to serve a district hit by the decline of coal mining. By improving facilities and road structure, creating jobs, renovating the townscape—all are elements of the French programs as well—the district will be able to sustain a population of 333,000 by the end of the century (present population of the five towns is 190,000). Already, an attractive new railroad station with shopping, social, and cultural facilities has been opened to serve the district. *The Times* of London devoted a four-page section to this redevelopment scheme in 1973.

The policies I am describing are designed to remove at least some of the pressures on existing metropolitan areas. If successful and on an appropriate scale, they would represent the difference between more expansion of existing cities, with inevitable suburban sprawl, and a stabilized population. No one suggests that the big cities will by these means cease to be big. Sometimes they too need to be, or to become, poles of attraction, to dissuade inhabitants from deserting them for already impossible suburbs.

Our cities have to be kept alive or be brought back to life. A book with the title *New York is Very Much Alive: A Manpower View* pleads for accommodating population within the city itself, and the official New York Master Plan advocates increased concentration in the central business district. There are signs that federal government policy in the United States will henceforth attach more importance to the health of inner cities while putting a brake on policies which favor suburban bungalow life. The growth of Planned Unit Developments allowing higher densities, business and residential units on the same site, now operative in a number of American cities, is one way back to city living.

Not only can we work in the middle of density, we can often live there, and better ,than elsewhere, providing that we maintain the escape hatch: fast transportation out. The same principle applies in the opposite way to the new districts being built in Europe, suburb-cities such as Sarcelles outside Paris, with a mix of high- and low-rise, shopping and business, and in-town suburbs such as Bijlmermeer in Amsterdam (described in the chapter on Randstad Holland): residents only a few minutes away on foot from fast transportation to the downtown districts of a major metropolis. Jean Gottmann mentions a third possibility, obtainable in Britain: One works in a central city office building close to a railroad station from which, in a short time, one can be whisked not to a suburb but to a genuine rural community. In San Francisco, the Bay Area Rapid Transit network, inaugurated in 1972, is one such attempt to deal with the automobile syndrome which has fostered suburban sprawl. A wide variety of innovative transportation systems are being experimented with both in Europe and Japan, and in the United States too, to help move more people faster. The right mix of transport, by bridging the distance between downtown and everybody's dream house in a remote countryside, could well make suburbs as we know them obsolete. It could at the very least prevent their proliferation.

II. PROBLEM CITIES

6. Venice as a Challenge

Whatever Venice's appeal for tourists—and of course it has been primarily a place to relax, a great urban playground—it exercises quite another attraction, often a passion, on lovers of the city. Indeed, Venice may be the urban space par excellence; it is a city in essence, almost a laboratory culture in which citizens have been planted and forced to thrive. Indeed, the Venetians were planted there: The earliest inhabitants transferred their experience of mainland communities which had grown by increment from crossroads and market places into what we know as the medieval city; they recreated these phenomena consciously as a group of islands.

Lewis Mumford saw Venice not only as a prototype of city planning which its contemporary cities failed to imitate, but as providing examples in urban layout for our own time *(The City in History)*. The ground-breaking report on automobile traffic prepared by Colin Buchanan for the British Ministry of Transport in 1963, *Traffic in Towns*, takes the hint and uses Venice to demonstrate a workable system of physical separation of vehicular and pedestrian movement. Le Corbusier had taken Venice as the model for his theory on the organization of cities. And at a meeting of the International Avisory Committee on Venice at UNESCO headquarters in Paris in 1973, Brazilian Ambassador Carlos Chagas, a member of this panel, said that "Venice is the only laboratory of urbanology that remains to help us solve problems that the future has in store for us"; he found it relevant even for Brazil. "Venice offers an ideal experimental field and a motive to expedite the study of the recycling and use of industrial wastes," added Dr. Roberto Frassetto, at the time the director of the national research institute concerned with the city's hydraulic problems. Reminding participants that a forward-looking American industrialist said that "pollution is business," he suggested internationalization of his laboratory so that the Venetian situation and solutions could be of help to other regions of the world.

If Venice is this laboratory, then we may be able to continue to think of it as the ideal city. What we can make of it we can duplicate elsewhere to revive urban living. Its failures portend failures everywhere.

Venice is also a lesson to us because it is one of the first urban areas whose perilous condition has aroused individuals and organizations in nations thousands of miles away, as well as their incipient world government. The fight to save it was initiated, as will be seen, by citizens of Venice, eventually reached the art and cultural élite outside, then the international organizations, and only later, and reluctantly, Italian authorities on the national and local levels. Here is a case history of what has been done by alarmed individuals to protect an urban environment threatened by nature, by industrial growth, by the greed of developers. While Venice may be almost too good a case history—isn't it stacking the cards to invoke Venice-saving when we are really concerned about Brownsville, Detroit, San Francisco, Montreal, and Quebec? —it may also offer a measure of consolation: If problems as vast and inherent as those of Venice can be dealt with, how can anyone say that we cannot cope with the far simpler problems—in scope, in cost—of our own neighborhoods?

Venice is an historical example as well. As an independent republic it possessed effective city planning, engineering skills, to deal with its peculiar geography (it lost the initiative when it lost its independence). There was a department responsible for navigation in the lagoon and canals of Venice in 1282, and in 1501 a *Magistrato alle Acque*, whose highly structured service functioned as supreme authority for dealing with problems arising from Venice's island position, up to the fall of the republic and beyond; it has a key role to play under the 1973 Special Law.

No one can say that humanity is not competent to deal with such problems all these centuries later.

To begin at the beginning: Venice, as we know it, is a downtown suffering from urban blight. Its wealthy continue to inhabit it, as wealthy New Yorkers do Manhattan Island; and so do the poor, until they can afford to move to newer neighborhoods. White-collar workers and young executives have moved to the suburbs (to the Lido, for example, or to new developments at the edges of the lagoon, more built-up settlements at Mestre, a mainland subdivision within city limits). The decay of Venice runs deeper than it does in any of our modern metropolitan centers, for it is more literal: the decay of rotten piles on which the city is built, the erosion of its stone, disintegration of its foundations and façades. Since many of these structures are palaces and monumental churches sheltering priceless works of art, they have not been torn down, as they would have been under other circumstances. But the art heritage has had one detrimental effect: Rescuing it has demanded all of our attention, all of the resources we wish to give it, at the expense of the attention that should also have been given to social questions, whereas in an American downtown (for example) economic and social interests would have predominated and all the buildings might have come down. The risk is that in our generation the social questions will not be resolved before all the blood has been drained out of a graciously embalmed body. Venice will be a museum, tastefully restored, but no longer a living city.

Many of those who opposed saving Venice the art historians' way had this fate in mind. From afar, this may not be as evident. We knew that industrial interests were lobbying for the development of a third industrial zone, highways into the lagoon, even a subway. We knew that their factories were polluting the atmosphere and that they were letting the city sink further as they pumped water from its subsoil, tampering with the ecology as well as the topography of the lagoon by digging deep-water channels for oil tankers, reclaiming low-lying lands which had served to reduce the effects of tidal flooding. And so the Italian government's Special Law for Venice was to deal first of all with physical Venice: protecting the lagoon, its banks, canals, and bridges, halting the sinking (subsidence) of the city (which may already have been checked, according to recent reports), putting a stop to flooding by narrowing and occasionally closing the entrances to the lagoon from the Adriatic Sea, reducing air and water pollution, the former contributing to the deterioration of buildings and monuments. This law would by no means be exclusive of the private efforts to provide first aid and total restoration of monuments and art treasures which might otherwise disappear before the effects of the long-range program for physical Venice were fully felt: One expert has said that the work might go on for fifty years.

But then one learned that the local Communists had opposed the Special Law on the grounds that any check on expansion of industrial Venice for ecological reasons would reduce employment.

Venice's mayor, far from being an instrument in the hands of reaction, headed a center-left coalition (that is, as a left Christian Democrat he governed with Socialists, Social Democrats, and Republicans), and yet he opposed the Special Law. In recognition of this defection, the new law provided for a minimum of decision-making on the municipal level. Venice is to be saved in spite of itself, or at least in spite of its elected leaders. A key figure in the save-Venice campaign wrote, after passage of the Special Law in April 1973:

> If the funds for saving Venice were given to the city, either they would remain in the bank, as happened—a little out of inefficiency, a little on purpose—with the money [previously] given by the national government, or they would be used to develop the mainland even further, thus for a purpose exactly contrary to that for which they were given. And legally there could be no objection because when one says Venice one means city of Venice, and in the city of Venice it is these industrial centers that are devouring Venice.

Thus the battle between parties and fractions of parties over these two years, a "dagger fight," brought to an end only through the force of national and international public opinion.

It is when one begins to ask questions that the assumptions of ten or fifteen years are shaken. And yet, did it really have to be a matter of either-or? Couldn't the salvation of physical Venice have been carried on concurrently with a social and economic program? There would have to be choices, of course: The subway beneath the lagoon, for example, advocated by those who believe that rapid urban transportation would retain population in the historic center while offering jobs in the industrial periphery, was nevertheless opposed by those fearful for the lagoon's ecology and for the rampant development it implied. If it could be demonstrated that the subway would do permanent damage to Venice's fragile infrastructure, then there should be no subway, of course. If the danger was imaginary, then it was up to the citizens who would continue to live and work there to decide. Surely both sides, assuming there to be no more than two, would agree to state the problem in these terms. But obviously they would not. The contending forces were on parallel courses, with divergent priorities: They had no intention of joining debate. More recently, a similar controversy has been raging over a proposed Munich-Venice super-highway. When I confronted one of the leaders of the fight to preserve Venice, Countess Anna Maria Cicogna Volpi, with the dilemma, she offered an alternative pattern of economic development: Venice as a commercial port rather than a polluting industrial one; recognition of its vocation as a governmental center, capital of its province; the possibility of making the city a headquarters for educational and cultural institutions both Italian and foreign.

The fact is that Venice is three-headed: island Venice, mainland Mestre, industrial Marghera. But: "One no longer says that Mestre and Marghera are the 'industrial suburb' of Venice; one says that Venice is the 'historical center' of Mestre and Marghera," a leader of the Venice campaign wrote recently. There are more people on the mainland than on the islands within city limits, while the political and cultural infrastructure is concentrated in the lagoon: city hall, provincial leadership, opera, libraries, museums. (The inhabitants of Mestre have been demanding an art museum of their own, evidence that they do not consider the world-famous museums across the causeway to be part of their world.) Proponents of the rapid transit system, to run as a subway beneath the lagoon, and then above ground on the mainland, feel that their project would put an end to this three-headed monster, allowing the island city to thrive as a cultural and administrative center, as well as a center for political, financial, and economic decision-making, while pursuing its activities in the crafts and the tourist industry. The new Le Corbusier hospital on the site of the slaughterhouse on island Venice will be an example of a facility of city-wide and even regional utility which the islands will maintain for the larger community.

The subway has been advocated by a committee of private citizens, many of them in fact leading public personalities, such as Mario Ferrari–Aggradi, member of parliament for the district, who has been a cabinet minister responsible for national planning for Venice. Dr. Simona Ganassi Sereni, a Socialist spokesman on city problems, is secretary of this Comitato d'Iniziativa per la Metropolitana Veneta. The committee was founded in June 1967 with the slogan "To save history restore life." As set forth in a pamphlet written by the committee's president, the argument is that a rapid transit line would eliminate the need for a surface road system that could destroy the Venetian landscape. The committee agreed that the priority was to save physical Venice, while Venice's economic health was of equal importance: The "stones of Venice" had to live. The proposed line would link the islands to Padua and Treviso, and to all the industrial, agricultural, and tourist centers between these cities. Venice itself, in the committee's view, would be the administrative capital of all northeast Italy, maritime capital of central Europe. The palaces of Venice would be resuscitated as office buildings.

The committe presentation concluded with an appendix offering the point of view of Italia Nostra's Venice chapter: The interurban transit system, underground in the lagoon, would be acceptable under certain conditions: (1) There would be no danger to Venice's buildings, and a study to ascertain this would have to be carried out more seriously than those undertaken for the deep-water channel at Malamocco or the implantation of the third industrial zone on the mainland. (2) The subway (Metropolitana) must carry railroad-type wagons only and no private vehicles, to obviate the smuggling in of motor-car civilization. (3) Property sales would be frozen, to head off real estate speculation near subway stations. Finally, Italia Nostra recommended the drafting of an alternative economic plan so that the city would not suffer from the immobility of its authorities while a decision was pending on the subway.

In support of its program, this committee for an interurban transit line published a study which reiterates the conviction of its experts that the problems of Venice can be dealt with only on a regional level. The transit system itself is seen as part of an overall plan including the renovation of old Venice and its physical preservation from the waters. As for the physical danger to Venice the subway might represent, the report asserts that vibrations and noise would not be felt or heard above ground either during construction of the line or later under operating conditions. There would be no damage to buildings; on the contrary, construction of the subway would provide opportunities to consolidate their foundations.

The committee did not claim omniscience. Soundings would be necessary along the route of the subway, which route could be plotted only after further studies were undertaken. The same would be true for the choice of construction methods. As for financing the system, options were wide open. There was a bill in parliament concerned with the construction of urban transit systems, in addition to the possibilities within the Special Law. The international prestige of Venice, Padua, and Treviso might make them attractive to foreign financial institutions, and some bankers had already expressed interest. Finally, if less relevant to the problem of Venice's own renaissance, the authors of the survey believe that the realization of an interurban system would represent for

Flood waters overflowing dikes and damaging the Piazza San Marco, Venice, November 4, 1966, focused world attention on the increasing frequency of destructive high tides.

The decay of Venice runs deeper than it does in modern metropolitan centers, for it is more literal: The factories and refineries of the industrial complex at Marghera, on the mainland, are polluting the atmosphere and causing the foundations and façades of old churches and palaces to erode and disintegrate.

Left: A canal in the old ghetto, Venice. The International Fund for Monuments has plans to restore the entire ghetto as a monument of Jewish "culture and courage." *Below:* A Venetian canal being drained in order to reinforce the foundations of nearby houses.

In Amsterdam, about 2,000 buildings, like these in the old Jordaan district, have been restored thanks to a combination of city, province, national, and private funds.

The corner of Vijzelgracht and Prinsengracht, Amsterdam, before and after restoration.

When workers cleaning a construction site for Marseilles's new downtown administrative center discovered a Greek harbor 2,300 years old, developers, municipal authorities, and many townspeople fighting for more parking space hoped to clear away the cumbersome archeological ruins and go on with the digging. The result was compromise: The new project was pursued around the excavation site.

The Jewish quarter of old Jerusalem, destroyed by the Arabs after their takeover in 1948, is being reconstructed. The overall effect is stark and contemporary, yet it is Jerusalem stone and "style."

Near the vast industrial and harbor complex at Fos-sur-Mer, near Marseilles, new housing was integrated around the walls of the ancient citadel without destroying their character, although from the top of the old walls one now sees oil tankers in the sea, refineries in the plain.

Just south of Paris, Emile Aillaud's new village, La Grande Borne, provides subsidized apartments for underprivileged laborers and their families. Some façades are subtle pastels, others blotches of violent color; walls are covered with mosaic portraits of Kafka and Rimbaud. Every such attempt to change the decor of the daily lives of those who can have no alternative to housing-project exile is a blow for humanity.

Public policy has preserved patches of green all over Stuttgart—even hillside vineyards (*opposite*). The winding Neue Weinsteige (New Wine Trail) is one of many scenic streets that lead from the hills down into the city center. Stuttgart's famous Weissenhof colony (*below*), zoned by Ludwig Mies van der Rohe in 1925, contains houses by Mies himself, as well as by Le Corbusier, Gropius, and other outstanding architects. In Bijlmermeer (*above*), a controversial development removed from Amsterdam's center and connected to it by subway, vehicular traffic is routed on a system of elevated roads. Interiors face garden areas and are equipped with hobby rooms, playrooms, nurseries, buffets, meeting halls, study and music rooms.

Conserving old city centers and caring for monuments has been a concern of the Dutch since 1918, when a governmental committee was set up to supervise an inventory. Depicted in black on the map (*above*) of Amsterdam are some 6,800 monuments designated in that city. Many of them may also be seen in the photograph (*below*).

The entire business and commercial center of Cologne is being turned over to pedestrians. Hohe Strasse, one of the two principal shopping streets, is an outstanding example of pedestrian-zone planning.

Outside the new Roman-German Museum, citizens of Cologne, seated in comfortable modern chairs, can partake of refreshments, look across the Domplatz at the soaring cathedral, or, through large glass panels at the front of the museum, examine the famous Roman mosaic displayed inside.

Around the corner from the museum is the Hohe Strasse pedestrian mall (*below*), with benches and potted plants where cars used to park. Munich's downtown pedestrian zone (*above*) contains a Richard Strauss Fountain as well as plantings.

In the past, pedestrians on their way to and from Munich's city hall had to face the rigors of traffic in the Marienplatz (*above*). Today, the square, closed to automobiles, contains planted areas, pleasant seating arrangements, and easy access for pedestrians.

Downtown does not need to mean blighted. Stockholm has found ways to bring more light and air into the city and has declared main streets off limits to private vehicles.

Paris has been losing its beauty, as speculators defile the peculiarly human scale. This structure, the tallest building in Europe, has ruined the intimate skyline of Montparnasse.

Often, new districts of German cities are attached to the old ones or built on the outskirts, as in the case of West Berlin's Hansa district (*above*), for which some of the world's greatest architects designed individual buildings, and Gropius-Stradt (*below*), with its structures of various heights and colors.

Like West Berlin's new districts, Bologna's low-cost public housing developments have been built along the city's periphery. But they are the last of their kind—for Bologna's revolutionary housing plan is predicated on the fact that suburbs are hell for the uprooted people condemned to long, tiring journeys to and from work.

Bologna's miles of arcaded streets are unique. To many Bolognese, a city without arcades doesn't seem a city at all. Plans therefore call for the renovation of such old neighborhoods.

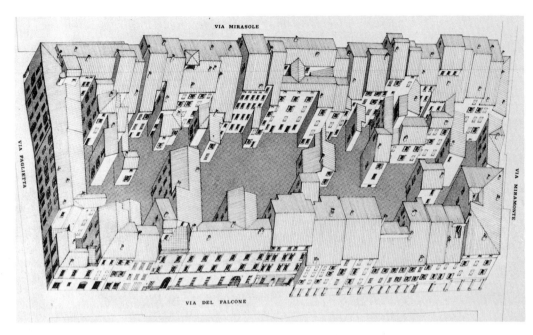

The present inhabitants of Bologna's deteriorated houses are guaranteed that they can remain in the same buildings after renovation and that their rent will be based on income. Meanwhile, they will be housed temporarily in new houses that are being built nearby. The block plans shown here attest to the fact that the new houses will conform to the style prevalent in the old neighborhoods. Soon they will be unrecognizable as new. The elevation (*below*) is of the arcaded street seen in the photograph overleaf.

the urban communities concerned a qualitative jump in their development, greater than the level of development possible for these communities considered individually, making them a stronger element in the national economy.

Professor Ganassi Sereni suggests that one can be a firm supporter of Venice, and an architect as well, while refusing to give priority to the saving of physical Venice, that is, refusing to allow the dissociation of physical and economic regeneration. Physical Venice happens to be the easiest to save. The problem that remains is to define the role of the city, for Venice once did have a role and a function. Dr. Ganassi Sereni has carried out a study commissioned by UNESCO on the economic future of Venice, which she feels has been alienated from its original reason for being: life on the water. The alienation had begun under the Austrian occupation; Austria didn't need Venice as a port and was suspicious of it. During that era, many canals were filled in, more bridges were built, and the use of a wide variety of boats for specific purposes was gradually forgotten. The Italians, when they took over, pursued this policy.

Venice became more interesting to the rest of the Italian nation when new sources of energy began to be exploited. While island Venice was becoming an ever-greater international tourist attraction, port installations were being developed at the other shore of the lagoon, notably the refineries, the industrial zones of Porto Marghera. The next step would have been a highway, and the filling in of more of the shallow water surrounding the old city. To save Venice, development had to be checked. The last significant "improvement" is Tronchetto, a 40-acre island reclaimed from the lagoon just behind the Piazzale Roma automobile zone, to add more parking space and other tourist facilities. Even more important are the 30,000 acres of lagoon surface which over the years have been closed off by private owners; they represent a quarter of the lagoon's total area.

The Special Law of 1973, in architect Ganassi Sereni's view, should have dealt with a larger territory than Venice's historical center, and it should have dealt with the economics of Venice. To save physical Venice without having a thought for what will happen in Venice is to open the gates to spontaneous development, that is, expansion of the tourist sector, which will reduce Venice to the "pathetic" role of manufacturer of nostalgia, comparable to America's Indian reservations. As for renovation, the likelihood is that only large companies and speculators will be able to make use of the borrowing provisions of the Special Law. Either you keep a patient alive with oxygen or you attempt to cure him. The Special Law, in this view, risks being mortal to Venice.

Signora Ganassi and her friends have no easy answer. To an outsider their proposals might even seem contradictory, until it is understood that distinctions are made between polluting industries and others, between activities requiring access to the sea and those which can indeed be decentralized; Venice can be the ruling center of the region without competing with or "humiliating" Padua, Verona, or Treviso.

Local authorities, and the left-wing parties, felt that the saving of Venice, in any case, was the job of local forces, using expropriation as a first step. Instead, the city level was bypassed in the Special Law, and the use of expropriation was excluded. Even the Communists showed excessive respect for private property in the alternative bill they introduced. "The result," Signora Ganassi wrote in an analysis of the draft Special Law published in the April 1972 issue of *Rivista Veneta*, was that "the battle for Venice was waged not only against conservative Venetian forces, against real estate speculation in the historic island center, but against all conservative forces anywhere in Italy who see profit in historic centers, expelling workers and their families."

More recently, the talk of a vast harbor development extending from the Po Delta all the way to Trieste, 60 miles long, covering an area comparable to the port of Rotterdam, provides an even wider context for the economic salvation of the city. Signora Ganassi speaks of the plan for a large port to be built at the mouth of the Po east of Rovigo, now largely an undeveloped area. It is even said that informed political leaders have already bought up land earmarked for development—it was cheap enough—and that this is what makes it easier for them to accept loss of the third industrial zone on the lagoon itself, which in principle has been frozen by the Special Law. Recent statistics, principally the Italian industrial census of 1971, confirm the shifting of economic strength to the Adriatic, whose provinces have had the highest rate of growth in numbers of industrial workers in the nation. The dichotomy is no longer between north and south only, but between east and west. The Veneto, for example, saw a 30% rise in industrial employment in a decade (Piedmont, only 12.27%; Lombardy, 10.2%).

One wonders, all the same, whether the city of Venice, left to itself, would have done very much about saving Venice, physically or economically. What did it accomplish in all these recent years while others were evolving policies on the national, even the international level? One is unlikely to be impressed with the infrastructure seen up close. The local newspaper, which covers the entire province, didn't refer to the passage of the Special Law at all during the week prior to the final vote, reporting the historic act only the day after it happened. Under the circumstances, what kind of public debate can have taken place? Even a casual tourist will have had some contact with the local tourist office, where he will have seen for himself the kinds of functionaries the town breeds (notable for their lack of interest in their city). In the early days of the campaign to save Venice, the city administration hardly made itself heard, being more involved with the development of industrial zones on the mainland where most of its electorate resides and votes. "The extent to which the interests of Venice are taken to heart by its leaders is demonstrated in the choice of industry to which they opened the door—petrochemicals, the most polluting," Venice's editorial protector Indro Montanelli wrote in *Corriere della Sera*. As for the national government, it set up a Venice committee in 1962 that accomplished almost nothing until the 1966 flood. Money was found to dig a deep-water channel for oil tankers highly destructive to the ecology of the lagoon and a potential danger to the water level, but not for a hydraulic model of the lagoon, considered at the time (before the introduction of computer models) as an essential first step in the study of what happens, for example, when one digs a deep-water channel for oil tankers. While the city slept, or defended itself against accusations that it slept, while higher echelons remained indifferent, citizens pursued the campaign, notably with a petition addressed to the president of the Italian Republic after the November 1966 floods: "Thus Venice dies. . . ."

And then a law was passed. Introduced nearly five years after the flood, nine years after formation of the government's first fact-finding committee, it took nearly two more years for a final vote. ("In Italy, two years of struggle to assure the triumph of a good cause is a cheap price to pay," commented Montanelli.) Cynics said that it would be another year before enabling regulations were promulgated, and many years before the financial appropriations began to make themselves felt. Actually, the cynics were this time understating the case.

Before the Special Law was passed in 1973, it was known that low-interest international loans had been arranged; UNESCO's role in the borrowing was said not to be negligible. The bulk of the funds was to be used for water and harbor works, restoration of public buildings, aqueducts and sewers, the former to allow the shutting of artesian wells responsible for lowering the level of the soil, the latter to allow occasional closing of the Adriatic flow by a system of locks yet to be devised. Money was also to be provided for renovation and restoration of landmarks and for water and air purification. At this writing, when not a lira of this money has been allocated or spent, inflation has already made most of the allocations provided for in the Special Law insufficient to carry out these works.

A commission was set up under the law chaired by the president of the regional government (this was a last-minute change under pressure from local authorities, for the chairman was originally to have been the *magistrato delle acque*, Venice's waterworks commissioner). A delegate of UNESCO was included in this commission for the safeguarding of Venice, an unusual provision in any national legislation, since the commission's decisions on urban development were to have the force of law until the adoption of an overall regional plan. Finally, the new law banned pursuit of development of the industrial zones on the mainland side of the lagoon, pending promulgation of the plan. Further encroachments on the lagoon were prohibited.

What was to be the last act in the international campaign to save Venice took place, fittingly enough, in the palatial Scuola Grande di San Giovanni Evangelista, a Gothic-Renaissance jewel painstakingly restored with donations raised by the Venice Committee of the International Fund for Monuments, whose Venice headquarters it is. The occasion was a reception which brought to a close a two-day meeting of private organizations involved in saving the monuments of Venice, with the simultaneous inauguration of a photographic exhibition of the work of the restoration committee in over a dozen different churches and palaces. (UNESCO has also published an illustrated brochure on private restoration efforts in Venice.)

It was also a victory celebration. The press that morning, April 14, 1973, carried the news that the Italian parliament had at last voted the controversial save-Venice bill, the Special Law providing funds for physical Venice, a bill that had been on the desks of the legislators since Easter 1971, where it was delayed by the fall of the government, weak coalition cabinets, and rear-guard resistance by private interests, and also by leftist political parties and by the Venice municipality.

Those attending the reception in the richly decorated rooms graced with paintings by Tintoretto and Tiepolo were leaders of the fight to save Venice; the mood was festive, for the battle seemed to be over. As they took their places in the narrow choir stalls for a concert of medieval music utilizing ancient instruments, one might have thought: But these are Henry James's people, titled Europeans and privileged Americans, incapable of a response to such questions as: What do you do with the buildings you will now be saving? How will you keep ordinary people in Venice, to prevent the city from becoming a museum?

It is easy to feel that one understood the circumstances when one was far from Venice, but on the scene confusion grew rapidly. Here one learned, for example, that in Venice being progressive didn't necessarily mean favoring city-saving: The center-left coalition which governed the city had fought the Special Law, just as the Italian Communist Party voted against it. It was said that the mayor was too permissive, that his team was working hand in glove with financial interests whose designs on the industrial zones were to be kept in check by the new law. The left replied that the conservationists had their own real estate speculation in mind. The latter noted that the mayor, elected by a population whose majority comes from mainland Mestre, gives priority to industrial development over preserving the historic center intact.

For if saving physical Venice is only half the job, conceding the justice or at least the good faith of the dissident position, it would seem to be the essential half. And none could deny that it was inspired and carried to the present stage by private citizens, many of them outside Italy, in a rare example of voluntary activity on an international scale. (The UNESCO effort for the Nile Valley temples had begun on a governmental level, as do most famine relief and earthquake disaster rescue efforts.) Although they never said in so many words that this is what they were doing, the international committees which met under UNESCO's flag were keeping Venice in the spotlight, applying the pressures of influential public opinion to a sovereign nation which was not theirs. The January 1973 meeting of the International Advisory Committee, held at UNESCO's Paris headquarters in the presence of its director general and of the then Italian cabinet minister Ferrari–Aggradi, had, for example, emitted the wish that the Special Law be passed "as rapidly as possible," and then it was passed. But the Committee also called for a continuation of international activity coordinated by UNESCO.

The defenders of Venice, an Italian journalist remarked, are a peculiar kind of international mafia. They are spread through many countries, in a score of private committees. They maintain a tight network of telephone and mail communications, possessing "friends" in the major American and European media. And whenever there is a threat to Venice, great or small, from whatever source, they make it known fast.

Such activity is now being carried out by private citizens in a number of countries through organizations such as the International Fund for Monuments' Venice Committee; Save Venice Inc.; the Italian Art and Archives Rescue Fund of Sir Ashley Clarke; the Venice in Peril Fund of Viscount Norwich; Friends of Venice in Dallas, Texas; the Stichting National Comite Nederland voor de Europese Culturele Samenwerking; the Comité Français pour la Sauvegarde de Venise. They have adopted particular buildings, or parts of them, and after restoration they try to find legitimate uses for them so that they become part of the living tissue of the city.

Before the 1966 flood, Italia Nostra had already undertaken the pilot restoration of a row of modest houses on the Calle Lanza as a demonstration that Venice could be made attractive to young people at the beginning of their careers who would otherwise flee the old city. At present, Venice's population is the oldest in Italy; it is the only city in Italy with a higher death than birth rate; a third of all apartments in Venice, two-thirds on the ground floor, are unfit for habitation.

The Cini Foundation had been working for years on the restoration of Palladio's church and monastery on the Isola San Giorgio just opposite the Piazza San Marco, and utilizes them as its main offices, research library, facilities for seminars, etc. The British Fund, now the Venice in Peril Fund, launched the first complete restoration carried out in Venice, at the Madonna dell'Orto church. A German educational foundation with Federal Republic financing restored the Palazzo Barbarigo on the Grand Canal and now uses it as an Institute of Germanic Studies. Sir Ashley Clarke, secretary general of Europa Nostra, has described some of the other major works in progress: restoration of the Palazzo Labia by the Italian government's television and radio network, for use as its regional headquarters; the rehabilitation of a disaffected Gothic church for use as a laboratory for the restoration of paintings.

The International Fund for Monuments, on a grant from the Edgar Kaufmann Charitable Trust, is cleaning and restoring the thirty-nine huge Tintorettos at the Scuola di San Rocco, one of Venice's principal treasures. The same Fund contributed to the restoration of the Ducal Palace "Golden Stairway," completed in May 1974. Its Chicago chapter raised money to restore the Canton synagogue in the Venetian ghetto and announced a long-range plan to restore the entire ghetto as a monument to Jewish "culture and courage," while Save Venice Inc. has taken responsibility for saving the Levantine synagogue, and an Italian fund for Venice has contributed to the restoration of a third of the ghetto temples. A Committee for the Jewish Historical Center of Venice, directed by Dr. Alberto Mortara in Milan, has since 1971 been in the fore-front of efforts to rescue this long-overlooked old district. (Mean-while, the International Fund for Monuments has published an attractive illustrated book on *Jewish Art Treasures in Venice*.)

The International Fund for Monuments, whose headquarters is in New York, had already been at work on the restoration of 800-year-old churches in Ethiopia and on archaeological research and preservation on mysterious Easter Island. Starting in 1968, the Fund became active in Venice, its first efforts being the façade of the Ca' d'Oro palace museum, and restoration of paint-ings in selected churches. The Fund's Venice Committee held its first meeting in February 1969, its premise being that "engineering problems" were the responsibility of the Italian government, whereas private organizations in collaboration with UNESCO and Italian authorities should and could raise funds for specific restora-tion and preservation activity.

These remarkable works are without doubt essential if com-plementary accompaniments to the engineering for which the Special Law is to provide funds. Indeed, they are the only works that have actually been carried out so far, for up to the middle of 1975 the Special Law had had no practical implementation. In no case could all of the old landmarks of Venice be restored by a public authority, national or international; it would have required a "billion billion billion," as was remarked after the 1966 floods. And when real estate promoters restore old buildings for resale or rental, as they are doing in old Rome, in old Paris, old London, old everywhere, the original tenants are priced out of their neigh-borhoods, driven to what has been called "asylum" on the main-land side of the lagoon, making Venice still less vital, robbing it of its future. This is where restoration becomes a political and a social issue.

That the restoration of palaces for artistic and cultural institu-tions, eventually for public and private companies, was a necessary first step should be easy to understand. Similar activity will have to go on for decades. Every contribution to the national and inter-national action groups is a worthy one, despite the fact that the Italian government continues to tax the spending by these groups (the I.V.A., or added-value tax) and the importation of equipment. The work of the International Advisory Committee, the achievements of the private organizations (seventeen of them participated in the January 1973 UNESCO meeting in Paris), are deserving of the highest praise. And these good men and women themselves demanded, in the recommendations voted at the close of their last meeting, that the preservation and restoration of Venice benefit all categories of the population. They even expressed satisfaction that the Special Law provided for improvement of sanitary conditions in houses in the historic center, "indispensable to improvement of the standard of living."

Yet fairly soon, lines will have to be drawn. It will be considered a corruption of social purpose to restore habitable buildings by turning out the present occupants and making it impossible for them to return. What does the Special Law do about this? It is too early to say, although its opponents expected the worst, that is, that slum clearance will once again signify poor-people clearance, that the historic center will be given over entirely to sterile tourist activities, but this time via a luxury tourist industry, with palaces for the international rich. In recent years, and despite Venice's declining role as a business and industrial center, the price of real estate has skyrocketed, along with rents for even modest apartments: grim confirmation of these fears.

After passage of the Special Law in April 1973, the city of Venice published a plan that divided the island city into a relatively untouchable historical area (Zone A) and all the rest where new building was possible (Zone B). Almost all of the island of Giudecca, for example, except for the façades visible from the center of Venice, was included in Zone B. An indignant press in Italy and abroad warned that Venice was an ensemble, so that no such arbitrary redistricting was conceivable. Fears were expressed that the city's planned renovations in Zone A, the protected zone, would drive out all but the wealthy, throwing back the charges originally made by pro-city forces against the international conservation bodies.

Meanwhile, the failure of the Italian government to carry out any major provisions of the Special Law led to a near-crisis with UNESCO, which virtually threatened to withdraw from the rescue program if the Italians didn't begin to carry out their promises. No money had yet been spent or even allocated by the end of 1974, and decrees to implement the law had not been issued. Rome sent an emissary to a meeting of the international Advisory

Committee held in Venice in July 1974 to promise that the necessary directives would be drafted and that money for urgent works
would be forthcoming. Regional and municipal authorities also
promised cooperation, but in fact the presence of the then-director
general of UNESCO, René Maheu, and of all those worried officials on the Italian side was testimony to the fact that nothing had
been done at all, and everything had become more confused, more
expensive, and dangerous.

Speakers at the July meeting, held in the monastery designed
by Palladio on Isola San Giorgio just opposite Piazza San Marco,
ranged from expressions of diplomatic regret to blunt criticism
of actions or failures to act. The Italian side—one Italian journalist
called them "the defendents"—also had their say. Venice's Mayor
Giorgo Longo insisted that his city must not become a museum
and that the people had to be considered first and foremost. Representatives of the regional government said that they would advance
funds for aqueducts to bring water to the industrial zones, thereby
eliminating the need for the destructive artesian wells (but also,
although they did not say so, encouraging industrial development).
After some polite arm-twisting by René Maheu, the prime minister's spokesman agreed that urgent public works would be initiated
without waiting for an overall territorial plan, which might take
years to draw up. Experts reported some progress in reducing air
pollution, the cause of much of the deterioration of Venice's stone-
work. It was decided to hold a technical meeting jointly sponsored
by UNESCO and the Council of Europe to find remedies for
deterioration of stone and damage caused by air pollution to works
of art.

But if the stones of Venice, inside and out, need to be saved,
what good would that do if the major public works to control the
environment are neglected? Each flood tide that sweeps into the
lagoon from the Adriatic, the effect of a combination of weather
and exceptional daily and lunar tides, destroys more of the vital
underpinnings of the city, deteriorates more façades and base-
ments. The frequency of these high-water days has been increasing annually, because of the gradual rise in average sea levels
and what is called subsidence, Venice's gradual sinking as its
supporting soil and water are pumped out, nearly eight inches so
far in this century, which added to the rise in sea level puts the
water surrounding Venice almost a foot higher than it was at the
turn of the century. No church or palace or private dwelling place
will be safe until the threat of *acqua alta* is vanquished.

The solution seemed to be a system yet to be devised for controlling the entry of the sea through the three existing openings to the Adriatic along the Lido, the strip of shoreline forming an unreliable dike against the high seas. Experts were hesitating among several possibilities: narrowing the width of the three channels so as to reduce the effect of the tides, a method preferred by public works engineers, with simultaneous construction of sewers to reduce water pollution which would be a consequence of reducing tidal flushing, or closing the channels altogether when the sea level reaches emergency proportions. If the first method would reduce the number of high-water days to no more than four a year, members of the Advisory Committee felt that this would provide no protection against extraordinary flooding. They preferred a system of locks that would shut completely, offering absolute protection.

In any case, Dr. Roberto Frassetto, who then headed the government-supported research center in Venice (with headquarters in a palace on the Grand Canal), assured the author in 1974 that the scientific know-how is now definitely available to preserve Venice, as soon as the political will and the funds come into being. (Dr. Frassetto has since left his post, having long since fallen out of favor with the bureaucrats because of his plain speaking.)

The July meeting was told, for example, that a technique was being tried out for raising the level of the city by subterranean injections of materials that solidify instantaneously. It was recommended that a deep-water channel that had been cut through the lagoon for large tankers in the days before Venice-saving was taken seriously be partly refilled. The experts politely reminded the Italian government that on these questions it should be consulting a technical and scientific committee provided for by the Special Law, but never appointed.

At the time of this writing, one could continue to hope that the hesitations and delays, the charges and the countercharges, were no more than reactions to the inevitability of progress: suspicion on the part of conservationists, sour grapes on the part of local forces. And yet there is sad confirmation of fears for the integrity of Venice in the history of renovation of other old cities. In this most spectacular renovation of them all, with the eyes of the world on these islands, isn't there a challenge to see that the worst doesn't happen?

Chronology of the fight to save Venice

March 1956: A law for Venice voted by Italian parliament provides 3 billion lire from the government and a 6-billion-lire loan authorization for city borrowing to restore bridges, foundations of buildings, canals (expires in 1966).

May 1958: Venice section of Italia Nostra founded. In a brochure, it attacks city's draft urban plan which calls for a highway crossing the lagoon. Brochure circulated in Italy and abroad.

May 1959: Government approves the city's urban plan. Italia Nostra submits objections, later (June 1960) issues a manifesto denouncing threats to the city.

March 1961: Italian Public Works Commission modifies Venice plan in line with objections by concerned citizens.

July 1966: A new law voted by parliament authorizes city borrowing for urgent public works (30-billion lire ceiling). In August, funds are voted to allow studies of Venice's needs.

November 4, 1966: Flood waters overflow dikes and damage Venice's center, focusing world attention on the increasing frequency of destructive high tides. Italian government asks UNESCO's assistance in preserving and restoring cultural property endangered by floods both in Venice and in Florence (whose catastrophic flooding occurred at the same time, creating even more damage and eliciting great response both internationally and locally).

March 1967: UNESCO's executive board authorizes a study on how UNESCO can help save Venice, in November of the same year joins with Italy in sponsoring an international meeting for the protection of the cultural property of Florence and Venice.

1968: Preparation of a UNESCO-sponsored inventory of Venetian landmarks lists 392 palaces, 86 churches, and 30 other buildings requiring restoration to cost $73.6 million; the inventory was in part based on material compiled by Italia Nostra.

July 1969: First meeting of International Advisory Committee for Venice sponsored by UNESCO indicates that it is up to Italy to produce a plan to save the city. UNESCO offers technical and moral assistance, while its director general urges a "speedy commitment" by the Italian government.

April 1970: UNESCO's director general sends the Italian government a confidential note recommending that a governmental body on the highest level be responsible for preparing and applying a plan to save Venice, taking into consideration the compatibility of the economic activities of the region and the city's cultural vocation.

September 1970: Second session of the International Advisory Committee.

April 1971: Legislation introduced into Italian parliament to protect Venice from tides and pollution, sinking and deterioration of its buildings (the new Special Law). Passed by the Senate in

December, it is sent to the House, but the fall of the government and dissolution of parliament in February 1972 lays it to rest until after the May 1972 elections.

October 1972: Italian Senate again passes Special Law and sends it to House.

January 1973: Meetings in Paris of International Advisory Committee (third session) and private organizations concerned with safeguarding Venice express hope that Special Law will be passed speedily, urge continuing international cooperation, but also recommend priority to restoration of life in the historic center of the city.

April 1973: Italian parliament at last votes law to authorize borrowing 300 billion lire. UNESCO announces opening of a liaison office in Venice headed by Joseph Martin, deputy director of the National Gallery in Ottawa (the law provides for a UNESCO representative to sit on the commission which will rule on all new development in the Venice region until an overall urban plan is approved).

February 1974: World press reveals a "secret" plan of Venice's city authorities which divides the historic center into Zone A and Zone B; in the latter zone, where there is no ancient construction, new buildings would be authorized provided that they blend into surrounding neighborhoods.

July 1974: In the fourth session of the International Advisory Committee, held in Venice and attended by UNESCO's director general, a further attempt is made to bring international moral pressure to bear on Italian authorities, so that at least the urgent work of rescuing Venice called for in the Special Law can be pursued. Italian government representative promises that the directives for implementation of the law (indirizzi), already a year overdue, will soon be issued.

March 1975: Italian cabinet approves directives for the drawing up of a regional plan for Venice, calling for a halt to polluting industries (but not to development of the third industrial zone for other kinds of industries), and also providing for the installation of flood-control locks at the lagoon entrances, the designing of which is to be the object of an international competition.

7. Rebuilding Jerusalem

One might have thought that the principle of saving historic old sites had entered into our mores, that never again would a surviving historical center be threatened by progress or speculation. And yet, despite lessons learned in hindsight, each new case requires a new battle. After the destruction of so much of what was old, graceful, and on the human scale in American and European cities, one still fights (often against heavy odds) to save Agrigento, Avignon, Bath, and why not Martha's Vineyard? One of the best-known statements of the case of the moderns vs. the ancients was Le Corbusier's *Charter of Athens,* in which the architect and his colleagues of the International Congress of Modern Architecture (CIAM) offered little more than sympathy to those who wished to preserve old cities. At best, they would allow token relics of the historic center to remain in place as an out-of-doors museum, bypassed by the modern city. But the progressive ideas of Le Corbusier seem strangely dated now. Everywhere, people are living in old neighborhoods without being prevented from living modern lives, thinking modern thoughts.

So it is something of a shock to discover that the perennial quarrel of progress vs. preservation has been revived in Jerusalem, of all places. Jerusalem, which if anything is a heritage, a tangible evidence of man's community, the great religions' birthplace and continued cohabitation, is now an involuntary testing ground for coexistence. Worse, the battle lines are ill-defined. All those involved profess to want to save Jerusalem. The question seems to be one of definition. Can you save an historic core while surrounding it with a contemporary city, Le Corbusier's way, if the latter becomes part of the landscape of the former? The conservationists say that you cannot.

And in Jerusalem the quarrel of the ancients and the moderns has been complicated by underlying needs for national identity. If Israelis need to make Jerusalem not only their capital but an Israeli city, how go about it? By bringing in Israelis, evidently; the same thing happened in Constantinople in 1453, for similar reasons. When the Israeli flag went up over a united Jerusalem after the Six-Day War, the city's population was 266,000. It is now 315,000 and is expected to reach half a million by 1985.

But where to house these new people, where put them to work? It is in the logic of urban planning to group them in the center, so as to avoid the desolation of urban sprawl. Developers obviously demand the best sites, the most desirable land, the broadest panoramas. In the name of growth, the city fathers have accepted high-rise buildings which now and presumably until the end of time will dominate a cityscape which had remained essentially the same for most of its constructed history. Until recently, there has been no policy at all for new building, few restrictions on where or how high they could go. An apartment development on French Hill changed the familiar low-lying Jerusalem cityscape for all time; a luxury skyscraper apartment-hotel put up in a central city park stands as a monument to a city without plans; a whole Manhattan skyline of high-rise buildings is on the drawing boards.

A city without plans? But Jerusalem has been planning for years, under the British, under the Jordanian authorities, under the responsibility of the present mayor. A splendid product of the most recent planners, *Planning Jerusalem: The Old City and Its Environs*, doubles as an illustrated album and guide to the historic walled city; it is a history of Jerusalem's people as well as of its architecture. Actually, it was to serve as the public presentation of the official town planning scheme, drawn up within the broad guidelines of Jerusalem's Master Plan of 1968, whose permissive attitude toward new building had disconcerted the eminent architects and art historians of the Jerusalem Committee, itself brought together by Mayor Teddy Kollek as his unofficial advisory board for the preservation of old Jerusalem.

For this is the hitch: *Planning Jerusalem* concerns itself with the Old City and a section of the newer districts immediately to the east—in all, it covers only 10% of the municipal area of Greater Jerusalem. It scarcely deals with, officially ignores, most of the western area of the city. The loving care with which this scheme has been produced cannot compensate for its failure to treat the old walled city as part of the larger entity. What good will it do to preserve the monuments of ten centuries if they can henceforth be seen only by the inhabitants of surrounding skyscrapers?

I had an opportunity for personal observation of the sympathy and concern which Jerusalem's mayor and his staff bring to the planning of their city. But at City Hall one also learns that the urban planning unit can give advice but has no power of decision. The City Council votes, but the national government's District Planning Commission makes the decisions, and the city is only a minority on this committee. While the city has managed to keep most green areas green, new buildings and developments are approved on a day-to-day ad hoc basis. Some of the decisions have startled: Meeting in Jerusalem in June 1973, Mayor Kollek's Jerusalem Committee, which included R. Buckminster Fuller, Isamu Noguchi, Louis I. Kahn, Sir Nikolaus Pevsner, and Professor Bruno Zevi, pronounced its "unqualified condemnation" of high-rise construction already completed, in progress, or in the planning stage. It criticized the machinery of governmental decision-making, pleaded for limits on building height, location, and surface utilized.

But as Dutch architect Jacob Bakema pointed out, not all the recommendations of the Jerusalem Committee were negative. It praised Jerusalem's planning unit, for example, and the Hebrew University campus being built on Mount Scopus, as well as Moshe Safdie's design for a new Western Wall plaza. "At the moment," Bakema said, "I cannot imagine that there is somewhere a government or a town which allows such open criticism by an international committee."

In response to this criticism, the city acted, within its power to do so. The City Council voted in August 1973 to limit building height: to three floors near the Old City walls, eight at the edge of modern Jerusalem, twelve in the business district. But the final decision, again, was in the hands of the District Planning Commission. Mayor Kollek was quoted as hoping that in the meantime the city's action would "influence" those who were building skyscrapers to reduce heights already approved. But the recently completed 17-story hotel, the 24-story office building, the other new scars on the horizon, would not be affected by the law or the hope. And as an example of what the higher echelon may do, the decision of the District Planning Commission to allow construction of a controversial eight-story hotel in the center of the city was not encouraging.

But what could one demand of this good mayor and his harried council? Is it their fault if they are at one and the same time at the head of the first city of the world and of the capital of a new nation which must prove its dynamism? The scheme presented in *Planning Jerusalem* has as its first object "To allow for the development of the area . . . while carefully preserving [the old city's] special character." Many see in the promised "development" a threat to the rest. Indeed, the city's own interim report on the 1968 Master Plan warned against "destruction of existing cultural and landscape assets" but also against the spread of construction to rural areas, that is, suburban sprawl. The mayor has been quoted as preferring high-rise construction to the mushrooming of suburbs.

By far the severest indictment of the present situation is a book in the form of a tract by a former planning officer of the Old City, who acknowledges the help of other members of the city's town planning unit. Arthur Kutcher's *The New Jerusalem: Planning and Politics* is another work of art. The 183 plans and drawings it contains are a recommended introduction to the architecture of Jerusalem and to the problems it has inspired. One of Kutcher's drawings, indeed, by demonstrating how a 23-story hotel would dominate the Old City, was responsible for cancellation of that project. When Jerusalem is subjected to visual analysis by a process of composite skyline diagrams, and this is Kutcher's method, one sees that it is a city of panoramas. A mosaic of cultures, it nevertheless has a visual harmony of its own. New buildings in the planning stage can be inserted into the skyline diagrams to see what effect they will have on the whole. And as it happens, in its June 1973 recommendations, voted after Kutcher's book had gone to the printers, the Jerusalem Committee declared that "planning *must* be studied in three dimensions—the three-dimensional visual character of the site and proposals for architecture and urban design in the landscape must parallel the more analytic studies of land use."

In conversations with Mayor Teddy Kollek and other officials responsible for the planning of Jerusalem, I discovered that the chief problem is not so much a failure of will as a lack of sufficiently powerful urban planning instruments. Jerusalem is hardly a metropolis; its population ranks it with Rochester, New York; Tampa, Florida; and Wichita, Kansas. It is also a very young city, in terms of the history of its present municipal authority. What Jerusalem's planners do can be undone at higher echelons, or something else can be done, so that even when the planners make a wise move it is often no more effective than a hope.

In the spring of 1975, a seminar of planners gathered at the resort beach of Netanya concluded that in matters of urban policy there was many a slip between the cup of decision and the lip of execution. The deputy mayor of Jerusalem, Meron Benevisti, noted that while his planners draw their zoning maps, the real decisions are being made by the national ministries. Jerusalem District Planner Mordechai Sahar added: "We're living with three systems. There's the morning norm, which is that of planners working in their office. There's the afternoon norm, which is that of political considerations. Then there's the norm of budget allocations." According to the Interior Ministry's chief planner Jacob Dash, many planners knew of the Jerusalem Hilton skyscraper, completed in 1975, only when they saw it rising in the air to become West Jerusalem's most prominent landmark.

Later, Deputy Mayor Benevisti confirmed to me that the city was not only a weak sister with respect to the national government, but it did not have the cash to pay compensation when it sought to block the construction of a projected building. He cited as an example an 18-story structure that was to go up near the recently opened Plaza Hotel. For lack of funds, the city "will have to accept it."

Also in the spring of 1975, the *Jerusalem Post* reported that the city could not veto the construction of a glass-front hotel opposite the Old City walls, which would also aggravate conditions at what has been clocked as the city's busiest traffic intersection, Kikar Zahal (formerly Allenby Square), since cancellation of the building permit would require compensation payments to the owners, and "Who'll give us the money for it?"

In an attempt to conclude with a more positive note, I visited the walled Old City with a member of the mayor's staff. A rather small, somewhat rectangular-shaped enclosure located near the center of the greater city, the Old City now has a population of 24,000, largely in depressed housing. The outline town planning scheme calls for thinning it down to 20,000 inhabitants in improved housing. Officially, old Jerusalem is divided into Muslim, Christian, Armenian, and Jewish quarters, but this last had been destroyed by the Arabs after their takeover in 1948. It is being restored now.

The scheme provides housing for 3,500 on the 35 acres of the Jewish quarter within the walls. This re-entry of the Jews into their historic neighborhood plus the thinning out of overall density will obviously reduce the Arab population there, including the 5,000 who lived more or less as squatters in what survived of the Jewish quarter. The plan allows for 10,000 Muslims inside the Old City and new neighborhoods for others outside the walls.

The visitor's shoes are quickly covered with white dust as he walks through the remarkable restoration-reconstruction in progress. The main achievement seems to be the cluster of four Sephardi synagogues dating from the 16th century, restored in a four-year effort after the Six-Day War, now visible and useable. The interiors gutted by the Arab Legion in 1948 have been refurnished, but the overall effect—because of the stone facing—is stark. The adjacent *yeshiva* (religious school) compound surprises by its contemporaneity, yet it is Jerusalem "style" and stone. Attention has been paid to street furniture; the lamps are quite 20th century but seemingly appropriate. The roofline profile is that of any old section of the city. The chief architect of the reconstruction, Shalom Gardi, who worked on the restoration of old Jaffa, explains the guiding principles: respect for the archeological findings discovered during rebuilding, preservation of existing structures of value, new construction where the original buildings were completely destroyed. Archeological digs, for example, sometimes require changes in plans, calling for open space beneath buildings to allow continued access. In one case, the overall layout was revised to keep the excavation open to the sky; it happened to be part of the Old Temple wall.

Not all the plans go down equally well. Louis I. Kahn designed a grandiose synagogue which some felt was out of keeping with the smaller masses of the other buildings of the area, old or new. Arthur Kutcher quotes a member of the Jerusalem Committee as describing the plans for the whole quarter as "fake kitsch."

Homes are being provided for 600 families, to be chosen because they lived in the Old City before 1948, because they fought for Jerusalem. To this one adds some 1,000–1,500 religious-school students. There are, Gardi says, many more people who wish to live here than there will be room for. At the time of my visit, fifty families had already moved in or moved back. Among the amenities they would discover: The quarter was a pedestrian zone. Small vehicles (the plan is for them to be electric) will be used for deliveries, garbage removal, to fight fires. Heights are limited to four stories for dwelling units. It is difficult not to be captivated by the simplicities here. The restraint shown in the reconstructed Jewish Quarter could serve as a model for those playing with the skyline.

8. Tokyo Forever

Is it the beginning of something, or the end? The visitor begins asking questions, of himself first of all, from the moment he arrives in Tokyo. The concentration of population might perhaps be greater somewhere else, he thinks, but surely never more random. There is an old joke about the American farmer with an oil well in his back yard; here in Tokyo, it often turns out to be a giant refinery. Do automobiles pollute the cityscape composed of private homes and shops, Buddhist shrines, and factories? In a traffic jam, it often seems that the primary victims of pollution are the motorists themselves, whose cars emit fewer noxious gases than the surrounding factories do.

This first impression lasts. The Tokyo city plan seems to have been to map out a grid system but then to fill the empty blocks with anything that came to mind. Small patches of more rational urbanism appear here and there, such as a smart business and government district surrounding the Imperial Palace and its parks, or a new office building center with some of the world's finest contemporary buildings in the Marunouchi district adjacent to the central railroad station, and one or two attempts at composing a new district (Shinjuku). Later on, discussion with informed persons suggests that Tokyo's plan is no plan at all, lacking as it does a necessary coordination with other nearby cities and the central government. (City and central government are ruled by opposing political parties, which have drawn up separate and often conflicting plans.) In Tokyo a governor is elected by the twenty-three districts that compose the city, each of which has its own elected mayor. Beyond the jurisdiction of these districts, the situation is said to be far worse. It is a Wild West, according to one old Tokyo hand, with industry coexisting in shocking promiscuity with densely populated residential areas, the dormitory towns which supply the labor force for the Tokyo region.

We are speaking of a nation roughly the size of California, much of it mountainous and therefore unable to serve people and their cities and factories, most of it not even useful for agriculture. Scarce real estate is of course dear; food produced on it is necessarily expensive, and to a degree unknown in the West. Most Japanese are concentrated on one of the islands of their archipelago, Honshu, in a 50-million-inhabitant megalopolis baptized Tokaido, which designates a linear alignment of Japan's largest cities, among them Tokyo, with 11.6 million inhabitants, one of the world's two or three largest cities no matter how boundaries are drawn; Yokohama with 2.1 million, Nagoya with 2 million, Kyoto with 1.4 million, Osaka with 3 million. Tokyo's region contains 30 million inhabitants. Overall, half of Japan's population is concentrated in urban areas covering 2% of the land surface of the nation (one-third is concentrated on only 1% of the land). Density reaches 730 persons to the square mile, one of the highest in the world (with the Netherlands, Belgium, and two other Far Eastern states). An American planner, Byron Hanke, formerly chief of the Land Environment Staff at the U.S. Department of Housing and Urban Development, noted the similarities between the Tokaido region and the United States Atlantic seaboard, although Tokaido's present population is already that of the American megalopolis of the year 2000, with about twice the density. Japan's urbanized areas, reflecting the chronic land shortage, have densities three times higher than those of the United States. Japan's economic intensity, furthermore, represented by the Gross National Product per liveable square mile, is fifteen times that of the United States.

Tokyo is the center of what the Japanese are now calling the National Capital Region, which covers a radius of 60 miles southeast and 90 miles northeast of the metropolitan area. Some 30 million people live here. "Tokyo's problems are magnified by the fact that it has more people, and more industry and commerce, than any other city in the world," a city report on urban renewal states. In Tokyo are to be found head offices of 60% of the nation's largest enterprises, 40% of the financial firms, 30% of the university graduates, 70% of the recognized intelligentsia. The state structure from the beginning of the Meiji era encouraged centralization in Tokyo; from the end of World War II to the present, the population of Tokyo has been increasing at a rate exceeded only by that of its nearest neighboring prefectures, indicating that the metropolitan area has been spreading. The city administration describes the pattern of growth as a doughnut, the center gradually thinning, surrounding areas becoming more dense. Between the beginning and the end of the 1960s, residential construction within a 12-mile radius of Tokyo's central railroad station diminished, while it increased beyond this radius.

The result of all this concentration? Certainly more production, perhaps more efficiency. There is simply nothing to do in the National Capital Region other than to work; to travel to work and then home again. What seems like fanatical dedication to one's business or firm may actually be that, but it is also the only course of behavior available. Home life is represented by apartments too small, an urban environment not conduicive to leisure-time activities, hardly any grass, few public parks. Many compete for little. Liberal resort to abortion (but so far not to contraceptive pills, outlawed except by medical prescription) has kept the birth rate down. One would guess that the sense of discipline and the promiscuity of family life are also factors. The overall population will rise to 130 million or more by the year 2000, but Japanese are more worried about declining population and the effect an aging labor force will have on the economy. (UN figures, from "World Population Prospects as Assessed in 1968," see the average annual rate of increase declining from the present 1.2% to 0.6% at the end of the century.)

In a public opinion survey carried out in October 1973 by the Tokyo metropolitan government, citizens listed among the merits of urban life as they knew it the variety of jobs available, the ability to be informed, the liveliness. But almost all (90% or more) complained of heavy traffic and environmental pollution, the scarcity of greenery and parks, high prices and poor housing, commuting problems (80%). On balance, 47% felt that urban life had more drawbacks than advantages, only 13% felt the contrary, and 34% were undecided. Earlier surveys summarized in Tokyo's daily *Asahi Shimbun* show that Tokyo's citizens complain of houses being too old or too small, of inner-city skyscrapers robbing them of sunlight, and of the unhappy alternative of a two-hour commuting train ride without a seat, twice a day. The lack of sewers, even of adequate garbage disposal and plumbing—58% of Tokyo still lacks flush toilets—is an unexpected but very real problem in an apparently modern city. The ever-present threat of fire to remaining wooden houses, and of earthquake to the rest, is never far from the minds of these city people under virtual siege.

The Japanese experience—one feels safe in saying Japanese for Tokaido or even Tokyo—is without doubt wholly dominated by considerations of space. The Japanese have been victims of their own success in concentrating population, in devising ever more efficient uses of their land for maximum economic return. It is as if they were scientists seeking to miniaturize equipment for use in the tight confines of space vehicles. Just as they are famous for the cultivation of dwarf trees, the Japanese have applied themselves to the cultivation of their own miniature lives in cities. Every public policy that can be identified as such tends to encourage intensive use. Thus, the acquisition of land for development is facilitated by the tax structure, by the publicity given to land available for purchase, by public participation in renewal projects. As a consequence, the forms taken by Tokyo's dense urban tissue are legendary: houses and apartments shared by entire families, subways designed for rush hours, with the famous muscular attendants stationed on platforms to push more people into trains. Everything that can be done to accommodate more people in the same space, or at different times, is attempted. Health standards are rigid, so that Japan is an Asian city without Asian diseases, despite the prevalence of open sewers. One is aware that more thought has been given to the daily problems of city living than is given in other world cities even older than Tokyo.

Even in the lesser details. Garages in new buildings are equipped with traffic lights and audible signals to warn and stop pedestrians when an automobile is about to emerge on to the street. The major subway stations are veritable underground cities with several levels, providing pedestrian alternatives below street level over considerable distances. The visitor strolling in the central business district was surprised to see people dropping from an office building through hoselike chutes. They were testing a means of escape from their high-rise, an example of planning for big-city catastrophe. Japanese architects devised means to build earthquake-resistant skyscrapers before they began to put them up in Tokyo. A visitor from America or Britain will constantly feel out-of-date in this city built to accommodate more and more people.

He will ride the monorail, just like any rubber-necking tourist. It is not an amusement park attraction here, but the surest means to get from Tokyo's Haneda Airport into the city, emerging from a tunnel under the runways, sliding past factories of an industrial zone, following a waterway, swooping under a bridge, paralleling elevated highways with their slow-moving traffic.

For intercity transport between metropolitan areas of the Tokaido alignment, the Japanese invented the Shinkansen system, with the world's fastest trains to link Tokyo with Osaka 320 miles away; the very fastest of these trains—which stop only at Nagoya, Kyoto, and Osaka, Japan's second largest city—move at maximum commercial speeds of 131 miles per hour. In 1975, a 240-mile extension was opened to Japan's southernmost island, Kyushu, with new trains clocking 150 miles per hour. These "bullet trains" are for businessmen, although including regular-fare cars utilized by everybody else. They are air-conditioned, with interior doors opening automatically; telephone service is available and (judging from the calls over the loudspeaker system to passengers) heavily used. What makes the Shinkansen trains a practical and universal means of transportation between the cities of Japan's megalopolis is the frequency of their service, with one leaving every twenty minutes from the special track in Tokyo's central station. (Platforms are marked to indicate the precise position of entrance doors, to allow queuing and fast loading.) An observer stationed anywhere along the line can see these long (sixteen-car) streamlined expresses racing by almost with the frequency of an intracity subway system.

If the density of Tokaido is attenuated by the discipline that has already been described in this chapter, and the movement of persons in and out of places with the dance-step precision of the Radio City Music Hall company, it is also being taken into account in urban planning. Thus, a new garbage incinerating plant for Tokyo, with a capacity of 1,600 tons of waste a day, was installed in Tokyo's Koto ward on reclaimed land known as Yume-no-Shima, Dream Island. But it is a clean plant, so that most of the ground surrounding it remains a green area. According to the *Asahi Evening News,* the city government will build, adjacent to the incinerator, a home for the aged and a rehabilitation center for the physically handicapped, while a short distance away there are to be a marine park, a gymnasium, a sports field, a hothouse for tropical plants, and a heated swimming pool (making use of the heat from the incinerator). Tokyo will indeed have its Dream Island, but it must coexist with Tokyo, the ultimate urban region.

Another way to attack the problem is to move people out of Tokyo and Tokaido, or to stop them from coming. That is being approached in two ways: breaking Tokyo into smaller and more manageable pieces, and then rethinking the entire Japanese land mass for its present and future inhabitants. The Tokyo metropolitan government itself has a plan called "Program to Create Open Space and Blue Sky in Tokyo," inaugurated in 1971 for the purpose of giving priority to urban amenities over industrial efficiency.

The central government's laissez-faire Liberal Democratic majority is too committed to the latter, in the opinion of the Socialist forces who run the city (and indeed who run all of Japan's big cities). The city claims that its own plan "represents a 180-degree turn in values from a capitalist to a popular base. It is the people—not its business and finance—that gives a city its heartbeat." In an effort to reduce the concentration of political, economic, and cultural activity in Tokyo, the metropolitan government program includes the building of a cluster of new towns in the Tama district to take the pressure off Tokyo: Business activity would be concentrated in Tokyo's center, the residential function in the Tama cities, in what Tokyo planners call a bipolar concept. There would be urban renewal of Tokyo's depressed eastern wards, increasing the capability of Shinjuku and other secondary downtowns to relieve pressures on the central business district, and general improvement of Tokyo's downtown environment, making use of reclaimed land in Tokyo Bay. But the Tokyo program requires a considerable degree of regional cooperation, for Tokyo cannot solve such problems as water supply from within its territorial limits, or relocate government offices, industry, or educational institutions outside the city without assistance from the rest of Japan.

Brakes would be put on industry under the city's program, while the towns in the Tama area would not only provide homes for 1.5 million of the city's population in a greener setting, but improve access (and reduce travel time) to jobs. Tama New Town itself was built for 410,000 persons on 7,400 acres, representing a density of 337 persons per acre in a "natural" and pollution-free landscape. The eastern section of the city earmarked for renewal is considered particularly vulnerable to earthquake damage, and here anti-disaster bases (streets of fireproof high-rise buildings with a total capacity of 1.5 million refugees) are being designed.

In the same spirit, the city is opposing a mammoth highway project for Tokyo Bay, again in the interest of priority to the needs of residents and downplaying development of industry within the city; the bay area, in the view of the metropolitan government, has gone as far as it can go.

An example of new neighborhood development for higher densities with increased amenities is Shinjuku, traditional entertainment district, although less known to foreigners than more central Ginza. Here Tokyo's three tallest skyscrapers are located, the Mitsui, the Keio Plaza, the Shinjuku Sumitomo buildings. (Renovation of the district was discussed in an earlier chapter.) The first renewal project under the Urban Redevelopment Law was completed in the Bunkyo ward in the summer of 1974, designed to improve living conditions in a slum area known as Edogawa-bashi, consisting of dingy row houses and rundown shops. In their place rose a twelve-story building with a third-floor roof garden and a basement floor linked to a new subway under construction. More remarkable: The occupants of the building will be former residents of the area, together with others who earned the right to move in by winning a lottery. A new law allows authorities to initiate a renewal project only after receiving the consent of at least two-thirds of the present occupants. According to *Asahi Shimbun*, these tenants formed a renewal association with a public corporation; work was financed by the corporation and the city (50% of whose subsidy came from the national government). Not only was use of available land increased and more decent living and commercial space provided, but residents were left where they apparently wished or needed to be. This was a small-scale effort, very much a prototype, now being visited by planners from other Japanese cities. But it is also based on law, new law, and therefore indicates the direction a good deal of future development of Tokyo may take. (Still, a major criticism of planning for density is that the city does not always plan for the increased pressures on available transportation, or on schools and other services.)

Other improvements for Tokyo will be in the direction of transportation. Studies are under way for the building of new monorail lines as the fastest, safest, and least polluting interurban system, and cheaper than subways. It is estimated that a municipal monorail system with 49 stations and four-car trains, operated at average intervals of four to five minutes, could carry 750,000 passengers a day (the existing monorail from airport to town runs at fifteen-minute intervals).

A more famous solution to the problems of Tokaido density is the Tanaka plan, "Proposals for Remodeling the Japanese Archipelago" (published in book form in English as *Building a New Japan*). Conceived by Kakuei Tanaka before he attained the position of prime minister of Japan, inspired by his own origins in the distant province where forest and mountain remain unspoiled, where peasants farm the land and the air is pure, the plan in essence moves industry, and people, to available land far from crowded Honshu Island. The receiving territories are now insufficiently developed; much of their able working force now migrates to Tokaido after the local harvest to supply needed and cheap labor for Japan's factories. "Public opinion calls for the simultaneous solution of overcrowding and underpopulation to live in comfort in a beautiful land of affluence and security," Tanaka wrote in the preface to his plan.

> Disparity between urban and rural areas, between the prosperous Pacific coast and the stagnating Japan Sea coast, can surely be eliminated by using levers such as relocating industries, making them more knowledge-intensive, constructing super-express railways and trunk expressways throughout the nation, and creating nation-wide information and communication networks.

Indeed, improvement of communication is an essential element of the Tanaka plan:

> A ready availability of information irrespective of location will make it possible to relocate not only manufacturing plants but also plan-ning, research, and managerial departments of business firms. Once this is done, graduates of local universities may choose to seek employment in their own locality. Corporations need not necessarily establish their headquarters in big cities.

The plan provides for the bolstering of smaller cities as growth poles, a solution that is already being applied elsewhere in the world. Tanaka also advocates the strengthening of the central functions of prefectural capitals which are also regional cores, improving the living environment and urban functions of medium-sized cities (by renewal of downtown areas, suburban improvement, and subway or monorail construction from intracity transport), and the creation of "quarter-million cities" having as their core industrial parks to be constructed in the process of industrial reloca-tion. The program as a whole must be situated in a context of steady decline in Japan's rural population, and in the population of smaller towns outside the Tokaido megalopolis. Between 1965 and 1970, according to the Tanaka report, 70% of all such cities, towns, and villages lost population.

Obviously, the Tanaka plan has its opponents. The chief criticism is that decentralization of industry will also decentralize pollution, so that what is left of Japan's beauty will be scarred by industrial and urban development and suffocated by fumes. There is also the argument that Tokyo's congestion is due not as much to industry, or at least recent growth cannot be blamed on it, as to the mush-rooming of governmental and transactional (quaternary) functions, the work of head offices of companies, and of the Japanese govern-ment. In any case, the Tanaka plan was not being implemented officially even when Tanaka became prime minister, although the areas earmarked for decentralization of Tokaido were known and real estate speculation in these areas was rampant. And Tanaka

himself later came under fire for his questionable business deal-
ings, with the implication that he might be financially involved
in the development of the rural regions.

Already in force since 1958, a more modest National Capital
Region Modernization Program (for Tokyo) worked out by the
national government, in distinction to the city government's own
projects already described, may be considered a complementary
plan, when it is not a contradictory one. In essence, it shifts new
development to the periphery, linked by high-speed transportation
to the old centers. Some functions that are presently centralized,
factories but also universities and high-rise developments, are
being moved to these subcenters. This national program has so
far been better financed than the city's own projects, but it seems
not to have reduced environmental pollution: the contrary is truer.

Pollution, indeed, has become a symbol of Japan to newspaper
readers in other nations, accustomed to frightening reports seeming to herald the future of us all—for example:

> Tokyo, July 5 [1974] (AP)—Thousands of Tokyo residents had
> bloodshot, painful or swollen eyes during the last two days because
> of sulfuric acid in intermittent misty rains, officials said today.

While the major causes of this pollution are industrial wastes and
the heating of office buildings, Japan's Environment Agency is now
concentrating its research on photochemical smog and on the possibility that chronic respiratory diseases are caused by the concentration of ozone, the principal property of this so-called "white
smog," which is apparently caused by automobile exhaust and has
a close cousin in Los Angeles. Yet Japan's automobile makers have
managed to win postponement of implementation in 1976 of Japan's
equivalent of the U.S. Muskie Act pollution ceilings, just as American standards have been relaxed. Half-hearted experiments have
been attempted with traffic-less zones, on car-less days (one Sunday each month); they did not last, and in any case they accounted
for little reduction in pollution. The traveler who flies into Haneda
Airport across the vast industrial zone so close to the city center
will not give much credit to attempts to reduce pollution by token
gestures of this kind. If the pedestrian streets of Tokyo are of use,
they are above all a civic amenity. The Sunday closing of the
principal shopping street of the Ginza links it to narrower permanent pedestrians-only streets for an 8½-mile car-free promenade.

Still another result of over-density and industrialization is Tokyo's
curious phenomenon of subsidence (sinking of ground level), similar to that of Venice, brought about by roughly the same causes:

uncontrolled pumping of underground water and mineral resources. In Tokyo, this problem affects almost all of the central business district and large parts of the rest of the city; over half of the area of Tokyo's wards sank one centimeter or more in 1971. As in Venice, the problem is being coped with by controls on pumping and by providing alternative sources of water, but the return of the land to its original level is felt to be impossible.

What, one wonders, happens to old Tokyo landmarks when the city improves its people-carrying capacity? Usually they go. Recently, a red-brick 19th-century building, seat of Japan's Supreme Court and a memento of the Meiji era, was doomed when its functions were transferred to a new building under construction. Tokyo citizens duly took photographs and made sketches to remember it, but no one tried to save it. Public campaigns to preserve other landmarks, such as the Frank Lloyd Wright Imperial Hotel or a row of London-like buildings of the Mitsubishi Company in the Marunouchi district, had failed; now no one bothers. Real estate interests began tearing down Tokyo's old buildings when they learned how to build earthquake-proof skyscrapers, an embittered resident of this district told me.

Tokyo remains a mixture of old and new. A patch of unexpected and uncared-for greenery through which a wooden house or two and a shrine can be perceived may coexist with surrounding high-rise business buildings. Of course, the Japanese will not touch the immense 250-acre park in the heart of the city, whose series of moats protect the Imperial Palace. (Simple citizens can enter the park only once a year, to sign New Year greeting registers for their emperor.) I have already spoken of some of the ways in which Tokyo is more modern than most major U.S. cities. Yet in the homes of Tokyo's inhabitants color television coexists with eating and sleeping on mats. Young girls work in electronic environments and then return home to perform the tea ceremony for their fiancés. The habits and the traditions remain; people insist on that.

Yet the need for more living and working space continues to remove the physical vestiges of the Japanese past. A symposium held in the ancient shrine cities of Kyoto and Nara under UNESCO sponsorship in 1970 found that there was little effective control over the surroundings of a monument or site in Japan; if the site itself survived, the reckless urbanism surrounding it almost neutralized its effect. The Tanaka plan calls for government subsidies for conservation of local art forms and historic monuments, as well as the construction (or renovation) of folk art museums and libraries, "not merely as a tourist attraction but more importantly as a symbol of local pride and a national treasure." Meanwhile, the danger grows that it is too late. "For the first time in the history of Japan," long-time resident Robert Guillain reports, "the evolution that it is undergoing is a revolution which razes and bulldozes what came before, which destroys cruelly, which cuts the links to the past."

III. SAVING PEOPLE

9. The Quality of City Life

The joys of rustic life have been celebrated far and wide. The singer of pastoral lays is our modern suburbanite; his idyl is a retreat from the blighted city—at least in the evening, after work. For this shepherd-suburbanite, time passed in the city is lost time; he endures it only long enough to earn his money. Home, home life, leisure-time activity, even shopping are where the heart is, in the uniform streets and pale façades of suburbia.

And yet if life is measured by its excitements, by the sensations we receive and the demands they make of us, it is clear that we live most keenly, if most desperately, in the jungle of the cities. We relax less, but more of our senses are engaged, our intelligence is challenged, we are bombarded with perceptions. If sometimes the tempo seems too much, the train or the automobile ride back to our pastures is our means of withdrawal from the real world, not to say our surrender. There, we abandon the promise of living at the height of our powers, confessing to a weakness for leafy trees.

Can the two sides of our nature be reconciled, and in a way that might reduce the land surface scarred by suburban sprawl, thereby also reducing the time required to travel to work and home again? Can the city itself become the site of our rest and leisure-time activity, as it once was? With the increasingly urban future we are promised, any solution in the sense of "the city beautiful," every additional amenity, such as making outdoor parlors of our squares and even of our humblest streets, would seem to go into the direction not only of idealism but of practical realism. How improve our cities? What do we mean by "improve"? What do we look for in our daily lives?

And yet there cannot be a single standard by which we say that city life is good for us. The same set of characteristics that drives some of us out of cities—not only of New York, Toronto, and London, but of Rome and Paris, too—represents an irresistible attraction to others. In Paris, the man in the street is apparently willing to accept substandard housing, incredible noise (of unpoliced motorcycles on narrow residential streets in the dead of night), anarchic priority traffic, and abusive but tolerated parking—and all this because of a pattern of living without a parallel elsewhere in that nation, a near-perfect symbiosis of business and living areas, the near-ideal mixture of spaces, allowing for constant and efficient use of all but a rich man's ghetto to the west and some new but still peripheral renovated districts, desolate and irrelevant to the Paris with which we are concerned.

People who like crowded city centers turn out to be manifesting a natural grouping tendency. (How much they suffer depends on how much we have managed to degrade these city centers.) Compare the average tourist's enthusiastic reaction to London with the following letter from a provincial Englishman to the editor of a London evening newspaper, which was printed on its front page under the headline "Why I Hate London So!"

> . . . You say London is big; you forget that size is not necessarily synonymous with greatness.
> You discount the fact that London is made up chiefly of sprawling miles of monotonous suburbs, and that the exciting "happenings" are in the main confined to a small area around Central London.
> London IS dirty, a fact to which many tourists would testify.
> It IS corrupt, but you have probably never been subjected to the fleecing gimmickry of the tourist traps.
> It can be lonely because its very size makes it impersonal—a place without a heart.
> Your bus services are the worst of any city I have visited.
> You are right to boast of your wonderful parks in Central London, but what about the lack of such parks in your suburbs, with a few exceptions? . . . Climb out of your ivory tower and look around this big city of yours. For every reason you can offer for boasting its greatness, there is a reason for lament. . . .

The letter concludes on a positive note, praising "the warmth, friendliness and hospitality of . . . ordinary folk," which is why the writer chooses to remain in a city which fails to enchant him.

Lately, we are increasingly conscious of attempts to measure our happiness. In the United States and Canada, as well as in Europe, there is growing utilization of social indicators, the purpose of which is to quantify those factors of well-being not covered in the more traditional economic indexes. People are being asked how they feel about various components of the social climate, but at the same time, more objective criteria are being evolved to obtain complementary information from sources believed to be scientifically reliable. We ask individual citizens whether they feel safe from violent crime, then ask them to what extent they have actually been victims of crime; but we also go to police and court statistics for information on the incidence and nature of crimes committed.

Attitudes toward the quality of life have been studied by the Institute for Social Research in Ann Arbor, Michigan, among other institutions, while in Washington, D.C., the Office of Management and Budget issued a compilation of social indicators for the first time in 1974 to document the trends in eight sectors of well-being: health, public safety, education, employment, income, housing, leisure, and population growth. Similar work being undertaken in Europe has often been more in the nature of public opinion polling carried out for the news media—for example, within the space of a few weeks, two French magazines published contradictory findings, based on the same national statistics, concerning which regions of France are best endowed and "happiest," in equipment, resources, even in their surviving customs.

Subjective questionnaires often produce surprising results. Thus a French opinion survey in fifteen of France's largest cities (except Paris) turned up the information that city dwellers especially appreciate the outskirts of their cities: parks and countryside, rather than the downtown scene or their own neighborhood environment. Objective surveys tend to be gloomy, underscoring the lack of opportunity to get close to fresh air and sunshine, inadequate fresh water, physical exercise, etc.

We can nevertheless pursue the attempt to quantify, if we are prepared for the inevitable contradictions—for example, the Parisian enamored of his increasingly unliveable city, and the irreducible cases, such as the "lower class" described in Professor Edward Banfield's *The Unheavenly City* which is attracted to slums by "the very qualities that make the slum repellent to others."

An example of the attempt to establish international norms in the utilization of social indicators, the program of the Organization for Economic Cooperation and Development (OECD) is worthy of attention. OECD, a grouping of the United States and Canada with major nations of Western Europe and Japan, has the benefit of a late start and so can profit from earlier mistakes. It is known, for example, that certain statistics on social happiness can be misleading: Better to measure health not by the increase in the number of hospital beds, or doctors per 10,000 inhabitants, but by people who are healthy, even the number of years of healthy life they lead. The working party of statisticians, economists, and sociologists, together with representatives of OECD member governments having their own national plans in mind, drew up a list of 24 fundamental social concerns chosen to represent identifiable and definable preoccupations of direct significance to human beings, formulated so as to show not only an absence of negative factors but the presence of positive ones. As approved by OECD, the fundamental social concerns are the following:

Health
    The probability of a healthy life through all stages of the life cycle.
    The impact of health impairments on individuals.

Individual development through learning
    The acquisition by children of the basic knowledge, skills and values necessary for their individual development and their successful functioning as citizens in their society.
    The availability of opportunities for continuing self-development and the propensity of individuals to use them.
    The maintenance and development by individuals of the knowledge, skills and flexibility required to fulfill their economic potential and to enable them to integrate themselves in the economic process if they wish to do so.
    The individual's satisfaction with the process of individual development through learning, while he is in the process.
    The maintenance and development of the cultural heritage relative to its positive contribution to the well-being of the members of various social groups.

Employment and quality of working life
    The availability of gainful employment for those who desire it.
    The quality of working life.
    Individual satisfaction with the experience of working life.

Time and leisure
    The availability of effective choices for the use of time.

Command over goods and services
    The personal command over goods and services.
    The number of individuals experiencing material deprivation.
    The extent of equity in the distribution of command over goods and services.
    The quality, range of choice and accessibility of private and public goods and services.
    The protection of individuals and families against economic hazards.

Physical environment
    Housing conditions.
    Population exposure to harmful and/or unpleasant pollutants.
    The benefit derived by the population from the use and management of the environment.

Personal safety and the administration of justice
   Violence, victimization and harassment suffered by individuals.
   Fairness and humanity of the administration of justice.
   The extent of confidence in the administration of justice.

Social opportunity and inequality
   The degree of social inequality.
   The extent of opportunity for participation in community life, institutions and decision-making.

The next step would be to develop sets of social indicators as such—that is, generally accepted yardsticks to determine levels of well-being in the areas defined above. These indicators would be statistical measurements allowing monitoring of levels and changes in levels over a period of time. Phase II is in progress at the time of this writing, a responsibility of the OECD Manpower and Social Affairs Directorate.

Meanwhile, the same organization's Environment Directorate was developing a separate set of indicators focusing on the urban and physical environment: housing, neighborhood, transport, access to jobs and urban services, but also weather, air, noise and vibration, space and condition of land, density. Here, too, the emphasis is on fundamental indicators of individual well-being; the number of tons of sulfur dioxide in the atmosphere, on the other hand, would not tell us how this kind of pollution affects individuals or how they may feel about it. These urban indicators will also be of both the subjective and objective kinds. On the question of noise, for example, it may be important to know both the number of people exposed to a certain level of noise at a certain hour of the day (objective) and the number of people who claim to be bothered by noise, perhaps close to an airport (subjective).

The urban indicator project of OECD is addressed to decision-makers, both on the national and municipal levels, but also to researchers and to public opinion at large. The working party sees as the functions of its indicators (*1*) to describe the present state of affairs, comparing situations from city to city and in time; (*2*) to attempt to understand the functioning of the urban system through relationships among indicators; (*3*) to act, eventually, on the situation as it is discovered, by getting the facts to decision-makers at the planning stage and by emitting danger signals when a condition seems to require immediate action.

Once these urban indicators are drawn up, they will be tested in a number of cities. The first findings are to be presented to the United Nations Conference on the Environment, whose theme is Human Settlement, in Vancouver in 1976. Suburbs enter into the study only to the extent that cities are broken down into districts, which may include outlying areas as well.

The quality of life in all this? The hope is that by measuring the totality of the positive and negative factors of city living, it will be possible for us to comprehend how people feel and perhaps to understand their behavior. National differences of course enter the equation, not on the level of descriptive and objective indicators, but on that of how people react to objective conditions.

Measuring happiness can have practical applications. Decisions can be made, even unmade, on the basis of how people are affected or even of how they feel. It doesn't always happen, but it can happen.

Precisely what do we feel about the quality of our urban lives? In this area we may be able to work out our own set of subjective indicators. And, as has already been suggested, the results may surprise us. Thus, the larger cities are characterized by a plethora of excitements, too much noise and movement perhaps, and too much density, but also too much of what we generally consider to be desirable features: people to talk to, signs to read along the streets, shops to browse in, variety in services. For the intellectual man or woman, the larger cities are characterized by the overabundance of sensations and of attractions. There are more theatrical performances, art shows, concerts, lectures, and conferences than there are days or nights of the week. The number of invitations to openings of expositions, new plays, or short-run events of whatever kind is sufficient to make the head turn. There are not only sufficient libraries and research institutions, there is a choice of them, and they duplicate or overlap in their holdings and services. Truly, we live at the height of our powers when we are lucky enough to find ourselves in such a city.

If we want to find ourselves there. For the city dweller can prefer silence and no activity, or (as indicated in the French study already referred to) everything about the city which is not the city: its outskirts, parks and countryside. Or, like Italians at the hour of the *passeggiata*, we can seek the very heart of the city, where buildings and people are at their highest density, to congregate with all the others every time we are free to do so. Some suggest that it is a matter, in Europe at least, of Latin outdoor urban life vs. the northern way (few public places indoors or out, respect for the sanctuary of one's fireside). But how, then, explain a Piccadilly Circus crowded with dancing couples in the cold nights leading to January 1? Or the outdoor forum in downtown

Stockholm? The cathedral square with its café tables in Cologne? Pubs in Dublin get as crowded as cafés in Marseilles.

If cities are inherently bad, as the puritan suggests, than we can go no further. If, however, cities can produce both humanity's most sublime moments and its furthest descent into hell—

> I wander thro' each charter'd street,
> Near where the charter'd Thames does flow,
> And mark in every face I meet
> Marks of weakness, marks of woe.
> (William Blake, "London")

—then we may look more closely at those elements of our lives within the city that are worth saving, even worth fighting for. If, though, the great cities of the world, including Amsterdam, Budapest, Geneva, London, Paris, Rome, Stockholm, Verona, and Zurich (to select from a list made by Le Corbusier), reflect contemporary disorder, stifle and crush their inhabitants, offering no saving graces (this we find in Le Corbusier's *Charter of Athens*), then we are wasting precious time talking about them.

Take streets. For Le Corbusier's *Charter of Athens*, ours are not adapted to today's world. There are too many cross streets, their width is insufficient. For Jane Jacobs, we live best on these narrow streets, their frequent crossings providing a variety of routes for walkers, favoring the proliferation of small specialty shops; they help keep us safe as well as contented. And truly, the quality of our city life, speaking subjectively, is enhanced in those old and congested downtown streets, just as all life vanishes (sometimes it meets a violent death) in the interminable streets of the modern garden city which the Le Corbusians theorized and then walked away from.

Of course, the stumbling block for the rational urban scientists who are represented by the *Charter of Athens* is the irrationality of human behavior. We like the disorder of our cities. The juxtaposition of the old and new housing allows a mixture of classes, a variety of professions, the survival of marginal businesses: small repair shops, specialty leather or button or spice shops, key-makers, shoe-repairers, bakeries, the ubiquitous candy stores of the American central city. The most expensive residential neighborhoods of our great cities include some of the oldest housing, renovated, sometimes (as in the Netherlands, France, the United Kingdom, increasingly in Italy, although only spottily in Spain) for use as banks and insurance companies and other businesses requiring prestige quarters. Amsterdam's old canals, London's West End,

Paris's left bank furnish many examples of the old street with bulging or tilting façades in which rental space is as expensive as in palaces. There must be reasons.

One of them is the pleasure we have in frequenting much-walked ground, buildings with a history of their own, streets that are busy and varied in their attractions. The suicidal boredom of suburbs finds preventive medicine here. Density, noise, and air pollution are also causes of suicide? But these can be dealt with in the old city centers, and with a minimum of adjustment, thanks to traffic bans or restrictions, pedestrian zones, strict regulations on levels of noise and pollution.

As an indication of the kind of subjective difficulty there must be in any attempt to gauge the quality of life in the city, compare the increasingly bitter attacks on Paris's declining amenity with the almost desperate loyalty to that city found among its oldest residents, as well as among many French provincials drawn to their capital temporarily or for a lifetime, and of course among foreigners. It would be easy to compile an anthology of press articles, chapters in books, even whole volumes, on the decline of the urban framework of that city. Paris is threatened, says one writer, by Pigalle-ization: cabarets replacing food shops in historical neighborhoods become tourist haunts. Ugliness pays. Paris will become a rich man's reserve by 1980, says an urbanist's angry book; its suburbs will resemble Los Angeles. One of France's best polemical writers on architecture and urbanism sums it up: "High cost of living, astronomical rents, persistent housing crisis, pollution, noise, nervous fatigue, incredible consumption of tranquilizers and sleeping pills, hateful congestion, power drills, construction projects, mud, dirt (Paris is becoming one of the world's dirtiest cities), the soul and body of the historical center sacrificed to the so-called necessities of automobile traffic." These things are true. Old and picturesque specialty shops have been driven out by false pubs and steak houses in the district of St. Germain des Prés, a center of intellectual and literary life; fine squares have become parking lots, when they are not traffic circles; other sites conserved over the centuries have in a matter of months been destroyed by a senseless policy of underground parking lots with very visible surface appendages.

To counter these horrors, one speaks of laws to guarantee better architecture, while the laws that are supposed to protect old and historic neighborhoods have been misused to prevent good contemporary building while encouraging nasty pastiches. There is to be an improvement in street furniture, certainly an enhancement

of any city scene, but which would have been considered super-
fluous in the Paris of a generation ago. Paris is to encourage a
policy of small parks, even opening some heretofore private gardens to the general public. Small offerings, but then there is still
enough of legendary Paris to hypnotize true city-lovers; if not,
they can refer to the legend. Every contribution to the city beautiful deserves encouragement, even pathetic contributions. The
plastic trees and flowers planted along Jefferson Boulevard in Los
Angeles were better than nothing at all.

Of course, any old city is an accretion, streets deriving from
existing streets, buildings attached to buildings, sometimes extra
floors and balconies added, often courtyards and alleys encumbered
with annexes. That is what people wanted: to be close to the convenient center and to each other, and that is what they got. But
at the same time, these positive things represent unhealthy living
when one looks inside the buildings. Housing quality is not always
on a par with the outdoor scene in those cities with the most
envied urban landscapes.

In France, 60% of dwelling units were built before World War
I (in Paris the figure is over 50%), 30% before the Franco-Prussian
War of 1870. One quarter of all French housing lacked running
water in 1960 (12.5% in Paris), 60% lacked toilets (43% in Paris),
and 72% bathing facilities (64% in Paris). A national housing survey
in 1967 updated this information. Fewer than half of Paris's apartments had all amenities (water, toilet, bathing and heating facilities), 4% had no water at all, 18% had only running water. The
young and the old, the poor of all ages, above all migrant workers
from southern Europe and Africa, occupied apartments too small
for them. And of course the situation in the older cities of the
provinces and in rural localities was worse in terms of facilities (if
better in terms of space).

In Rome, an increasing proportion of the population lives in
shantytowns spotted around the periphery, while, more deceptively,
large numbers live in what look like proper houses, but which,
built in defiance of zoning rules and in the absence of urban facilities such as fresh water and sewers, are in effect high-rise cement
shacks. Some 70,000 persons in a population of 2.6 million are said
to be living in what is euphemistically called "substandard" quarters of this kind.

What happens, of course, is that a dual society develops in these
great cities. The crowded downtown with its noise and bustle is
a kind of champagne to the well-to-do visitor or to the native
living in comfort; one may even live in Paris's bourgeois western

neighborhoods or on Rome's airier hills and make it a practice to return to the historic center for an outdoor lunch or an evening of theater or strolling on winding streets among centuries-old buildings. In Paris and Rome, and even in The Hague, visitor and native alike can utilize the life-enhancing features of the old downtown while remaining indifferent, even ignorant, with respect to conditions faced by those living behind the old walls. More and more, these popular old districts are renovated, becoming high-rent areas for the middle classes determined to spend *all* of their time there.

So that, one way or another, these conflicting situations converge: Old need not mean uncomfortable, downtown need not mean blighted. If we can live at the height of our powers only in the city center, it ought to be possible for us to do this without suffering for it, and for more of us to do it. Nor do we need to chase out the present inhabitants; we can save the center, improve their quarters, and find sufficient space in once-derelict buildings for ourselves, too.

We can also find ways to bring more air and light into the city, since people seem to want that, and it may be a way to keep them from longing for the suburbs. There are limits to what can be done; do we sacrifice an historic neighborhood or even a single row of ancient dwellings to make a park? There is an alternate view that cities should consist of built-up areas, with the nearby countryside as everybody's escape hatch.

But where open spaces exist, they should be spared. Rome, again, provides examples of many fine parks within city limits closed and even surrounded by high walls. When open areas exist and are under the apparent protection of the city, they get built up anyway: Rome's press provides almost daily examples of this, with photographic evidence. Paris has begun to open pocket parks; public opinion, usually dormant in cities such as this one largely ruled from above and by decree, has protested the destruction of trees during the digging for underground parking or highways crossing the city, and has even won promises that the trees will be protected or replaced. On another scale, the history of Chicago has been one of constant struggle for the lakefront, speculators on one hand, the local inhabitants on the other. In Stuttgart, a major industrial center, public policy has preserved patches of green all over the city, even hillside vineyards within walking distance of the central business district when they are not inside it. One would think that Stockholm could live without trees, in that country of forests, and yet there have been violent skirmishes between citizens and builders about the removal of trees for building or road construction. "Trees are necessary to life, automobiles are not," read the protest signs.

Some urbanists will reason that cities can't be gardens, that large open spaces preempt ground needed to house people who otherwise must travel farther and farther away from the center, increasing the time it takes to get to work and home again, filling the nearby green belt with endless suburbs, adding to costs of urbanization of new suburbs. Better to use cities for city folks, saving the areas immediately surrounding them for recreation. Even the enlightened planners of Bologna have opted for this solution.

The geographer Jean Gottmann sees little hope for greening the city with high-density areas, while suburbia is only a temporary solution: "But as more people crowded into suburban areas, the density thickened there too. The lawns and gardens around the dwellings of many millions of the suburbanites became miniaturized themselves." Mixing city and countryside eventually "loses its quality and turns into a source of landscape pollution; and the rising costs of services and environmental control increase as the numbers, and therefore the density, of suburban establishments rise." Professor Gottmann sees a combination of small green areas in cities and increasing utilization of large, distant rural areas, "managed in a way that does not interfere with the production functions of these areas" (*Challenge for Survival,* 1970).

When a Central Park exists, and this was the savior of New York's central business district, or the Bois de Boulogne and Bois de Vincennes to the west and east of central Paris, do not let an acre of them be covered with cement. A 1973 decree in France protects all green spaces over 500 square meters in dimension in urban areas, bans destruction of any urban wooded area of any size, requires that promoters include gardens on 10% of the land being developed. In France, the beach resort of Deauville may have provided the last example of the rape of the beachfront by promoters (of an artificial port and residential community); since approving it, the French government has yielded to public protests against further alienation of the coastline.

It all depends, of course, on what our priorities are. Not always what we say that we want, but what we do with what we have. In consequence, the studies in progress on the quality of life, particularly in the urban context which is the milieu for a constantly growing proportion of the world's population, are important in that they will help guide the planners who draw the lines on city maps. But we also decide, by moving in and out, voting with our feet in the American expression. If we move out, turning our backs on the large city, the city can only decline. Nobody will remain who cares to make it more comfortable for all segments of the population. If we stay and look for ways to improve the quality of life around us, we are likely to be moving with history. Most of us will never escape from cities; they grow out until they find us.

10. Public Housing for Private People

From the air, the buildings are a snake, following the sinuous track of a pedestrians-only roadway; from the ground, bright cubes with a splash of color suggestive of serpentine form. But whether sinuous or straight, the rows of three- to five-story structures stand on a disconcerting series of planes, so that one walks uphill and down as well as in and around the labyrinth. And if the buildings don't get you, the spaces between them will. A paved piazza may buckle into a series of small mounds for children to climb. It might contain the body of a giant, a Gulliver in stone partly concealed in sand (which is a sand lot for children). Farther along stands an obelisk sundial, outrageously large ceramic apples and pears. On the village's main square, ceramic tile trees and flower boxes reveal human features.

Façades change color rapidly. Some are subtle pastels, others blotches of violent color. One windowless building wall is covered with a mosaic portrait of Franz Kafka; the poet Rimbaud stares fixedly from another, a plaintive donkey's head from a third. Finally, a pair of guileless pigeons as tall as dinosaurs guard the square in front of the local police station. Streets bear names such as Minotaur and Labyrinth.

Vacation village for the jet set on a Mediterranean isle? Posh suburb? In fact, La Grande Borne, designed by French architect Emile Aillaud, was put up by a public building authority, its subsidized rentals tailored to households earning under $3,700 annually. Many of La Grande Borne's 15,000 tenants are Arab and Portuguese migrant laborers, the French equivalent of America's underprivileged black and Spanish-speaking minorities. Monthly rents begin at $50 for three rooms plus kitchen. The village is only minutes south of Paris, just off a major north-south expressway.

Its closest neighbor happens to be the antithesis of La Grande Borne, a conventional high-rise apartment co-op simulating luxury, bringing the drearier side of urban living to the suburbs, further evidence of the improverishment of academic French architecture dominated by the stifling traditions of the Ecole des Beaux-Arts. Aillaud's village may indeed be a rare exception to the rule, in the light of a recent decree banning housing projects of over 1,000 units in agglomerations containing less than 50,000 inhabitants, or 2,000 units in larger cities, in reaction to the dismal urban/suburban skyline the so-called *grands ensembles* have created.

As a rule, and apparently because architects and planners think that they cannot afford to do it any other way, low-income housing in France has been particularly grim. The program called HLM, for *habitations à loyer modéré,* contains nothing else as remarkable as La Grande Borne, and yet maverick Emile Aillaud's village remains within the HLM budget per square meter of housing. His secret, of course, was imagination, what the architect himself called a return to the "mystery" of the city, its complexity, even irrationality. The 3,500 dwelling units are divided into seven neighborhoods, 20 small squares. The masons who paved the streets were told to improvise patterns. Automobiles are conspicuously absent, although parking is never more than 160 yards from any apartment.

Expectedly, many of La Grande Borne's lower-income residents are disoriented, vaguely unquiet. They expected bureaucratic gray; are they being discriminated against? Aillaud said frankly that his village was built for children; it remains difficult for adults to live in "at present." But if it is cut off from the rest of the world by an expressway, by surrounding vacant lots, and even by a local prison, it is hardly the architect's fault, since he had to work with what he was given. The working-class inhabitants are unable to support all the shops originally planned; only half of them were open a year after completion of the project. There is insufficient community life, equipment, and the same shortage of nursery facilities for working mothers which prevails in other districts old or new. The architect was unable or chose not to do anything about these things. He is quoted: "It's easy to say: What good is a Rimbaud or a Kafka in mosaic to a Portuguese worker who gets up at five in the morning to walk to the railroad station? Nothing, of course, except that it isn't Rimbaud who deprives him of bus service."

La Grande Borne, its best friends admit, is far from being perfect. Seeking to innovate in design, hoping that the plastic beauty of the result would somehow stimulate the inner fantasies and therefore compensate for the isolation of all such developments and the poverty of its facilities, Emile Aillaud, now 70, has not answered all our questions. But every such attempt to change the decor of the daily lives of those who can have no alternative to public-housing-project exile is a blow for humanity. And it must be carried out, for this is the real challenge, with funds normally available for government-assisted housing. It cannot be so costly as to outrage the taxpayers; indeed, it should not be more expensive than the grim garrisons which are usually reserved for the poor and the ill-housed.

What do we see around us, say in the housing of the past decade, when the advanced industrialized nations had moved sufficiently beyond the post-World War II era so as not to be able to use "postwar" as an excuse? We see comparable budgets being spent to build horrors, veritable prisons for that segment of the population sentenced to urban renewal, and then, alongside them, usually on a far smaller scale, a gem of a project which an architect or urban planner created in order to change the daily lives of inhabitants, at least a little. Housing shortages are a universal phenomenon, even in nations without bread or water shortages, few nations having succeeded in satisfying the present needs of their populations on all income levels. Everywhere the problem is insufficient venture capital and a lack of public funds, but nearly everywhere there has also been some imaginative building. So that the money excuse is no good; if the need to construct cheaply and quickly makes light of humane and esthetic considerations, it is the choice of the builder, and the failure of his talent.

Today, in several places, an effort is under way to break this syndrome. In France, competitions with a strong esthetic orientation are being carried out before contracts are awarded to architects of new towns or satellites of the major cities. Young architects see their chance in open contests of this sort, and they can apply their new concepts, starting from the cell or the module, outward, thinking of the individual dwellers, but then also looking at the ensemble of the modules the way an inhabitant of the new project will look at it: Will he feel he is going back to a dormitory at the end of the day? Will the surroundings add to or diminish the despair of wives and others confined to the project all day and every day? What will young people think about, and do about, their environment? The investigators know that people from inner-city slums who move to a large project within the same city or in the periphery are at first too bedazzled by the newly acquired comforts to be critical. Often they have sacrificed the intensity of street life, stimulations of an old busy block, to come here, but they are not quite ready to notice what is missing from their lives. Hot water and inside toilets are too exciting.

In France, where public housing, like all state-sponsored architecture, was among the least innovative, least adapted to contemporary living, central government (from which all policy derives) has declared it important that people live in more interesting buildings. A program of new architecture, PAN (for *programme d'architecture nouvelle*), has been introduced by the Construction Ministry. A government official is responsible for encouraging innovative design, offering the results of the research and small-scale experimental building to contractors in the private sector. But then the state backs up its theories with orders for public housing conceived by PAN: 50,000 "new-style" dwelling units, representing a tenth of those under construction, were approved for 1975. "New" means breaking up the rigidly rectangular lines of building projects, adding balconies and terraces, varying heights.

In the Munich suburb of Perlach, in a plan for large-scale construction of public housing (25,000 units for 80,000 residents) an attempt has been made to avoid monotony by grouping the housing into smaller units of 1,500 to 2,500 residents. Units vary in their architecture, providing variety and camouflaging the comparatively high densities called for in the scheme. The overall plan is that of a contemporary garden city: Pedestrian lanes connect residential areas to schools and shopping, to malls, small parks, and playgrounds. Indeed, only the Netherlands in Western Europe seems not to have changed its policies with respect to the institutional appearance of public housing, presumably because space is so much a factor there, and the Dutch (who know this so well) accept the situation as just one more constraint required of good citizens. The Soviet Union has no such space problem, but there is a continuing housing crisis, requiring—and getting—ever greater standardization in designs and structural units. Nearly half of all dwelling units in that nation are being built as fully prefabricated concrete and reinforced concrete units; another 36% of new units (1969) utilize large-panel construction. That is now the main type of construction in such cities as Moscow, Leningrad, and Kiev. No room for fantasy there.

Both in the United States and in the United Kingdom, there is now ample public encouragement of new design in public housing. If British projects are less exciting, there are also more constraints, both in funds and in space, within or close to existing agglomerations. The U.S. Department of Housing and Urban Development has been giving biennial awards for design, while HUD's Operation Breakthrough, to encourage industrialized housing units, is not only demanding technical innovations to meet America's housing needs, but it has seen the building of attractive housing, nuclei of liveable neighborhoods. In New York State the Urban Development Corporation's untypical projects have received several local prizes; one award-winning pair of buildings in New York City's Harlem brought a comment from *Building Design and Construction* that "tight budgets don't have to be synonymous with unimaginative design." In a UDC project in New York City, imaginative design is the key to the new satellite town, Roosevelt Island, in the East River. The form of the island, long and narrow, allows more people to enjoy views and access to the waterfront, breaking up what might otherwise be another monolithic housing scheme planned for 18,000 persons in 5,000 apartments. For one of the persistent criticisms of public housing is that the projects are too big.

How big is too big? The French have been engaged in a nonstop program to provide housing for their shamefully ill-housed workers and lower middle classes, a program which involves a wide range of options including subsidized low-rental HLMs and obligatory employer contributions to housing funds. But another kind of malaise began to be felt, brought about by the bleak aspect of much of this new housing. It wasn't only a lack of architectural talent: The most famous architect who ever built a project house in France, Le Corbusier, was criticized for the mass, impersonality, and inappropriate siting of his Cité Radieuse in Marseilles. The mammoth dimensions of many of the new development sites were getting people down. Frenchmen, like Americans, preferred individual houses with gardens, and the kind of public housing that was being built for them was unlikely to persuade them to change their minds.

In 1973, the French government decided to call a halt to the proliferation of giant projects. "The urbanization of our country is going to continue for many years. It is time to act or the *grand ensemble* (large housing development) will become the rule in our cityscape," declared the minister for territorial planning of the time, Olivier Guichard. Housing projects in France may be undertaken within the framework of a "zone of concerted planning" (ZAC, for *zone d'aménagement concertée*), in which the national or local government or a public housing corporation builds, or orders from a private contractor, controlled rental or purchase (co-op) housing. Most developments in France are carried out under this system.

Under the Guichard regulations, future ZACs may contain no more than 1,000 dwelling units in cities of under 50,000 inhabitants, no more than 2,000 in cities of over 50,000 (with the exception of designated new towns). As written, the rule sees these as maximums; actually, the number of dwelling units must not exceed the number built in the course of the previous two years in the same city. The whole project must be completed within a six-year period (to avoid condemning early tenants to dismal years of walking through mud and under scaffolding). To reduce the social segregation which projects always exacerbate, it was decided that in developments containing over 1,000 units, at least 20% but no more than 50% must be subsidized and controlled rentals—HLM. The same percentages will be sought in the smaller projects as well, without this being a rule. The ceiling on numbers of units, and the linkage to existing new developments in the urban agglomeration, are designed to avoid unbalanced development of a town, with financing also remaining within the realm of the possible.

Other provisions of the Guichard circular, as it is called, provide for more equitable distribution of public housing to avoid segregation by rental. Apartments are to be set aside for the aged, for single tenants, for the handicapped. Inhabitants are encouraged to participate in the management of their projects and the organization of their surroundings. Diversity of architecture and techniques are to be encouraged as well, to break with the uniformity and monotony so familiar to residents, even to casual visitors, of such projects. (No more than 500 dwelling units on the same site in a subsidized project can henceforth be designed by the same architect.) More nonresidential activities will be brought to the sites of public housing: sports facilities, public services, commercial functions.

This defiance of decades of practice in every advanced nation was not to be carried out without controversy. Its motivation seemed to be improvement of the quality of life, the increasing need of rank-and-file dwellers to turn to the new developments for want of reasonable alternatives. Traditional architects—the vested interests—protested the Guichard circular. They felt it would increase red tape and slow down building, encourage smaller promoters less scrupulous of building regulations, and thus lead to a disorderly, undisciplined urbanism. It was felt to be less economical, and would make it more difficult to finance public services which are usually conceived for larger populations. As for the attempt to reduce social and economic segregation which the quota on cheap subsidized housing units within a single project was to accomplish, the feeling was that "people don't like to mix," the rich desiring to remain apart from the poor, but also vice versa.

The French parliament indicated in its discussion of the decree that many aspects of it were upsetting. Already eight major developments in the Paris region have been blocked, or modified; in all, forty such projects were to be suspended, as funds became available to buy up the properties as government land reserves. Minister Guichard also indicated that the government would not pursue the development of new towns, although it would carry out the ones already being built in the Paris region. In the same way, it was too late to do anything about the oversized projects that had actually been built, and which were proving a trying experience to their new and unsuspecting residents. For projects already under way, public officials were urged to negotiate a voluntary scaling down of their dimensions.

That the government of France meant what it was saying was to be demonstrated only a short while later, when a ZAC on the outskirts of Dieppe was vetoed despite the fact that its designer was an architect of international reputation, Oscar Niemeyer (who had planned Brasilia). The Niemeyer scheme called for 3,000 units, publicly financed, in a pattern showing the originality one might have expected from Niemeyer. The new neighborhood would have the shape of a heart, with ten undulating buildings on pilotis, each to contain 300 inhabitants, spread out like a fan among greenery. A central square, from which motor vehicles were excluded, would concentrate public services such as a school and a swimming pool.

Each of the Niemeyer houses was 150 meters long; a limit of 60 meters had been put into effect in 1971 by a predecessor of Minister Guichard.

An attempt was made to win an exemption from the Guichard and 1971 decrees, but the national authorities stood firm against the city of Dieppe and Niemeyer. The city, whose mayor is a Communist (Niemeyer himself designed the Paris headquarters of the French Communist Party), charged political discrimination. It claimed that the size of the city was immaterial and that Dieppe would become even smaller if denied the right to build cheap new housing and industrial zones. The government wished to improve the quality of major housing projects, ran the argument, but it is precisely when Dieppe got the best architect and urbanist possible that its plan was vetoed. "Great names don't excuse great errors," Guichard replied. "Don't Dieppe's workers have a right to beauty?" its mayor asked. "You can't blame the minister," an editorial in the daily *Le Monde* commented, "for wanting to avoid an exemption that could have served as an alibi for mediocre builders."

Both sides were right, of course; it is a good day when a country may choose between a good rule and a good design; usually the choices are of another order. Emile Aillaud, the innovative architect of La Grande Borne, got into similar difficulty with Chanteloup-les-Vignes, a subsidized (HLM) project of 4,000 units near Versailles which introduced many of his controversial ideas, such as a mix of buildings, an absence of grass around the buildings, and a heavy density. Accused of overcrowding the site with the risk of creating another low-income ghetto, Aillaud's project was suspended after completion of 1,600 apartments; it has been in litigation ever since.

A nation of some 52 million inhabitants, France has been building half a million new housing units a year, most of them with HLM or other public funds, a fifth financed by obligatory contributions by private companies. Some day the inconsistencies will be worked out of the new French crusade against size; already it appears that innovations will be accepted more readily. Meanwhile, in a world of nations which continue to produce barracks for our inner cities only slightly better barracks for the rich but barracks all the same, these imperfect, sometimes clumsy attempts to change it all, while they cannot show all their effects overnight, are making life less painful for the new and inevitable urbanites.

11. Defenses Against the Automobile

On one hand, the city redesigned for the movement of private motor cars, roads become highways, overpasses when they are most practical or economical, underpasses when strictly necessary. Neighborhoods cut in half or isolated by expressways. Residential areas losing their character as they are cut up, sometimes piece by piece over a period of time, as in an ancient form of torture. Automobiles parked on sidewalks when roadways are insufficient, parked on pedestrian crosswalks, on the center alleys of wide boulevards, under trees, forming a wall around churches and monuments. Gracious squares designed for walking humans now serving as parking lots.

On the other hand, the automobile kept at a respectable distance from the city dweller, if not from the city. No highway into town; on the contrary, a system of one-way streets discouraging driving, preventing traffic through and across the city center. Car-free zones arranged as pedestrian malls. Parking permitted only in designated off-street garages, preferably out of the center though close to public transportation. Above all, strict enforcement of parking and traffic rules, a strong will to prevent abuses and a sufficient force of patrolmen to carry out the will.

Both kinds of city exist. If Paris continues to widen its roadways, further reducing already narrow sidewalks, London has widened pedestrian sidewalks at the expense of motor roadway: Busy, commercial Oxford Street now provides lanes for public buses and taxis only. If Paris opens its tree-lined boulevards to "tolerated" parking, London withdraws already installed downtown parking meters to discourage the use of automobiles and to enable it to ban parking on these streets. The number of parking spaces in central London was reduced by over 50% in a decade;

few other cities are prepared to boast about that. At present, 10% of London's suburban dwellers use private automobiles to get into central London, against 20% in the Paris region. Parking fines are lower in Paris than in any other major city.

So that if Paris allows parking abuses in its tourist centers to the prejudice of local inhabitants who happen to use these same streets and squares, other cities pay particular attention to policing these areas; they have been turned into car-free zones. The civilized Londoner has learned that he can survive without a private vehicle in the city. He walks to work and to shop, or uses a convenient bus or tube; he may taxi to the theater. The Parisian apparently feels disgraced if he can't use his car in the city center the way he would use it on his farm. Not without reason: His public transportation is deteriorating, with underground transit at saturation, surface buses unable to move during peak hours, and hardly to be found at other times.

Paris destroyed one of its riverside walks, the right bank of the Seine, with a speedway, along about the time that London was rediscovering its own river. And in 1974, in the teeth of protests from environmental groups, it seemed that Paris would begin construction of a highway on what had been the left-bank quais of the Seine, after rejecting alternative plans for a tunnel beneath the river; it required the authority of a newly elected president of the republic anxious to innovate to call a halt to work already in progress, like the queen's messenger stopping the execution of the hero in "The Threepenny Opera."

Does one design a city for automobiles, should one oblige a city to adapt to maximum circulation? Isn't this what influential citizens really want? A recent French president had suggested that automobiles took priority over esthetics in Paris, and the structure of that capital's government gave him the power of decision which elsewhere in France would belong to local authorities. Should we isolate the automobile, control its use within the city? It is a concept that has been dealt with in Munich and in Milan, as I shall show in a later chapter, and it is in the works for many metropolitan areas, including New York City, which has proposed a controversial transportation plan to take effect before this book is published, and St. Louis, as part of a downtown development plan to be implemented over the course of the next fifteen years. Where highways have been built in downtown areas, fewer and fewer citizens are found to be proud of the achievement. Those who are familiar with Los Angeles, which of course got that way for historical reasons having nothing to do with the typical urban morphology, worry about the danger of "Los Angelization" of their own cities.

Actually Los Angeles was created by its highways, just as there is a point of view that Las Vegas is better for its Strip. But it doesn't take much automobile-adapting to destroy the tissue of an old city. The nine countries of Europe's Economic Community (the Common Market) possess some of the world's oldest and most valued metropolitan areas. But it is in this EEC region that the automobile is doing the most damage. Noise and motor exhaust pollute in a more acute manner, other things being equal, an ancient and narrow street than a modern boulevard of generous proportions; the old winding lanes designed for medieval man are also the least adaptable to motor traffic. The nine countries of EEC, which had 75 million private automobiles at the beginning of the 1970s, will have an estimated 85.7 million in 1980 (France leading the pack with 348 per 1,000 inhabitants, followed by Germany, Italy, Great Britain—this last with 307; compare the 1970 figure for the United States: 433). In Paris alone, a 1970 estimate was for twice as many cars by 1985 (both estimates were made before the threat of worldwide scarcity and higher prices of the oil-producing nations).

There are those who feel, with British traffic expert Colin Buchanan, that automobiles go with buildings. You can take steps to channel traffic, but you cannot prevent it from coming at all:

> We conclude that the motor vehicle (or some equivalent machine) is a beneficial invention with an assured future, largely on account of the great advantages it offers for door-to-door travel and transporation. . . .
> We think a constructive approach to the problem of accommodating it in towns and cities is both required and justified. (from "General Conclusions," *Traffic in Towns,* 1963)

Apparently nothing can be done to limit the total number of automobiles in circulation (we do not know what the result of oil scarcity and/or higher fuel prices will be). As fast as they are able to, nations still relatively free of automobiles such as the Soviet Union and its East European neighbors, and the developing world, augment their number, both as a means to promote the many industries which combine to produce automobile civilization, and to satisfy citizen-consumers; the desire for prestige is not missing from the equation. Congestion, air and noise pollution, danger of accidents and not least of it the wear and tear on the nerves of drivers and their pedestrian adversaries, are necessary concomitants to national growth.

Still, many countries now plan to tighten regulations on safety, emissions of carbon monoxide and hydrocarbons, noise. These are functions of the amount of money that manufacturers and consumers will pay for this protection, itself a function of popular willingness to make the sacrifices necessary, reflected in the resolution of governments. The oil shortage which began to be felt in 1974, more accurately a money shortage, was used as an excuse, valid or not, to postpone rigid new standards for automobile exhaust in many countries. Where least is done is in the restricting of urban traffic by both enforcement of existing regulations and the availability of alternatives such as mass transit and peripheral parking. And so we have a situation where some of our most vulnerable and precious centers continue to be assaulted by the highway builders. Paris is the worst but not the only example.

An American architect has suggested that pedestrian engineering become a city agency, to give pedestrians a voice against the traditional city departments concerned with motor traffic. Indeed, the problem is being seen in the more enlightened municipal administrations as an overall one: If you limit automobile traffic, you are almost certain to improve public transportation at the same time. It remains to city authorities to provide edge-of-city parking and rapid transit from that parking to the places to which people need to go. Simply to ban street traffic and create pedestrian malls while allowing as much incoming traffic as before results in chaotic traffic conditions. One solution is to arrange one-way and closed streets in such a manner that automobiles simply can't go from one sector to another through the center. They must remain in the limited sector they have entered, perhaps from a ring road, and find their way out again the same way. Rome has been planning such a system; Munich is further advanced in the same direction. It has been suggested that motorists desiring to enter the downtown city (London) during the working day pay a special fee, just as New York City has been experimenting with the use of dissuasive tolls on tunnels and bridges entering the city. Moscow has announced that when the number of private automobiles owned by city residents reaches one million, no further sales of vehicles will be made; anyone insisting on possessing one will have to try to move elsewhere.

Well-governed cities such as London have carried out detailed surveys and listened to every possible remedy. The French are developing comprehensive traffic plans including reserved lanes for buses, two-wheeled vehicles, and pedestrians, as well as parking restrictions, coordinated traffic signals. The intention is to make plans which can be put into effect with a minimum investment in infrastructure, such as ring roads or new subway or streetcar lines. A group of French towns is serving as a pilot for rational investment in traffic control, and the seventh French five-year plan will include the concept of a comprehensive traffic package, with all echelons contributing to a single "envelope" from which public expenditures will be drawn. Meanwhile, the existing budget structure leans the other way: Local authorities can get more government help for highways into the city than for ring roads or public transportation.

What is certain is that every large city has its teams studying automobile traffic. Remedies may be forthcoming on a piecemeal basis, such as new systems of traffic signalization and new parking restrictions, or on a long-term basis, such as building of underground parking lots or new rapid transit lines. The surprise is that not every metropolitan area has decided to limit automobile traffic. In some cases, it remains a matter of laissez-faire, the battle of pressure groups of drivers or walkers for possession of the streets. The idea that every major choice is resolved in this way, with city officials as arbiters and executors of decisions supported by the most powerful or vocal of its citizens, did not die in the 19th century.

A balanced if not a final word comes from the Organization for Economic Cooperation and Development (OECD), grouping twenty-three major countries of Europe, Japan, and the United States. The OECD's Environment Directorate has studied "Environmental Implications of Options in Urban Mobility." Its conclusions on automobiles in the city dismiss the likelihood that these machines will be dispensed with entirely, as no more politically feasible or operationally useful than the idea of making private vehicles the exclusive means of urban transportation.

Neither massive investment in urban highways nor an expensive, high-capacity subway system may be necessary to solve the transportation problems of a city. Instead, the ideal solution may be innovative, low-cost improvements in existing systems, such as bus priority lanes, and what is called a semi-metro: trains or lighter rail cars running on their own tracks above or below ground, as well as a public automobile service (collective or shared taxis). Each of these solutions would require a parallel reduction in the use of private vehicles in the center of the city: It always comes back to that.

The means to keep cars out vary. At the time of publication of the OECD report just referred to (November 1973), London, Zurich, Stockholm, Amsterdam, and Minneapolis had declared main streets off limits to private vehicles, while continuing to permit the operation of public transit on these streets. Geneva had experimented with a ban on automobiles in a large area of the city center; Milan's experience is described elsewhere in this book. The practice of dividing cities into sectors for the purpose of interdicting through-traffic had been put into effect in Bremen, Göteborg, Bologna, Liverpool, and the inner suburbs of Stockholm, and was being planned for Besançon in France. Restriction on automobile use by deliberate reduction in the number of available parking places or by raising parking fees or imposing other restrictions was operative in Bologna, Newcastle, Hamburg, The Hague, London, and Glasgow.

Of course, there can never be enough parking spaces in a city for all who live and work in it. The old cities have had to improvise, with ancient cellars and sometimes even churches converted into garages. The other options, if motor cars really have to be where people are, include the demolition of a building that might otherwise have survived into perpetuity as part of the tissue of the historic center, for surface or silo parking, or to dig up old squares for underground parking, covering them over with cement and replanted greenery. Why not? asked Lord Mancroft, president of the London Tourist Board, who advocates ignoring "the protests of the preservationists" because "City trees are tougher than you think." In truth, the roofs of underground parking lots which now cover Paris do not—it was discovered too late—support big trees.

Easy parking attracts motorists. Some underground parking lots remain empty while the streets above them are encumbered with illegally parked vehicles. Even if motorists are satisfied, everyone else suffers when a sea of vehicles covers a once majestic public place, or a familiar cityscape is marred by access roads and entrances to underground parking lots, or by the view of a concrete silo garage. Whatever the solution, surface or underground, silo or cellar, the end result is to encourage the possession and utilization of automobiles in the city, so that in a short while there are as many vehicles as ever in the places they were no longer expected to occupy.

In the 1960s, the city of Paris tore up its heart to acquire 10,000 new parking places, defacing public squares such as the one in front of the ancient church of St. Germain l'Auxerrois opposite the Louvre Museum, removing great and ancient trees which were replaced with anemic plants when the job was done. In all, the Paris program would offer shelter to 35,000 vehicles, while more new cars were being acquired by Parisians during the period of their construction than they were designed to handle. Paris had 700,000 cars to park in 1970, 330,000 of which had to find room on streets or on sidewalks. Traffic has augmented 10% a year since then.

One French city known for innovation is at this writing studying means to re-introduce bicycles as a major inner-city means of transportation, with an infrastructure adapted to it: marked bicycle paths, specially adapted traffic priorities, parking facilities for two-wheelers on streets and in buildings. The technicians of Grenoble have gone to the Netherlands to see how the Dutch do it. In January 1974, an Association for the Development of Public Transport, Bicycle and Pedestrian Lanes was founded to put pressure on the authorities to change what many felt to be policies too favorable to the automobile.

The two extremes are the city as highway and the city as pedestrian mall. It has come to that. A motorized army of influential citizens with homes or offices outside the downtown area prefers not to be told that access highways should not penetrate the city center. They are duplicating the Los Angeles way of life in places where no Los Angeles had existed, or (as in Tokyo) they are gradually replacing the last remaining open spaces with congested roadways. Lyons has put a highway along its river; the same fate threatens, or has been visited on, Rouen, Bordeaux, Toulouse, Grenoble, Reims, and Orléans.

Read the appeal of the Committee for Safeguarding the Banks of the Seine, a coalition including Friends of the Earth, the Association for the Rights of the Pedestrian, the National Association for Protection of Art Cities, and other groups which have tried to block the left-bank highway for east-west traffic, opposite the existing right-bank highway for west-east traffic:

- It will not help solve the general traffic problem, but on the contrary in encouraging more motorists to enter an already saturated Paris, will contribute to the bottlenecks, noise and pollution.

- It will destroy the equilibrium of one of the world's finest urban landscapes which should have been set aside for leisure and strolling. . . .

Compare the decision of the United States government to refuse funds for a highway that would have marred the historic French Quarter of New Orleans; even the solution of a depressed road-way was rejected as disruptive as well as expensive.

But even those roads that circle a city, or provide a bypass for ongoing traffic, require considerable study. Ring roads or peripheral roads often destroy neighborhoods, too. They may suggest a traffic mobility which doesn't really exist, and therefore congest those sections of the city they touch, or lead to a demand for still more of the same. And then in Paris the peripheral highway was obsolete before it was completed, and already during its infancy there are demands for doubling its capacity with an upper deck. When they are good, ring roads help keep regional traffic far from city limits, while allowing those motorists who need to come into town to pinpoint their place of entry, and so to use as little of the metropolitan street network for as short a time as possible.

The one sure way to stop traffic in its tracks, as I shall suggest in another chapter, is the pedestrian zone. Motor vehicles come up against no-entry signs or, better because less vulnerable to abuse, a wall of trees or potted plants, raised sidewalks, if necessary chains or tank traps. An OECD study confirms the Munich experience, described in a later chapter, that these zones have positive effects on local business; in notable cases they have reduced air pollution as well. Only when a city is dominated by shopkeepers' fear (Brussels and Paris are sad examples) are pedestrian zones slow in coming: In Brussels, the Grand'Place was given back to parked cars at public demand; in Paris, pedestrian-zone experiments have been so poorly organized and enforced that it is next to impossible to know that one is walking in one of them. If there is not yet much public demand for pedestrian streets in places where they have not been tested, it is undoubtedly because not enough citizens have seen successful examples elsewhere, not enough shopkeepers have bothered to learn of the effects of such zones on business.

The automobile cannot move without a driver. Fortunately, drivers are also sometimes pedestrians, and need fresh air, too, and perhaps the peace that comes with a transformed urban environment. It may be the only hope for the big city.

Paris

It is temporarily a paradox that the metropolitan area with the least respect for its walking citizens is the birthplace and national headquarters of an organization for defense of pedestrian rights —or perhaps the one explains the other? Parking fines are lower in Paris than in most places; the police are more tolerant of traffic and parking violations, often on instructions. Paris was once warned by its highest authority, as I have already indicated, that it would have to adapt to the automobile age. And so mothers wheeling baby carriages, pregnant women, old people and children, not to speak of the rest of the population, climb over automobiles not only to cross Paris streets but to walk along their sidewalks.

Actually, Paris is not the only offender. Everywhere, the problem of what to do with automobiles is or should be a national as well as a municipal priority. In Europe alone, the universal tendency to increase urbanization is accompanied by a growth of the automobile population. Highways move into the cities, so that motorists drive through city streets at country speeds.

In Paris, the Association for the Rights of the Pedestrian (Les Droits du Piéton) has been attempting to do something about the automobile invasion for the fifteen years of its existence. In an unending flow of letters to authorities, communiqués for the press, public meetings, but especially and most conspicuously eye-catching handbills and leaflets, the Association has been unique and often alone in its fight for the men and women who must live in an urban environment which others have taken as their highway and their garage. One can be both a driver and a member of this Association, for this is no anti-alcoholic-beverage league, where a drinker has no place. The point is to be a considerate driver. Presumably few members of the organization are as active as the founder-president, but then it must be recalled that the French tradition has found little place for the voluntary association so dear to the Anglo-American tradition. Few private foundations exist, and the habit of unpaid activity in an organization which promises no personal profit for its members is not a very widespread one. So that the Association's president Roger Lapeyre fights not only against the automobile lobby, complacent municipal governments, selfish motorists, but against apathy on the part of people who should be furnishing him his troops.

Droits du Piéton manifests itself in Paris in many ways. In tiny yellow handbills, convenient for tucking under the windshield wipers of an offending automobile: "Think of us." The drawing is of a mother pushing a baby carriage, another child walking alongside. "For a humane city," says the tract, "join Droits du Piéton."

"Reject the absurd," demands another sticker half the size (no larger, in fact, than an auto tax stamp). The drawing is of a traffic jam filling every possible inch of an intersection.

"I don't respect pedestrian rights," announces another small yellow handbill. The drawing is of a rather *méchant* motorist parked on a crosswalk, and on the sidewalk, where a pedestrian is attempting to cross.

Other flyers for sticking under windshield wipers of offending vehicles or distributing on streets warn motorists: "Leave sidewalks free" (photo shows an old woman forced to walk in the roadway because an automobile is parked on the only available sidewalk). "If an accident occurred to this lady," the tract warns, "or if she had caused an accident, the driver who parked his car on the sidewalk would be criminally responsible." The date of an appeals court verdict confirming this rule is given. Another leaflet of similar format reminds drivers that

> To park
>   on sidewalks
>   on protected crosswalks
>   at bus stops
>   is a sign of selfish behavior. Don't take advantage of the impotence or negligence of the authorities: You would commit a bad deed.

On the reverse side of these larger handbills, usually containing comic-strip-type drawings to reinforce their message, there is more room to describe the broader aims of the Association. "We don't want to oppose normal progress stupidly." But man must not become a slave to his machines. The Association demands more protected crossings, traffic lights directed to pedestrians, sidewalks free of automobiles, underpasses, better road safety, priority for urban transit and collective taxis, protection of green space, leisure areas, pedestrian streets, suppression of noise and pollution, construction of new towns where pedestrian and motor traffic are separated.

Roger Lapeyre was an officer in France's Ministry of Transportation, an inspector responsible for security of workers and passengers on public transportation systems. Until 1974, he was also secretary general of a trade union of government employees, the Fédération de Travaux Publics et de Transport. His work taught him that automobile owners were adequately represented by their lobbies, while no one spoke for pedestrians. At the beginning, it was a matter of the very evident needs for protected crosswalks and elimination of accidents, which led to a concern for movement of people, and the defense of the city dweller in general (for example, green parks for those without secondary residences). From then on, it was obvious that the whole area of environmental and urban planning was involved; the Association had to broaden its scope to include the totality of transportation and urban policies. Since 1965, the group has lengthened its name to "Pour la Cité Humaine—Les Droits du Piéton" (For the Humane City—Pedestrian Rights). "It was more than a change of name," insists Lapeyre, "it was a change in philosophy. As an association we are reacting against the absurdity of the modern world in the city. We're not against automobiles, but we consider that the abuses of motor traffic in urban centers with heavy density create conditions of life we deplore."

In the early years after its founding (in April 1959), the difficulties seemed greater than the rewards. Now there are 12,500 enrolled members, but also 75 affiliated organizations, including local community defense groups, retired workers, the crippled. These organizations make use of Droits du Piéton literature relevant to their problems or their regions. Through them, the Association reaches an audience estimated at 500,000 Frenchmen. Lapeyre feels that his primary role is to see that his movement and its aims become known to larger and larger groups of people; one way to accomplish this is to participate in meetings and seminars devoted to urban and particularly traffic problems.

"When we started our work we weren't taken very seriously," he recalls. "It was said that we were opposed to progress. The most difficult thing was to convince people that we represent a serious interest group. Lately we have made a breakthrough among young people. They now make up half our membership, whereas we began with an older group. Our new members are considering that it is a matter of human rights within the city." It is said that while 80% of the members own automobiles, they are in the main professional people who are aware of the problems created by their vehicles; for the working class, the private automobile continues to signify social advancement.

Since its beginnings, when Roger Lapeyre may have seemed a Don Quixote, the Association has acquired standing in official and quasi-governmental circles. He represents his group on an official Paris Traffic Commission, and he is a committee member of the National Organization for Road Safety. He is also president of the International Federation of Pedestrians, now a decade old, whose secretariat is at the headquarters of the Dutch pedestrian association in The Hague. The principal component of the international group is a British organization which dates back to pre-World War I days. Roger Lapeyre has taken the initiative for the body, which now has sections in the United Kingdom, France, the Netherlands, West Germany and West Berlin, Switzerland, and Israel, with individual correspondents in Italy. At this writing, a new association had been founded in the United States but had not yet joined the international group.

In France itself, Lapeyre's association is best organized in the south and southeast (Rhone Valley, Dijon, Bourg, Valence, Nice, Marseilles, Montpellier, Toulouse, Bordeaux)—but also in Rennes in Brittany, although the movement has failed to interest the north and the east of the country. Sections are organized on the departmental level, which shares the dues (now a minimum of 10 francs annually per member) with national headquarters. Departmental sections also publish their own tracts and make better use of the local press than national headquarters can do with the Paris press.

"We aren't an official body; it is not our mission to educate pedestrians," Lapeyre says. "We want to remain a fighting organization—to oppose inhuman regulations. We refuse to integrate into the system."

Is the Association successful in its mission? "If you look at the parking situation in Paris, you would say that we haven't accomplished much. But we can't carry out a revolution in behavior. Those who believe that the private automobile is the solution to all problems aren't going to understand right away that all problems come from the automobile."

He includes among the achievements of the Association the growing awareness that pedestrians exist. In twenty French cities, the government is to subsidize pedestrian programs when the local authorities have drawn up appropriate plans. "Nobody jokes about the pedestrian any more." In specific cases, the group can point to a major, even an historic achievement. For example, it was one of the bodies which moved energetically to save the right-bank quais in Paris from the highway running along the Seine. After protests, the segment cutting through the historical center was put into a tunnel. The Association also joined other groups in a successful campaign against a parking lot that was to have been built under the park alongside Notre Dame Cathedral. The concept of material obstacles against abusive parking was launched by the Association, although Lapeyre is not happy with the concrete posts being installed on some sidewalks to keep automobiles away. And if a few narrow lanes in Paris are closed to motor traffic on certain days, Les Droits du Piéton deserves some of the credit.

Examination of Droits du Piéton newsletters, bulletins, press releases produced over the years suggests how much a dedicated group in a clearly defined area can accomplish. Recently, the Association allied itself with other organizations to save the older neighborhoods of Paris from renovation, from more highways into the city, from an upper level to be added to the ring road around Paris, and in particular from a new land-use plan which would allow more development and more skyscrapers in Paris. A public meeting in Paris brought Roger Lapeyre together with leaders of a federation of public transit passengers, a movement called S.O.S. Paris, and the initiator of a nature charter. Several other groups were co-sponsors: Friends of the Earth, some neighborhood defense groups—sixteen organizations in all. The meeting drew a crowd of 2,000, reportedly the largest gathering on environmental problems held until that time. The authorities, one newspaper commented, could no longer claim that the defense groups are general staffs without troops, nor were they preaching in the desert.

In most recent times, Droits du Piéton has been paying attention to in-town speed limits, advocates lower speed limits for trucks on highways and a ban on truck traffic in urban areas when alternate routes are available. At its 1974 general assembly, the Association agreed to demand a "reconquest" of sidewalks by pedestrians. It attacked the program of highways into and through the city as an encouragement of downtown traffic, called attention to the increasing use of sidewalks by two-wheeled vehicles. A special corps of traffic police was proposed, along with priority for collective transportation.

On the occasion of France's presidential election in 1974, the Association wrote each candidate:

> If you are convinced that among the problems preoccupying Frenchmen that of everyday existence is one of the foremost, can you give us the assurance that you will demand of the new government that a working group including representatives of the administrations, local elected officials, and the most representative national associations offer you the principles of a general policy of urban traffic?

The successful candidate, Valéry Giscard d'Estaing, pledged to examine the project for a left-bank highway and for an upper deck on Paris's peripheral boulevard, and added that only "indispensable" highways belonged in the city. He also indicated that he would reexamine urban renewal. Indeed, in his first months in office he stopped the left-bank expressway and other major urban renewal projects.

A random examination of leaflets available at Droits du Piéton headquarters, where they are printed in the basement of the Louis XV building housing Lapeyre's office, includes the 1973 appeal for a "day without automobiles," which coincided with World Environment Day (June 5). A number of illustrated handbills make the point that motor vehicles carrying single passengers take more of the community's roadway than they have a right to. There is an attack on the vandalism represented by certain high-rise constructions, parking lots, destruction of trees, roads built inside public parks, as well as the mushrooming of winter resorts on once-wild mountains.

Highlights of earlier years:

1959: Under the 1901 law on private organizations, Droits du Piéton filed its statement with the Paris Prefecture of Police. Its purpose: "to defend and protect the rights of pedestrians, to inform and instruct them on the servitudes of motor traffic, to assist them on all levels, to protect rest, residential, and play areas, to improve the protection of pedestrians in their movements, while facilitating traffic." Early actions included letters to authorities calling attention to traffic abuses, needed traffic signals—and these letters were answered. Warnings were also addressed to pedestrians on how to walk on roads and at night. There was emphasis on accident statistics in the bulletin of the association.

1961: The second issue of the association's bulletin recorded a number of examples of public response to the group's initiatives, as well as favorable (though sometimes noncommittal) responses by public officials. "The technical services, the prefectures, leave none of our requests without a reply," wrote Lapeyre. "It sometimes happens that a 'no' is followed by a 'yes.'"

1962: Droits du Piéton published a statement attacking the proposed Seine River highway, continued to demand traffic lights at dangerous crossings and improvement of public transportation, fought abusive parking, demanded pedestrian streets for Paris similar to those opened in other cities.

1963: Droits du Piéton designed an "ideal" bus possessing features useful to passengers such as a lower doorstep, leather hand straps for standing passengers, better lighting.

1964: Pursuit of the campaign for pedestrian streets, distribution of do's and don't's for pedestrians. Lapeyre took part in a seminar on accident insurance. Appeals were addressed during the course of the year to the Ministries of Interior, Justice, Public Works, and Transportation, as well as to mayors, prefects, city councillors.

1965: The Association sent a letter to candidates in the Paris municipal elections asking for their views and soliciting their support in protecting the historic center of Paris from the (left-bank) Seine highway, demanding that it be hidden in a tunnel between the Louvre and the Ile St. Louis.

1967: Droits du Piéton went to court to oppose a police ordinance granting a "tolerance" for parking on certain sidewalks, which the Association feared would lead to parking on all sidewalks. (After seven years of litigation, the supreme administrative court, the Conseil d'Etat, ruled against the pedestrian group on the grounds that the law doesn't set aside any particular space for them.)

1969: The Association approved the opinion of the prefect of police that "the private automobile is incompatible with contemporary urban life." But it asked that the city's acts conform to this opinion.

Each year since then has seen the number of actions grow, along with the Association's membership. Nevertheless, one can be skeptical about voluntary activity in France and predict that Droits du Piéton will last only as long as Roger Lapeyre does. Or one can be positive and congratulate the French for producing a Roger Lapeyre. The structure and activity of his group is a logical and a valid one; it has achieved significant results.

12. Islands in the Cities

I was talking with an official of the Prefecture of Paris about all the automobiles that are making life unbearable for Paris's inhabitants and their visitors. The official is a friend, so he displayed unusual patience as he reviewed the key features on a map of Paris parking facilities. The map showed that St. Germain des Prés, a noisy, polluted neighborhood, filled with traffic day and night (all the world's intellectuals come here for distraction), was soon to have an underground parking lot for 680 automobiles. There would be another at nearby Place St. Sulpice, and a third a short distance away. When completed, they would store some 2,200 vehicles; many of the spaces would be rented by the month or year, reducing the number available for transients.

"What good will it be when it's all done?" I asked. "You get tens of thousands of automobiles every day. With the promise of easy underground parking, you'll draw even more. They park on the narrow sidewalks right up to the building edge so that you can't walk past them, they block crosswalks so that you can't cross over, and the police tolerate it."

"There will be no solution," my friend agreed, "until the government adopts a policy of discouraging private ownership of automobiles. And that won't happen soon."

There is another remedy, I began to tell him, a radical one, but one that a strong city government could impose. It has worked elsewhere. But by that time, the noise had started again: They were digging another underground parking lot on the square behind the Hôtel de Ville, and the hammering would go on for months, so that they could shelter another platoon of the army of vehicles that invades this busy downtown district each day. My friend didn't hear the rest of what I had to say.

In this, Paris is like an American city. It is too big, too torn
by divergent interests, to have time for the human element that
was once so important there. I should have liked to tell my friend
about certain other streets and squares where cars have been pronounced incompatible with humans, and not only at those sites
where tourist considerations are primary, the Piazza Navona in
Rome, for example, or all of Venice, but in equally busy, commercially minded cities like Copenhagen, whose most interesting
shopping street, Strøget, is isolated from motor traffic, or Amsterdam, where Kalverstraat and Leidsestraat had also been judged
too important to be abandoned to the increasing chaos of motor
traffic. Similarly, when the Dutch rebuilt Rotterdam, a city totally
destroyed in World War II, they designed the attractive Lijnbaan
shopping street exclusively for pedestrians, with overhangs to keep
out Holland's 365 days of annual rainfall, benches for bright spells,
and flower pots to help keep everybody smiling in either case.
Lijnbaan is rather like The Pantiles, that charming 17th-century
shopping street of Tunbridge Wells, which is arcaded to parry the
English weather. Munich is another example, and I shall describe
that achievement in detail later in this chapter. Budapest has long
experience with a car-free shopping street in the heart of the central business district.

In Japan, as I have already noted, the main shopping street of
Tokyo becomes a pedestrian mall on Sundays, linked to existing
pedestrians-only market streets to make what is perhaps the long-
est pedestrian promenade of its kind, while two of Japan's shrine
cities, Kyoto and Kamakura, now enforce pedestrian zones around
major religious sites (in Kamakura on Sundays and holidays only).

Another notable example of urban planning for pedestrians,
which results in the creation of a zone of inner and outer peace,
is of course Cologne, whose downtown station and cathedral neighborhood has been redesigned over a span of two decades, repairing
not only World War II damage but also the urban renewal of the
19th century which had put the central station alongside the Gothic
cathedral in the first place, thus preparing the area as a 20th-
century traffic circle. But today motor traffic is being evicted from
the center of Cologne; even a bridge across the Rhine was removed
from the highway system since it brought motor traffic right up to
the edge of the old city. Little by little, the entire business and
commercial center of Cologne is being turned over to pedestrians;
it is becoming a park, but a park of stone rather than trees.

Naturally enough, new towns provide the best opportunities to
isolate pedestrians (it would probably be more human to speak

of isolating automobiles), as in Farsta and Vällingby, the planned suburbs along the subway line just outside of Stockholm. But nothing prevents the oldest part of a city from offering itself as an experiment, once the local shopkeepers are won over. One year, at roughly the same time, a nearly identical controversy was going on over Nassau Street in lower Manhattan, New York City, and the Plaza Mayor in the heart of old Madrid. On Nassau Street, traffic was cut off for the three-hour lunch period, 11 a.m. to 2 p.m., and the crowds took over. The Spanish plan was more ambitious: The historic plaza, once a mad arena of cars and people, was permanently retired from the machine age. Automobiles were sentenced to an underground dungeon if they wanted to stay, or to a tunnel running beneath the square if they were in transit. Local shopkeepers protested; it was inconvenient for their motorized customers, who liked to park within inches of the merchandise they wanted to examine. On Nassau Street, New Yorkers walked in the middle of the street, no longer rubbing up against the storefronts, and some merchants were ready with a percentage estimate of trade lost thereby. Nevertheless, the experiment seems to have worked in both cities.

Rome is more beautiful than any of the cities I have mentioned so far. It is also the least acceptable as a living place; one needs to spend time in a New York or a Paris as basic training for living in Rome. So that when the Roman municipality, despite a history of impotence and incompetence, proposed shutting off some streets, presumably the reasoning was that since neither motor nor pedestrian traffic was viable in those places, one might as well be cut off in the interest of longer life for the other.

The stakes were high. Some 860,000 vehicles crowd the streets of Rome at present, representing more than one for every three citizens. Each year, another 120,000 little Fiats are added, not to mention the still noisier contingent of 70,000 motorcycles of various styles and sizes. Because of the difficulty of building the limited subway system (too many archeological treasures below the surface) and the increased use of private transportation by newcomers to the middle class (who naturally prefer being stalled in a Fiat 600 of their own, seated, to being jammed, standing, in a blocked bus during rush hours), the point has been reached where the public welfare is in peril: Police cars and ambulances, for example, can't get to the scene of an emergency in time to be of use.

To save a little of Rome's honor, the city fathers selected a few squares, some of which are among the most beautiful in Europe, and banned all traffic from them, giving the streets as well as the sidewalks to the people. Tradesmen blocked the first bold experiment on the Piazza di Spagna and adjacent streets, but in other places the idea was given a chance to succeed. Rome's splendid Piazza Navona, boasting a Bernini fountain and a remarkable baroque church among the 17th-century palaces, is now what the Italians call an *isola pedonale,* a pedestrian island. So are the delightful Piazza Santa Maria in Trastevere, in the center of a typical quarter of trattoria and caffè life, the area around the Trevi fountain, and a small square near the city hall on Capitoline Hill. I have been watching this experiment from the first days, when blocking the Piazza Navona seemed a Sisyphean task, and when through-traffic seemed necessary in the narrow, winding alleys of Santa Maria in Trastevere. It wasn't, after all. Now, Rome's 860,000 automobiles have that much less space to move or stand still, perhaps aggravating the problem in other quarters. But who cares, now that there are islands in the sun on which to take refuge in that headache-inducing, otherwise lovely city?

The question of which comes first, the restricted area for pedestrians or the reduction in absolute numbers of automobiles, is obviously primordial. But if we wait for the latter, we shall wait a long time; no industrial nation is ready to discourage its automobile industry. Then can we discourage the people who drive automobiles? That may come, when all the desirable areas are accessible only on foot, and when the remaining space is too constricted to tempt sane men and women.

Verona

Verona is small as cities go, with only 250,000 inhabitants. The center of an enchanting countryside of choice vineyards, it is known to tourists for a hypothetical Romeo and Juliet whose very real balcony can be visited. There are superb monuments of the medieval Ghibelline period and of the Renaissance, and in summer, outdoor opera is performed in the well-preserved Roman amphitheater. From the more commercial downtown area surrounding the arena on the Piazza Bra, narrow streets run back toward the historical core centered on the Piazza delle Erbe, whose market stalls are covered by umbrellas, and the adjoining Piazza dei Signori, with the Scaligeri tombs and a Caffè Dante, whose customers play chess all afternoon oblivious of the business that might be transpiring in the courts and government buildings housed in ancient palaces on the same square. The streets of this quarter are reasonably rectangular, but they are narrow and numerous.

It was on November 12, 1968, that the mayor of Verona, after long debate in the Consiglio Comunale, in the press, and among business interests, closed this historic area to motor traffic. The running story deserves retelling because it is an example of how a single-minded city government, responsible both to pressures and to its better instincts, can resist premature protests and ad hoc committees. The decision followed an earlier experiment that had failed: a total ban on parking. Such a procedure seldom works in a country where respect for the law extends to the outer range of the policeman's eye, where parking tickets are never worried about and seldom paid. Underground parking lots were planned within the restricted perimeter and just outside, but the most important thing was that the city closed the area first, not waiting for the great day when parking space would become available. The automobile population of Verona had been increasing by some 3,000 cars a month, and the old center of the city was already saturated.

It was understood, and necessary, that public transportation would continue to operate on the boundaries of the zone and taxis, hired cars, and other vehicles taking guests to hotels, or the dead to be buried, would be allowed to enter. Various public services would have access to the perimeter, as would delivery trucks.

By the time Verona's *isola pedonale* was set up, most merchants were resigned to it or hoarse from protesting. Some took the expected position that cars equaled movement and movement meant customers, but a few echoed the sentiments of a caffè proprietor who said he supported the restriction, "first of all because I value my health and think that in eliminating cars we also eliminate noise and gasoline exhaust, and because I think too much traffic helps nobody."

When the great day came, forty-nine traffic patrolmen and four city officials guarded their newly conquered island. On my inadequate map I counted seven streets across and about three over; the next stage, when parking lots were ready and minibuses would convey passengers from private cars to their destinations, would cut off the entire old city from the Vias Roma and Pàllone to the river.

In the weeks immediately following the ban, the shopkeepers' protests grew louder. It seemed easy to obtain the necessary sticker to become a delivery man. The president of the Automobile Club urged that the ban be limited to four hours a day; newspapers ran photographs of deserted streets. The business community then issued a manifesto protesting the blocking off of the area before the necessary preliminary steps had been effected. (All 67 merchants on the Piazza delle Erbe had objected. Even the owner of the venerable Caffè Dante declared that he needed the tourist buses and the business they brought.) The mayor asked for patience; businessmen replied with an automobile parade with posters and blowing of horns.

Part of the Piazza delle Erbe was eventually opened for traffic cutting through the old quarter to connect the governmental offices to the downtown business area. Shopkeepers lost an appeal to the national government, then tried an occupation of the city hall. A reader of the local daily suggested in a letter to the editor that townspeople boycott shopkeepers who protested so clamorously.

What was the result of all this? Verona counts its tourists in the millions. When I last visited the city, out of the tourist season, I found the Piazza delle Erbe crowded; there were so many strollers on the traditional evening *passeggiata* along the Via Manzini (about 14 to 18 feet across at different points) that it was hard to walk without colliding with the people immediately preceding. Voting with their feet, the Veronese clearly favored safe passage among brightly lit shops. Cars approaching the perimeter saw red-bordered disks:

> *Excluse le autovetture dei turisti diretti agli alberghi e quelle autorizzati al transporto promiscuo di persone e cose.*

(There was nothing about "promiscuous transport" in the English translation just below. It merely said: "Cars directed to hotels can go.")

Bologna

The reader who has never been to the old city of Bologna has a treat in store. The Gothic and Renaissance façades will remind the visitor of Venice, a Venice without summer people. Among Bologna's other inherited advantages are the variety of piazzas and the streets that (apart from the area within the 11th-century limits) are seldom too narrow for modern uses. The arcades are carried on in many new buildings designed in the most contemporary of styles, and old *palazzi* continue to be used for commercial and public purposes. On the ancient Piazza Mercanzia, within 50 feet of the two strange family towers that are Bologna's symbol, I found an ultracontemporary tea room and an aggressively contemporary optician's shop, but I was not shocked by them. How Bologna is caring for its historic center and the people it contains is the subject of a later chapter.

As a prosperous city, Bologna was an early victim of automobile saturation. In 1968, within city limits, there were 120,000 automobiles (in ten years the number of inhabitants per vehicle had dropped from 13 to 3.6). It was in the middle of 1968 that a first proposal for *pedonalizione* was prepared by Bologna's traffic office. The existing historical centers could not be modified for cultural and financial reasons, but neither could they continue to receive all the traffic that converged on them. Above all, these old quarters could no longer be used as avenues for through traffic. The area earmarked for the ban, the Piazzas Maggiore and Nettuno and Via d'Azeglio, site of an admirable ensemble of monuments, one of the happiest surviving examples of urban space, was worth preserving just as it was. Via d'Azeglio, as it happened, was one of the busiest streets of the central city, with buses as well as private automobiles and preoccupied walkers. Alternative routes were provided for the traffic, new bus itineraries were mapped. The ban was put into effect in September 1968.

The city has produced a series of useful and attractive progress reports, an early example being *Un Anno di Isola Pedonale,* with abundant photographic and graphic illustrations. With respect to motor traffic, it had been decided that streets and squares used mainly by pedestrians would be transformed for exclusive pedestrian use, all through-traffic to be diverted, while encumbered intersections would be eliminated by changing the traffic patterns. All future uses of land and buildings within the medieval area would be studied to avoid aggravation of traffic conditions, parking facilities would be developed, public services assured and, if possible, public transportation augmented in the area. As corollary measures, a zone was reserved for parking commercial vehicles, certain streets were designated for public transport, and new one-way streets were mapped.

The first year passed. In its evaluation of what happened, the municipality of Bologna admitted that one could not measure the new sense of pride and freedom of its citizens, who for the first time could now really use the Piazza Maggiore, whether to admire their heritage, window-shop, gossip, or simply look at each other. Now other Bolognese streets and squares have been given back to the people, sometimes just by eliminating a supposedly sacrosanct parking lot from the front of a church or from a small public garden. What is more, there is a program of activities on the liberated central square, concerts and ballets in summer, the carabinieri band in early autumn. Finally, if the texts of messages and resolutions in the report are representative of opinion, even a part of the business community was reasonably well disposed to what has been done and will be done.

Later on, Florence joined Verona, Bologna, Siena, Pavia, and Rome in this dangerous experiment. The area covered in Florence is the historical center, between the Arno River and the Duomo, from the Via Tornabuoni with its fashionable shops to the Uffizi Gallery. Once again, establishment of the zone was resisted at first by shopkeepers. Local merchants once more asked that parking lots be built first, that minibuses begin their routes first, that decentralization take place before cars were removed from the *centro storico*. No one is ever ready for a pedestrian island, so it always comes as a happy surprise when we shipwreck onto one.

Munich

In Munich, a fast-growing city of 1.3 million inhabitants, third largest in the Federal Republic after Berlin and Hamburg, the experimental phase has ended. A vast center-city artery was given to pedestrians without prejudice to business or traffic; it worked so well that it will be extended.

The visitor is attracted to a display of picture postcards just opposite the Rathaus (city hall), and he selects a few that he would like to buy. As usual in tourist shops, the cards on sale are not recent views. In the poor color reproduction the visitor recognizes the city hall square, Marienplatz, crowded with automobiles, while streetcars roam the narrow Kaufingerstrasse. Then he turns around.

Where are the automobiles and the trams shown on the postcards? The Rathaus is now the centerpiece of a vast terrace with garden furniture, large pots of flowers, outdoor cafés whose tables and chairs invade the center of the square. There are no automobiles or trams, of course, for where would they be able to go? Decorative paving stones have replaced the asphalt. Indeed, the last streetcar ride through Kaufingerstrasse and Neuhauser Strasse took place on April 20, 1968, now a date for the history books. A shield of trees newly planted across the Kaufingerstrasse, where the trams used to run, announces defiantly Munich's intention that this pedestrian island be a permanent one. Sitting in a comfortable chair marked "City of Munich" in dead center of Marienplatz, waiting for the carillon chimes and the glockenspiel automatons of the Rathaus clock tower, the visitor thinks of that other outdoor salon, Venice's Piazza San Marco. With a momentary feeling of disloyalty to Venice, he decides that Munich's is a more satisfying urban amenity: Here the chairs are free.

The urban specialist has another thought: Munich's municipal authorities have now proved that major downtown business areas can be permanently closed to traffic without prejudice to the life of the city. Very much to the contrary, banning traffic can be an asset to business.

Tests of the interaction of users of these streets and the streets themselves culminated in a 1965 study which found that Munich's downtown shopping area was supported by pedestrians: 72,000 persons were counted using the main street in one day, from 7 a.m. to 7 p.m. Through and local traffic, on the other hand, was a disturbing influence rather than a support. Munich's city council adopted the pedestrian-zone concept a year later. But the execution of the new policy was geared to the creation of a mass transit network, whose pivot would be the Marienplatz. Both pedestrian-zone and rapid-transit link were timed to the 1972 Olympic Games. A competition for the design of Munich's pedestrian zone, open to architects, landscape and garden designers, sculptors and painters, was won by a private architect, Bernhard Winkler, and by Siegfried Meschederu, then a 32-year-old city architect. Their plan was discussed in open meetings, described at length in the press, submitted to public opinion.

The area covered in phase one is 50,000 square meters; the length of the traffic-free zone from Marienplatz to Karlsplatz is 840 meters, with two traffic crossings, plus a north-south pedestrian street (Weinstrasse and Rosenstrasse) adding 280 meters. The average width of streets in the zone is 20 meters. Compare Copenhagen's Strøget, which is 1,100 meters long, crossed three times by motorways. Essen has 1,400 meters of pedestrian streets; Cologne's Hohe Strasse and Schildergasse zone, 1,500 meters.

The visitor may observe certain patterns of use of these streets: On a holiday evening in Munich when shops are closed, with the exception of a few restaurants and cafés—there are eighteen in all along the promenade—the pedestrian zone is nevertheless crowded. About one stroller in three is observed to be using the very center of the street rather than walking alongside the shop windows or the independent display cases adjacent to shops whose façades are hidden by arcades. Next morning, a normal working day, the crowds return to shop. On the same morning, on nearby Maximilianstrasse, a principal artery with good shopping and normal automobile and tram traffic, the sidewalks are deserted at 10 a.m., at the very hour that the pedestrian zone and its contiguous cross streets and alleys are jammed. The observer fails to discover traffic congestion either on the Maximilianstrasse and the streets parallel to the pedestrian Marienplatz-Karlsplatz axis, or for that matter on the streets immediately surrounding the pedestrian zone, where one would expect a certain amount of frustrated automobile activity. There are parking facilities, apparently ample, at the edges of the zone, and a seemingly adequate supply of taxis standing at the pedestrian zone terminals. (Taxi drivers seem to have no strong complaints, although they say that traffic movement is difficult at rush hours.) The city is afraid to make parking too easy, for this would draw still more traffic, and these streets "cannot be broadened endlessly."

Street furniture is abundant and varied. Vast cement flower pots are grouped in oases equipped with a generous supply of white plastic chairs marked Stadt-München, although in good weather, frequent enough in the Bavarian capital, it is difficult to find an empty seat on Marienplatz or the extension west along Kaufingerstrasse and Neuhauser Strasse. The chairs are taken in during the winter months, but the flowers remain, and on warm chairless days off-season there is a certain amount of sitting on the edges of the flower pots.

"When we put out 500 chairs, we expected 200 of them to be stolen," recalls city planner Gerhard Meighörner. "Actually, we have lost only six of them. Now a second lot of 500 chairs has been put in place." They and the plants and pots are city equipment. "If we had been more optimistic about the success of the zone," confesses Meighörner, "we'd have asked the shopkeepers to pay for them. And for all the expenses incurred in establishing the pedestrian zone."

The lamp posts are attractively designed (elliptical spheres, two to a column). A few traditional fountains, the famous Richard Strauss and Buberl fountains among them, have been augmented by contemporary models, for a total of eight. Newspaper kiosks, outdoor shops, and fruit stalls are literally besieged during daytime shopping hours, and the visitor also finds that he can actually smell the seasonal fruits from a considerable distance, since no automobile exhaust intrudes. The trees standing in dead center, where tram tracks used to run, cannot fail to impress Munich's citizens with the change that has come over the city, and its permanence. Fussgängerzone ends with a splash: A fountain display on Karlsplatz effectively screens the view of heavy traffic on the square and the avenues beyond. In fact, it was designed to deflect automobile exhaust from the grand entrance to the zone, the Karlstor.

And then, one does not have to cross the dangerous-looking Karlsplatz at all, for stairs and escalators descend from the sidewalk to a large underground shopping plaza, with other exits served by escalators all around the square and the adjacent streets. This is also a station on the subway line. But up and out beyond the Karlsplatz, the familiar big-city traffic flow confronts the walker. After all, this municipality of 1.3 million is the nucleus of an urban conglomeration of 2.6 million. Munich's inner city alone contains 500,000 inhabitants, 400,000 jobs (its diameter: 3.7 miles). The Alte Stadt, the area bisected by the Fussgängerbereiche (as it is called in official documents), contains no more than 40,000 inhabitants (its diameter: 0.6 mile).

What is the effect of a pedestrian zone as ambitious as this one on local business? And what happens when the city's major artery, its city hall square and immediate surroundings, are closed to automobile traffic? Those involved in the Munich experiment, city officials responsive to public opinion and commercial interests, have had to be concerned with the answers to these questions. Two particularities were observed in Munich: For one thing, the traffic on these streets had been so intense that it hindered pedestrian movement, therefore discouraged shopping. It is difficult to recall what two-way on narrow Kaufingerstrasse was like, with streetcars added; one finds it hard to understand why civilized people would have wanted to live that way—now that trees and plants cover the roadway. For another, the entire length of the pedestrian zone had been torn up for construction of the subway line, a 4.2-kilometer underground link between the Central and East stations; work began in 1966 and was completed in 1972. The visitor recalls staying in a hotel on the Karlsplatz in that period and waking at night to the sound of roaring engines. Opening a curtain on what he assumed to be a quiet street, he stared down into a vast excavation which in its volume and eerie light resembled a volcanic crater. The night shift was digging the subway. This midnight vision became a daily fact of life for Munich's residents, to the point that it later became difficult to compare business results before and after installation of the pedestrian zone; the area had been a battlefield scene for so long.

Regierungsbaumeister Siegfried Meschederu, who remains in charge of pedestrian zone design, recalls the condition of the downtown area during subway construction. Not a few merchants sought compensation for the loss in trade. A restaurant opposite the Rathaus whose main asset was its agreeable site received DM 100,000. At the same time, business improved on streets near the construction site where it was easy to shop. And when the pedestrian precinct opened, there was a 66% rise in foot traffic.

Meschederu, a Romanian-born architect who migrated to Germany with his parents in 1939 and has lived in Munich since 1946, describes the workings of the zone. The ban on automobile traffic is partially lifted each day for deliveries from 10:30 p.m. to 9:45 a.m. Still, in all but eight cases, deliveries are carried out not on the main street but at the rear entrances of buildings. Because no back-door deliveries are possible in the area surrounding Munich's cathedral church, the Frauenkirche, motor traffic is given three extra hours each day, to 12:45 p.m. As if to compensate pedestrians for this, they have an extraordinary new fountain with ample stone benches arranged as if at random in an arena—the impression is of an abstract Fontana di Trevi—a much-frequented spot in good weather. (For emergency use, a traffic lane 7 meters wide is available, and is used by occasional police vehicles, from time to time by moving vans.)

If there was some criticism of the pedestrian zone when it opened (the style of the street lamps, the fact that some shops were given extra display space on the public promenade to compensate for their unfavorable location under arcades less likely to be frequented, now that pedestrians had the whole road for themselves), the overwhelming response has been positive. Merchants, who as will be seen, were involved in the planning of the zone, are now asking for more. Expansion has been requested north of City Hall, along the Dienerstrasse and nearby streets, including the famous Theatinerstrasse, and south from the zone's present terminal on Rosenstrasse to take in Sendlinger Strasse. Already a small pedestrian zone exists at Sendlinger Tor, at the foot of Sendlinger Strasse, with the familiar pots of flowers and garden chairs. This extension will require further study, since backdoor deliveries are not possible here.

Meanwhile, the Viktualienmarkt is being prepared as Munich's next pedestrian zone. A colorful food and flower market area in the heart of the city, utilized daily by shoppers, visited and photographed by tourists, this is actually a 20,000-square-meter extension of the first zone, separated only by a narrow traffic crossing. Siegfried Meschederu believes that pedestrian zones are only taking their baby steps. They will grow, and he plans to stay with them.

How and where the zones are to be implanted are matters decided by the city's Planning Department on nearby Blumenstrasse. Here, Gerhard Meighörner, head of Inner City Planning Management, is mapping out a second generation of pedestrian zones for the city. Munich's famous interior passages are one of Meighörner's preferred solutions. He pursues their extension, in a complex including the existing and planned pedestrian zones, largely by persuading private owners to allow the opening of new passageways between buildings. And he believes that if Munich's pedestrian zone is considered one of the most successful of its kind it is thanks to pre-existing spatial and environmental qualities: the attractive old buildings, the sequence and variety of small squares along the pedestrian itinerary. Now, with the demands for extension of the zone, the real problems begin. Among them is the question, Does the city have the right to plan a pedestrian zone which will increase profits of retail businesses along the route at the expense of other retailers on adjacent streets which are not being closed to motor traffic? Profits in the pedestrian zone increased 40% to 60%, for example, while they were said to have dropped 20% to 30% on a parallel street.

From the onset of construction of the underground transit line, explained Meighörner, motor traffic became rare along the axis later to become the pedestrian zone. Actually, the decrease in profits during the upheaval of construction was less than had been predicted. Townspeople seemed to enjoy visiting the site and then go shopping. The open pit of the subway site also served as a signal that the area was undergoing transformation. "We tell people: When you want to open a pedestrian zone, first open a construction site." Indeed, in another Munich neighborhood where subway construction will soon be underway, Gerhard Meighörner's department is considering following it up with a pedestrian zone, "which is just the opposite of the way we should be planning."

They are also planning the right way. Henceforth, proposed pedestrian precincts will call for serious economic and sociological research, and the decision, pedestrian zone or no pedestrian zone, will not be certain until all returns are in. It is also possible to envisage a compromise between the traditional street and a pure pedestrian zone, limited to tram traffic only, for example (as has been carried out on the Leidsestraat in Amsterdam). "People now know that installing a pedestrian zone is a serious affair, not a matter of intuition," says Meighörner. One proposal, for example, is for a pedestrian zone on a street and square in a moderate-income neighborhood some distance from Munich's center, Weissenburger Platz and the short street leading into it. The area was selected because its business "lives" on pedestrian traffic. At present, the Stadtplanung people are studying the area, and neighborhood residents have already had an opportunity to see and discuss the plans, just as citizen discussions are in progress on the Viktualienmarkt plan, with an information center displaying a scale model close to the site. Once the city planning department gives its approval, it is the job of Siegfried Meschederu's unit to execute the work.

The success of the pedestrian zone has led to another demand from commercial interests, according to Meighörner. Given that traffic-free streets are now known to be better for business, shopkeepers would like some less popular streets to be closed so as to attract business. Pressure for pedestrian streets is coming from local political leaders and private groups. Why, one is tempted to ask the city planners, do your streets work, while a city such as Rome, whose spatial environment is no less favorable, cannot convince its business sector to accept a ban on automobiles in a commercial zone? Meighörner replies that in the Bavarian city many organizations are eager to show that they do not think only of profit; they too have a *Münchnerherz*, a "Munich heart." Measures that would not have a chance elsewhere can succeed here; persuasion is often sufficient where no law can be applied. Munich also happens to be a Socialist city. "Politics," an old Münchner resident told me, "is the art of leading people to desire to go the way you want them to go."

Meighörner's thesis was tested by a visit to the Bavarian retail trade association, Landesverband des Bayerischen Einzelhandels, where one official was found to be specializing in problems connected with the pedestrian zone. This official noted that, from the beginning, the projected Marienplatz-Karlsplatz traffic-free area was of concern to merchants. It was true they had felt that a street without automobiles or trams would become very quiet; during construction of the subway, the retail trade association received daily telephone calls of complaint. But as soon as the pedestrian zone opened in 1972, it was a success. Spot checks by telephone indicated an immediate increase of business of up to 25%. (An average of 40,900 pedestrians used the zone each day between 4 and 5 p.m.—rush hour—in 1972.) A recent paper on the pedestrian zone prepared by the trade association set forth its advantages and disadvantages, concluded with a recommendation for more of the same. Because of the adverse effects on business just outside the zone, where streets become less appealing (in addition to which they must support extra traffic delivering goods to the interdicted zone), there is pressure to widen the zones. The retail trade group represented business interests in the Arbeitsgemeinschaft Fussgängerzone München, a now-disbanded association of citizens, including users and trade groups, set up in 1969 to deal with day-to-day problems connected with the planning of the zone.

City planner Meighörner explains that a new Arbeitsgemeinschaft Offene Planung Fussgängerzone with a different mix of members representing economic as well as social interests was organized in May 1973, with the mayor as chairman, to take part in earmarking and planning new traffic-free areas. Its sessions are open to press and public. Meanwhile, the city is examining the overall pattern of existing and future motor traffic, and it is likely that in the next phase automobiles will be limited to a small quarter of the old city; that is, they will have to leave the inner city by a street adjacent to the one used to enter it, and will be unable to cross to another sector.

Meanwhile, the subway system continues to grow. Begun in 1965, the U-Bahn will cover 56 miles by 1990, 25 miles underground. The first completed section is 7.5 miles long, while the S-Bahn (the underground connection of the Federal Railway lines), which opened in May 1972, extends another 2.5 miles. Until adequate mass transportation can replace all private motor traffic in town, air pollution is not likely to be reduced significantly. Meschederu points out that if pollution has been decreasing in the pedestrian zone, this is not true of all Munich. "The automobiles are just changing streets but not the town."

Munich's planning is a multilevel affair. District councils covering areas of 40,000 to 60,000 inhabitants meet once a month to discuss local problems. An official in the mayor's office collects their demands and routes them to appropriate city departments. These district councils, composed of from fifteen to forty members, can also meet directly with city planning officials. The city council must act on a district petition within three months, justifying its decision, and at least once a year in each district a citizens' meeting is organized under the chairmanship of the mayor himself. In all instances, final decisions are made by the city council, but the tendency is to accept all such humane measures because the "Munich heart" takes precedence over other considerations. And in Gerhard Meighörner's opinion, a city untroubled by economic problems, with full employment, continuing prosperity—although having its share of trouble spots—can and must give priority to what hard-deaded urbanists would call the sentimental factor.

In the case of the Viktualienmarkt, Munich's second projected pedestrian zone, the city planners provided the sociological research, a separate research department did the economic study, and then the representative organization of citizens and business interests, the Arbeitsgemeinschaft, had its say. The district council directly concerned is also represented in the Arbeitsgemeinschaft, but could operate independently if it so wished. Finally, the city council would make the irrevocable decision. In the case of projected zone three, Weissenburger Platz and Strasse, the decision will also depend on whether the planners believe that the area will be of some significance to the future development of the city.

I was in Munich for the first official birthday of the Fussgänger-bereiche. Officially opened in June 1972, it was in fact in partial use for a number of months before that, but without the pedestrian pavement which spelled the symbolic as well as the practical end to automobile traffic. On the square before the flag-decked city hall, the event was appropriately celebrated by a performance of the famous glockenspiel—the automatons in the tower, a concert of a young people's symphony orchestra and ballet. There were speeches, notably by the mayor. But above all there was a *joie de vivre* throughout the zone, from Karlsplatz to Marienplatz and over to the Frauenkirche. Elsewhere, there have been complaints that a pedestrian zone in a shopping area dies when the shops close down for the day. Siegfried Meschederu sees his zone as an alternative to old Schwabing, Munich's Montparnasse. The mayor is convinced that to be successful the zone must be "animated." A number of street fairs and festivals such as the annual Christmas Market have been organized here, or transferred here from other neighborhoods. The life of each new pedestrian zone will depend on such animation: This is a final lesson to be learned from the Munich experiment.

Milan

Few seem to recall that a pioneer city planner for Milan was Leonardo da Vinci, who is believed to have gone there first at the age of 30 as court artist to Lodovico Sforza. In between paintings, he worked on the famous notebooks treating engineering and the natural sciences. He also designed and built for his Sforza patrons, although today we are more aware of his interior decoration than of his architecture. He returned to Milan again under French King Louis XII as an architect and engineer, from 1506 to 1513.

Leonardo did not, apparently, ever devote himself to designing a city in its entirety. He focused his attention on particular features: public buildings, communications on land and water, sanitation, fortifications. His attitude, according to a leading Renaissance scholar, Eugenio Garin, was common in his time: The city and its evils compared unfavorably with the contemplative calm of pastoral life. Many of the amenities he advocated were designed to compensate for these evils, or to bring the country into the city.

One civilizing suggestion went into Leonardo's notebooks—in Codex B, now in the possession of the Institut de France—but there is no evidence that execution of the idea ever began during the artist's lifetime. Leonardo drew the plan for a pedestrian street, which was a raised platform designed for gentlemen who would be on foot. A lower street was reserved for carts and vehicles, as well as for *l'uso e comodità del popolo*. Delivery of goods, such as wood and wine, was to be carried out through gateways on the lower level. Leonardo's drawings of the scheme were accompanied by an idea of the measurements of these streets. (In modern times, a scale model of Leonardo's ideal city, bringing together his various proposals such as pedestrian streets, has been constructed, and it can be seen in Milan at the Museum of Science and Techniques.)

Of course, Leonardo's plan is criticized as elitist, although some scholars have preferred to see in the two-level street only a separation by function. Leonardo made the class distinction clear in his own notes, and his attitude was certainly appropriate to his time. In our own time, the separation of vehicular and pedestrian traffic derives from a new humanism. "The pedestrian must be able to follow other paths than that of the automobile," Le Corbusier wrote in *The Charter of Athens* (1941). If some anti-humane situations grow out of modern urbanism (for example, the poor on foot in Brasilia to their discomfort and danger, while the broad long avenues are enjoyed by those who can afford to drive), the intention is generally in the interest of the community of man.

Nearly five hundred years after Leonardo, in any case, Milan seems to have adopted an egalitarian variation of his scheme. The streets in the town center, on the Piazza del Duomo and its immediate surroundings, have been closed to all but pedestrian traffic. They are adjacent to a larger half-way area, in which streets are shared by pedestrians and local traffic (delivery vehicles, taxis and buses, and automobiles belonging to residents of the neighborhood who can prove they possess off-street parking space). If the plan has been put into effect after construction of a subway line, the fact is that in contrast to Leonardo's plan, Milan's plebian population has access both to the gentleman's upper level and to the underground passages, as well as to the trains of the Metropolitana.

Indeed, a wide area beneath the cathedral square is covered by galleries lined with shops and leading to the ticket windows of the subway line. Similar shopping and service areas exist at other stations. There are now two Metro lines serving Milan, the first about 7 miles long, the second only partly opened but already connecting the first.

With a functioning subway, and the same automobile hysteria that affects every large Western city despite the growing oil problem, Milan took the step of banning traffic from its busiest downtown space in May 1973. It is interesting to observe that cities which make decisions of this kind often have a history of humane planning. Thus Milan already possessed a network of arcaded streets (similar to, if less extensive than, that of Bologna), but also a series of "galleries," large interior passages such as the landmark Galleria Vittorio Emanuele II with its skylight cupola.

Milan's intention was to arrest urban decay before it got started. Pollution, noise, ugliness, blocked traffic accompanied the automobile wherever it could move in the central business district. All these afflictions could be gotten rid of at once by closing streets to unrestricted driving. The point was also to allow citizens to exercise the freedom to get to where they wished to go on foot, or by surface public transportation moving at ease on streets freed of private vehicular traffic. And when the arrangements were in place, it was found that there was no diminution of activity in the zone. Those services which might have been disrupted or inconvenienced were brought into the planning process; citizens, speaking through the press, seemed to approve what was happening.

The zone earmarked for closing to traffic was the city's biggest drawing-card, containing famous landmarks but also the entertainment district, and there happened to be a high level of existing public transportation. The 114 acres of the zone represent 16% of the entire *centro storico*. Once it had been ascertained that most traffic in the zone was in transit and that off-street space could be found for the automobiles of bona fide residents, the rest was easy. As for the districts immediately surrounding the restricted zone, the traffic police found that the situation conformed to past experience—that is, to the capacity of private motorists to adapt to the space available for driving and parking. In adjacent districts, the early days after the closing of 114 acres saw traffic congestion which gradually subsided to previous levels. The police called it self-regulation. At the beginning, too, shopkeepers were afraid of what might happen to their trade; they asked for special tax relief. But shoppers continued to come. It is said that shopkeepers on a street just outside the zone, the Via Monte Napoleone, are now demanding a pedestrian street of their own.

In a report on Milan's pedestrian zone by the commissioner of transport, traffic, and roadways, the following functional criteria have been defined:

(1) To reserve routes for pedestrians, so as to create a network of means of access to the points of major interest throughout the historical center.

(2) To allow private cars into the center without letting them drive across it, that is, forbidding radial crossing; parking facilities to exist at the periphery.

(3) Liberate public transport lanes from interference by private cars.

(4) Allow private traffic only on those streets wide enough to contain them in lanes independent of public transport.

(5) Abolish parking on traffic streets, allowing parking by frequent rotation on the periphery of the zone.

(6) Review parking and traffic rules to avoid radical variations in regulations in contiguous zones.

(7) Rationalize the itineraries of public transportation, with more transfer points.

(8) Extend the new system in the historical center to other parts of the city with analogous characteristics or particular problems of traffic control.

In fact, Milan's new pedestrian zone is divided into three segments:

Zone A1 (32 acres): No private cars. Public transport and taxis, except where streets are physically closed by stone barriers in the area surrounding the cathedral. Within a radius of 250 meters there are 18 separate transport lines, including route number one of the Metropolitana.

Zone A2 (55 acres), northeast of the cathedral: Access by cars of residents with off-street parking, and for deliveries at stated hours. Some 1,200 to 1,500 automobiles were issued permits to enter.

Zone A3 (26 acres), east of the cathedral: Traffic allowed but no parking, except from 8 p.m. to 3 a.m. This zone has many restaurants, cinemas, theaters, night clubs. Speed limit of 12 miles per hour.

Another area, Zone C, west of the cathedral, containing many narrow streets and old buildings, is also being studied as a future pedestrian zone. But it lacks a subway line, and it is not well served by public transportation on the surface, either. There is, finally, a project involving the street furniture of the cathedral neighborhood, and a competition will be launched for designs and ideas. "Many feel that the removal of motor traffic laid bare the ugliness of much of our neighborhood," a police department planner observed. Tram tracks now running along the south side of the Duomo will probably be shifted a block away, along the periphery of Zone A1.

13. Cleaner Air

Other cities have attacked the causes of air pollution with varying degrees of success. If we are particularly drawn to the London achievement, it is first because of the very dimensions of that city, one of the giants of the earth, and because London's air pollution was more than a problem, it was a legend, pea-soup fogs being a part of the English literary heritage. And it was leading toward disaster, with 4,000 reported deaths after one notable attack of smog two decades ago.

The London weather was the backdrop for centuries of literature, the grimy London of Blake's chimney sweepers, Wilde's

> The yellow fog came creeping down
> The bridges, till the house's walls
> Seemed changed to shadows, and St. Paul's
> Loomed like a bubble o'er the town.
> (*Impression du Matin*)

The scientific reality confirmed the legend. London's annual sunshine was one of the lowest of any world capital: 33% of the possible. Only Edinburgh had less (New York 60%, Tokyo 49%, Paris 37%). "Would experience more sunshine," as an old *Encyclopedia Britannica* had it, "but for the pall of smoke that sometimes shuts out the sky in the winter half of the year." Attempts had been made to cope with the problem for years, for the city of Francis Bacon had little difficulty in establishing the causal relationships. As early as the 13th century, it was forbidden to burn coal in London town; a royal decree in 1306 made it a capital offense. Over the centuries, many ineffective attempts were made to deal with the causes of London's bad air. In 1952, a giant fog was blamed for killing those 4,000 city dwellers in the space of a few days.

The eternal condition, "a London particular," as a character in *Bleak House* put it, had suddenly attained the dimensions of crisis. And crisis—it is almost a cliché—is something with which the British can cope. It is a point of pride with them. Parliament voted the Clean Air Act in 1956, carrying three principal provisions:

(1) Dark smoke could be emitted only during specially permitted periods or special circumstances, while all new furnaces would be adjusted to emit a minimum of smoke.

(2) Means were to be devised to prevent grit and dust.

(3) Local authorities were authorized to set up "smoke control" areas, subject to ministerial approval. It would be a punishable offense to allow smoke to be emitted from any chimney in a smoke-control area. Owners or tenants were to be reimbursed 70% of the cost of adapting their fireplaces; the British government would in turn reimburse four-sevenths (about 57%) of the local municipality's expenses.

Anyone who has visited London in recent years, and has had occasion to enter one of the great houses of the West End whose rooms are dominated by their fireplaces, is aware of the change brought about in London's life style. In the center of the ancient fireplace, beside heavy brass fixtures, one finds a sad little pile of imitation wood concealing a gas burner. One stares incredulously into the fireplace, attracted by the colored bulb simulating flames. In an old hotel near Piccadilly, one of London's largest, converting to gas was apparently too hard a job; each room now contains a portable electric heater.

London is divided into boroughs. Each would approach the task independently. By the end of 1968, over 60% of all the homes of London, covering 50% of the greater city's total acreage, was included in smoke control orders; by 1978, the whole of Greater London is to be covered, although this projection was made before the effects of the the world oil crisis began to be felt in 1974. Elsewhere in England and Wales, parallel activity was being pursued, with slower but presumably steady progress. By mid-1965, 28% of the total of inhabited places in England and Wales was covered or waiting for a decision, against 47% at that time in London itself.

By 1971, according to the Greater London Council scientific adviser's report for that year, the average concentration of smoke in the air of Inner London was only a quarter of the estimated level for 1955-56, before the introduction of the Clean Air Act. Since 1962, the emission of smoke in Greater London has declined by over 60%, and it is considered likely that the reduction since 1958 is 75%. Some of the figures:

TREND OF AIR POLLUTION IN CENTRAL LONDON
(averages of seven volumetric recording stations)

WINTER OF	SMOKE	SULFUR DIOXIDE
	(micrograms per cubic meter)	
1958/59	309	340
1959/60	206	275
1960/61	200	277
1961/62	182	302
1962/63	173	365
1963/64	136	299
1964/65	126	293
1965/66	100	243
1966/67	87	214
1967/68	68	203
1968/69	61	205

The consequences were gratifying, and almost immediate. The reduction of smoke appears to have increased the duration of winter sunshine since 1958 by 50%, according to the records of London's Weather Centre. "It is possible that the substantial reduction in smoke concentration has led to a change in the local meteorology of London," reported the Greater London Council's Research and Intelligence Unit. "The removal of the 'smoke blanket' over London is allowing more sunshine to penetrate to ground level and this is leading to the more effective breaking up of temperature inversions and dispersal of pollution."

Specifically, for central London there was a substantial increase in the hours of sunshine from September to March (November, 40% increase; December, 73%; January, 55%). Still more recent information communicated by the London Weather Centre's Meteorological Office puts the increase of sunshine in December, in the decade 1964-73, at 69%. The Weather Office has produced a comparison of the amounts of winter sunshine in central London with amounts in outlying Kew, Wisley, and Rothamsted (Kew is 9 to 10 miles from central London, in a park surrounded by suburban development; Wisley and Rothamsted are rural sites 20 to 25 miles from London). Whereas in the 1940s, central London received an average of 30 to 50 minutes less sunshine per day from December to February than the three peripheral sites, the differences have virtually disappeared. Lately, indeed, it has been sunnier in central London than at Rothamsted.

Less complete information is available on fog frequency. There were decreases in the average number of hours of fog at three meteorological stations, central London (Kingsway), Kew, and Heathrow, except for dense fog at Heathrow, based on measurements taken between 1947-50 and 1959-62 (decrease in dense fog for the three stations: 52%, 23%, and 5%; in thick fog: 24%, 22%, and 12%). In a report on the progress of smoke control compiled by the Greater London Council's Research and Intelligence Unit in 1970, the marked decrease in the frequency of fog in central London, compared with the city's suburbs, was believed to be due to the substantial decrease in smoke pollution in London's center. Indeed, 65% of the observations of dense fog at the Kingsway station in central London from 1947 to 1962 were associated with calm weather; the wind was at one knot or less in 77% of the reports of dense fog, leading to the conclusion that locally produced pollution may be more important than drifting pollution from outlying areas.

There is no certainty about any of this, although the fact that smoke control began earlier and progressed faster in central London than around Kew and Heathrow may explain the disparity in the figures. And "it is a fact that there has been no major fog in London for seven years" (that is, from 1963 to 1970).

When the air clears, everyone seems to benefit. Esthetically: The newly cleaned buildings are not getting grimy again as fast as they might have. More plants are growing in the city center; birds are coming back—138 identifiable species against half that number a decade earlier. There has been a dramatic increase in visibility; on an average winter day, a Londoner can now see nearly three times farther than he could in 1958. Finally, there seems to be a reduction in laundry bills. Shirts don't get dirty as fast. Paint lasts longer.

But "finally" should refer to the health of citizens. Official London is reluctant to proclaim results in this area, but there are encouraging signs. Reductions in mortality and hospital admissions have been noted, while reduced smoke levels have benefited bronchitic patients. One problem has been that the Clean Air Act contained no direct provisions against the emissions of oxides of sulfur, and sulfur dioxide is a major danger to health. While concentrations of it have been decreasing steadily, the more rapid fall of smoke concentrations produced a situation where sulfur dioxide concentrations were three times as important as smoke concentrations (see the table reproduced earlier). It was even feared by critics of the Clean Air Act that its failure to include sulfur dioxide emissions would lead to an increase in sulfur dioxide air pollution as fuel users converted to smokeless fuels, a fear that in the end seemed not to have been justified.

But in 1971, the City of London Various Powers Act filled the gap by limiting the sulfur content of fuel oil burnt in new furnaces to 1% in the one-square-mile area of the old City. It was not felt that it would be practicable for similar legislation to cover all areas, although it might be the way to reduce sulfur dioxide levels in the centers of large cities. On the whole, the general downward trend of pollution would result in a decrease in the emission of sulfur dioxide, too. Chimneys are taller, for one thing, more widely dispersed, and there is a growing use of natural gas as an alternative fuel. It was always felt to be a little unreal to discuss air pollution in terms of emissions, since a large proportion of pollutants rise into the upper atmosphere, and weather has a lot to do with that.

The Greater London Council requires its Scientific Branch to maintain continuous monitoring of pollution and to advise on new measures to be taken. It has also helped the Council reply to the many requests for detailed information from elsewhere in Britain and abroad on how London did the job. The London boroughs exercise responsibility under the Clean Air Acts of 1956 and 1968, the Public Health Act of 1936, and the 1964 Housing Act, while the central government watches particular industries under the Alkali Act first enacted in 1863, and enforces legislation on automobile exhaust. The city's routine measurements conform to a National Survey of Air Pollution carried out by a laboratory of the Department of Trade and Industry.

What does it cost to clear the air? Not as much as pessimists suggest. The London borough spent £6.8 million on smoke control up to the end of March 1969, representing an expenditure of some £0.88 per citizen for an effort spanning a period of thirteen years, or one old shilling and four old pence per head per annum, with the central government spending a fraction more, for a total public expenditure of three old shillings per capita per year. This has been compared to public expenditures on sewerage and sewerage disposal: £1.56 per capita per year.

There has also been a change in habits. The amount of coal consumed for domestic use in London fell by 80% between 1958 and 1968. It has resulted in the big bare fireplace of West End already mentioned: Christmas cheer around a gas burner.

In Pittsburgh, which had 520,000 inhabitants in 1970, a reputation as the Smoky City may be attributed to industrial pollution. One fifth of the steelmaking capacity of the United States is concentrated in the metropolitan area of that city, while nearby mines produce 40 million tons of bituminous coal each year. Steel fur naces, some within city limits, situated only 2 or 3 miles from the downtown area, emitted so much smoke and dust that it was a rare day when townspeople could see the sun. In the city center, street lights were needed at midday.

The city had begun to attack the problem as early as 1895, when an ordinance was passed (which did not produce results). In 1938, a WPA project set up air sampling stations, and in 1941 a new ordinance was passed, but enforcement had to be postponed until after World War II. Controls began to be enforced against industry in 1946 and in households a year after that, for 90% of homes in Allegheny County were heated by coal. (The county has 1,590,000 inhabitants, including Pittsburgh and 128 other municipalities.) Additional legislation was enacted in 1946 and 1949, county-wide regulations were put into effect in 1960, and there were contributing factors: lengthy coal strikes, the availability of gas for home heating thanks to a private utility company's acquisition of a war surplus pipeline. It cost the householders of Allegheny County an estimated $82 million to convert to gas or to install smoke prevention fuel burners, a little over $50 per home. (In London, householders were responsible for 30% of the cost of transforming their furnaces, the central government paid 40%, and local authorities 30%. One quarter of homes in Britain are covered by smoke control regulations, which were not designed to reach all households in the country, some areas burning so little coal that smoke is not a problem.)

Pittsburgh also changed its weather. Fog was reduced, laundry kept clean longer (although environmentalists say that Pittsburgh still has a long way to go). The Smoky City became known as Cinderella City. But the burden of the pollution, and its liquidation, came from industry, while London had troubled its air without steel factories and had to track down the sources of pollution from household to household. Without diminishing Pittsburgh's achievement, the London effort was compressed into a shorter time span, involved the effort of a larger number of individual citizens. However, the individual cost to Pittsburghers was possibly greater. That they still have a long way to go is suggested in a recent report by a local environmental group that Pittsburgh's air remains the dirtiest of any major American city, followed by Detroit's, Cleveland's, St. Louis's, Buffalo's, and New York's. In Paris some 100,000 cubic meters of sulfurous acid (H_2SO_3) and 10 tons of sulfuric acid (H_2SO_4) descend on the agglomeration each day. Only the rapid evacuation of these gases has kept Parisians alive. Pollution destroys stone cathedrals everywhere, even endangers the Swiss in their lakeside cities. If in the United States, down-town air pollution has the same effect on the breathing human being as smoking one pack of cigarettes a day, what must it be like for the inhabitant of Madrid, who finds it hard to distinguish detail in a painting in the Prado Museum at a distance of 50 feet, so heavy is the haze within that building? Or for the inhabitant of Milan who can't see the spire of the Duomo for a good many winter weeks at a stretch?

If the world turned a corner in October 1973 with the Arab attack on Israel and the oil blockade, environmental progress was widely believed to be one of its first victims. What nation could afford to pick and choose among sources of energy? The United States postponed polluting criteria, particularly built-in anti-pollution devices for new automobiles. The talk in London was somewhat pessimistic: Could a cold population be asked not to burn soft fuels, such as domestically produced wood and coal?

Experience, however, suggested that there might be reasons for optimism. Even before October 1973, there were periods of temporary shortage of authorized (that is, smokeless) fuels in Britain. In the winter of 1970/71, a large number of smoke control orders were suspended, yet the annual averages of smoke concentration for 1970 and 1971 were about 8% lower than for 1969. But it may be difficult, henceforth, to measure visibility in the good old ways, by climbing to the roof of County Hall for instance. London's scientists have discovered that the thick forest of high-rise buildings in downtown London has made it impossible for them to see as far as they used to be able to see. So they have begun making their observations from the roof of a neighborhing skyscraper, by courtesy of its owners, the Shell International Petroleum Co. Ltd.

14. Urban Peace

Crime in or out of cities, mostly in, would seem to be a function of tradition. There is demonstrably little crime in Japan; Tokyo, one of the two largest cities in the world, has the lowest crime rate of any metropolis. The Japanese seem to respect their laws and the men who make them, not to mention those who enforce them. The visitor who walks through a neighborhood of Tokyo famous for its dangers—rowdies and pickpockets, gangsters lurking in the shadows, according to the guide book—won't even know it (unless, as I did, he reads about it afterward in the guide book). There are other reasons for Tokyo's urban peace, like the ubiquitous police booths in strategic places, but I shall return to that.

Another tradition is that of the gun-toting citizen and his frontier justice (and then frontier injustice), exacerbated by racial tensions and drugs, leading to the tragedies of unorganized crime. For it is not organized crime that worries the man on the street. The kinds of violence that affect most Americans are the gratuitous, random ones: mugging, small-time burglary of home or automobile, vandalism. A Gallup poll published in 1973 showed that one American in five was a victim of one or more crimes, but in the inner cities the percentage was 33%, or one in three. More recent data indicate the predictable phenomenon that violence and other crime have been growing at a greater rate in the suburbs than in the cities (10% against 5% for serious crimes, 13% against 3% for violent ones). One does not have to accept any particular set of statistics, city police or FBI, to agree that there is good grounding for the fears of ordinary men and women.

If crime is a big-city, big-suburb phenomenon, growing as prosperity grows, growing with easy money and automobile civilization and its tensions, racial diversity and its tensions, then one should find a certain amount of it in other advanced societies as well. And, in fact, one does, in London and Paris, but usually without the drama that accompanies it in the streets of America's cities. In Paris, a comparatively light incidence of vandalism and subway crimes, and random muggings in dark streets, has become a favorite newspaper subject and a frequent theme of word-of-mouth exchanges of experience. The traveler himself will note the number of public telephones that have been vandalized in Paris and London. When Paris finally got outdoor telephone booths, decades after the rest of the major communicating countries, it also got telephone vandalism, so that it often seems that most of the public phones in the city have been visited by vandals.

Neither Paris nor London has the racial diversity of many American cities. Yet in some sections of both places the population of immigrant workers with darker skins than the native population reaches proportions similar to those in the United States. A dormitory suburb of Paris might be 50% or more black African or Arab North African, migrant workers living in cramped conditions, in shared rooms or shantytowns, most often without their families. All the potential for tension among races exists. It's another subject of scare headlines and frightened whispers.

But neither in Paris or London, nor in Amsterdam with its own large and growing colony of dark-skinned residents, do the relatively infrequent outbursts of racial tension make crime in the streets the concern it is in the United States. A skeptic will continue to say that the situations are different, and of course they are. No two countries share the same history. But there may be other factors to make a city like Paris so safe to walk through, that a visitor unaware of the headlines in the tabloid press and unable to converse with its inhabitants may consider it to be another Tokyo, where seeming racial homeogeneity obtains.

Tokyo, of course, is not made up exclusively of middle-class Japanese. There is a working class from the northern islands, from Korea, and as I shall show further in this chapter, even a home-grown untouchable class, all discriminated against, and conscious of discrimination. Meanwhile Japan has that policeman in his booth visible at every intersection. Those policemen assigned to a particular booth, or *koban,* are responsible for patroling the neighborhood, dealing with its quotidian administrative questions, knowing who lives where. They keep in touch with the people in Tokyo, a city of nearly 12 million.

In France, the organization of the national and municipal police may confuse a foreigner, and it confuses many Frenchmen, too. The French system derives from a long tradition of centralized government, whose central feature is national control. Even Paris's *police municipale* is part of the national police system, ultimately the responsibility of the Ministry of the Interior. In Paris the *Préfecture de Police* rules a vast empire, part of which covers the neighboring *départements* (districts, corresponding to American states). There is also a *police judiciaire* to investigate crime, and a patrol force called *police de voie publique*.

The municipal police force is responsible in Paris for maintaining public order, watching the streets. The 11,000 uniformed men available for this activity are called *gardiens de la paix*. They have 2,300 (*brigadiers*) who in turn are supervised by 300 *officiers de paix;* 40 *commissaires* run special departments. Over 300 women auxiliary police and 500 contract patrolmen (often retired policemen) are assigned to duty at street crossings outside schools and enforce parking regulations. (At this writing, a plan has been approved to swear in several hundred inspectors of the public transportation network so that they can write parking tickets for automobiles parked in designated bus lanes.)

Each of Paris's twenty *arrondissements* (wards) is the responsibility of a *commissaire de voie publique* commanding a company of *gardiens de la paix*—an average of 250 per ward. They are the infantry of this highly centralized police department, responsible for safeguarding the streets, surrounding a neighborhood or blocking off a road after a reported crime, spot checks of identity papers. They dispose of radio cars for general patroling, but they also stand outside the sensitive spots: housing projects, street fairs, entertainment districts. They include a famous bicycle patrol, *Les Hirondelles* (literally, "sparrows").

To bolster this system, a new corps of *îlotiers* (literally, "islanders"), neighborhood patrolmen, was organized in 1972 to be on constant duty in an effort to prevent minor crimes, or to arrive in the nick of time to catch bicycle thieves, stray minors, shoplifters, but also violators of traffic laws, those responsible for excessive noise, unlicensed or abusive commerce. The new block men stick to a neighborhood and become familiar with its habits; often a summons will be replaced by a verbal warning, and the *îlotier* is there to see that the promise is honored.

As a starter, Paris selected the hottest streets, neighborhoods of greatest density, to begin the *îlotier* experiment. Technically, the *îlot* itself is a new concept in Paris. So far, there are 129 of these small districts, to which 400 *gardiens de la paix* were assigned on launching of the new scheme (the men had been attached to central services before that). In each ward, twelve to twenty men were assigned to six to ten *îlots* in the daytime, from one to three at night.

But even before implementation of the neighborhood patrols, Paris had been known for its safe streets. The omnipresence of the neighborhood *commissariat* made the stroller feel that he would come upon the open door of a police station around every corner. The *brigades de nuit* already numbered 1,800 uniformed policemen, and included police cars and bicycle patrols, with occasional road blocks—a characteristic of Parisian night life— for spot checks of motorists and pedestrians, facilitated by the system of national identity cards. The police are aware of the unlikelihood of catching a criminal in the act with a noisy patrol car; the emphasis is on catching them on tiptoe if necessary. Special night crime teams, ERSN (for *équipes de répression spéciale de nuit*), move in groups of three with no other mission than to sniff out crimes in the making, notably car thefts. Other groups in uniform or plain clothes—about 250 men in all—circulate from 9 p.m. to 6 a.m. on regular itineraries. In 1974, the new minister of the interior instituted a system of surprise and massive night raids against selected neighborhoods known as problem areas. "Operation Fist," as it was called, uncovered few major crimes in the making, but apparently did purge certain neighborhoods of potential criminals.

The labyrinthine subway system of Paris has presented new problems with the gradual elimination of conductors on the trains who were responsible for operating doors in non-automated cars, and the elimination for reasons of economy of subway platform booths where station supervisors were available both for traffic problems and to report or prevent acts of crime or vandalism. The long corridors of the subways, particularly at the frequent transfer points between the lines that crisscross the city, provide opportunities not only for illicit peddling and begging, but for purse snatching or worse. Stations are being equipped with closed-circuit television and alarm systems with two-way voice communication to which the general public has access. The incidents of crime and aggression, while they are not on the rise (less than two a day, when 100 million trips are made on the system each month), have been getting attention in the press; the police have reinforced their surveillance.

Comparing the American situation to that of any other country is certain to bring the reproach that there is a difference: the racial heterogeneity of the American population, giving black Americans, many of them rural migrants of recent vintage, a majority in the inner cities, not to speak of the Spanish-speaking minorities. The idea that there is a hard core of citizens in basic disharmony, often in open hostility, to the surrounding dominant culture is supposed to render impossible any attempt at reinstating civilized relations in major American cities. The implication is that countries with a good record of urban peace in downtown areas do not experience such disparities.

Of course, as I have already suggested, the facts are quite different. In France, for example, the demand for laborers willing to do the dirty jobs in an economy of full employment has opened the door to migrants from former colonies in Arab and black Africa and migrant workers from depressed Spain and Portugal. These workers man the street-cleaning services of metropolian areas, the construction sites, the restaurant kitchens. In districts of Paris and Marseilles, in whole communities of the Paris suburbs, they may even form the majority. France in 1973 was host to 800,000 Algerians, 200,000 Moroccans, 120,000 Tunisians, and large numbers of black Africans from the former French colonies. The foreign population is concentrated in the Paris region (1.4 million), the Marseilles-Mediterranean coastal region (500,000), and the Riviera (400,000). Some 12% of the population of Paris is non-French (these from the Southern Hemisphere, but also 750,000 Portuguese, 570,000 Spaniards, 570,000 Italians—usually unskilled laborers from rural areas). There are occasional outbursts of racial violence in France against laborers, particularly from Arab North Africa (in cities such as Marseilles with large communities of Frenchmen repatriated from France's former North African territories).

In Epinay-sous-Sénart, a town of 13,500 in the Paris region, an estimated 55% of the population consists of migrants, many of them refugees from urban renewal of depressed neighborhoods of Paris. If ever there was a situation ripe for trouble, Epinay's should have been it. Actually this particular town prepared itself, augmented its social welfare staff, built sports and other leisure-time facilities specifically tailored to neighborhood mix and to reduction of potential tensions. First results suggest that such communities will survive.

In neighboring Belgium, the foreign population of 720,000 represented 7% of the total population in 1971, although only a few thousand of the strangers were dark-skinned. Belgium's tensions come from the ever more serious schism between its Flemish and

Walloon populations, characterized by continual "racial" agitation in press and public pronouncements, occasional neighborhood fighting, sometimes a confrontation taking on the proportions of race riot. New segregation here based on language has introduced a situation where half the population is treated as foreign in the other half of the country.

City life in Britain, of course, is now characterized by an immigrant colony representing 5% of the total population, a "coloured" community from several Commonwealth countries numbered in the millions, concentrated in a few cities where they happen to have maximum visibility. In West Germany, 6% of the population is now foreign (96,000 Turks, 75,000 Yugoslavs, 4,000 Moroccans in 1972). Denmark has 30,000 foreign workers to absorb into a total population of 5 million.

A newspaper reporter noted in 1973 the pervasiveness of national differences in Europe, including and especially involving prejudice against other natives of one's own country. Often there is a north-south distinction, internal colonialism manifesting itself in lower salaries and menial jobs for the people of the south migrating north (in Sweden, as in Japan, it happens to be a migration from north to south, but the problems are the same).

In several European states, racial tension has led to what are called racial crimes, or outright racial rioting. It has happened in the United Kingdom, but also in the Netherlands, a nation which has absorbed its brown-skinned East Indian population of 200,000, while racism of increasing gravity is directed against the black Surinamese (from Dutch Guiana), with discrimination noted in employment, in housing, in public places. There are now 50,000 Surinamese in the Netherlands, with new arrivals daily; some 10% of them are unemployed, and ghettos already exist in such cities as Rotterdam.

In all these places, the migrant workers, be they black, brown, or white, must compete for housing and civic space with the lowest income groups of the indigenous population, which often include a high percentage of internal immigrants from rural areas. And so there are black and brown ghettos in Europe; the economic laws which oblige new arrivals in lower income groups to congregate in declining neighborhoods see to that.

What has kept the urban peace, taking into account the kind of incidents that have already been cited, is the determination of the host peoples that city life will continue. Some states are supplementing augmented police forces with the introduction of more humane policies, such as inexpensive housing reserved for migrant laborers. The Swedish way is being taken as a model; there, a government agency acts in defense of the rights of immigrants. A report on *The Dutch Plural Society* by Christopher Bagley makes the point that the Dutch are at home with tolerance; they are tolerant of each other, first of all, despite the existence of religious blocs as rigid as racial blocs elsewhere. They are prepared to spend the money necessary to take care of their new population. Bagley's work contains figures which demonstrate that the crime rates of dark-skinned peoples in the Netherlands are far from alarming; indeed, there are more crimes proportionately among other foreign groups (for example, Germans) in that country.

There are few European countries without a racial, a religious, or a "national" problem; some have all three. In fact, the natives of several French provinces—Brittany, the Basque country, Corsica, Provence—have been campaigning against discrimination practiced toward their national languages, which are virtually outlawed, and their cultures. Many of the more militant groups also complain of economic underdevelopment and tie the two, cultural and economic colonialism, together. National and religious differences, north and south differences, even the less publicized town vs. country rivalry, have become war in Ireland, street fighting in Belgium, isolated terrorist raids and bombings in France and Spain. German and Austrian persecution of Jews is only a generation past. (In Japan, as I have already noted, where the population seems ideally homogeneous to the superficial observer, the *burakumin* are an untouchable caste living in ghettos of their own, unable to marry or even to associate with other Japanese, and there are three million of them in Tokyo. The Koreans of Japan, who are also discriminated against, often attempt to dissimulate their origins.

Usually these differences—in Europe, in Japan—do not carry over into the streets as readily as they do in the United States. This does not mean that the silent suffering is less, or the disguised segregation and veiled hostility less harmful.) Yet it would seem that Americans have not yet found the recipe for at least this outward form of coexistence. And when the time comes for an explosion of violence, perhaps Americans have not given the right orders to the policemen on the beat or don't have the right policemen.

There is, for example, a whole repertory of tactics, and even architectural techniques, to reduce vandalism, but they require a program of community relations to accompany them, or they are useless.

Saving American cities for Americans, from Americans, is probably going to require a good deal more effort than it has involved in other nations whose traditional attitudes to law and order, or whose restrictions on ownership of firearms, are so different. Yet it should be clear from the foregoing that the basic elements of the American urban scene are found in many other metropolitan areas, even—almost—in scale. Americans did not invent crime, or pillaging, or even hating neighbors. America's heritage was imported, even the negative elements of it. Conceivably, Americans can shop around among the best foreign antidotes as well.

IV. CITY MODELS

15. Saving the Past: Bologna

If urban renewal follows similar, predictable patterns in most developed areas, whether in Europe, the United States, or Japan, Bologna may be turning the clock back. Or is it forward? This old-new city has declared war on growth. When the Japanese architect of international reputation Kenzo Tange drew up plans for a new city on Bologna's periphery to house deportees from the center, Bologna vetoed Tange, and then went on to draft an unprecedented program to keep citizens in their neighborhoods. Now in the first stage of execution, this program to renovate old neighborhoods and (with public money which otherwise goes to dormitory housing in ever-expanding suburbs) to retain the original inhabitants—tenants but also owner-occupants, shopkeepers, artisans—will be a testing ground for the rest of Italy. It could be a testing ground for the rest of the universe.

"Slum removal is poor people removal" has been the eternal equation of urban renewal. Nearly all great city centers are in the process of being rehabilitated. At the very least, decrees and ordinances protecting landmarks have frozen the existing cityscape. In all significant cases, as I have already shown, restored buildings are priced out of the market for the original inhabitants. It happened yesterday in London's West End, New York's West Village, Boston's South End; it is happening today in Rome's Renaissance quarters and Trastevere, in Milan's vestigial old neighborhoods, in Paris's Marais and Latin Quarter. It may happen tomorrow in Venice. The scenario is predictable: A speculator buys a building or acquires individual apartments in it one by one; inhabitants are forced or persuaded to leave (the law usually authorizes a system of bribes). They learn that they cannot find equivalent rents in a city where the renewal process is everywhere the same, although escape to an expanding suburb is possible. New roads will be built for them, along with new water pipes and sewers. There will have to be a system of public transportation, costly but nevertheless requiring additional hours of travel to and from places of work. Meanwhile, in the center, the renovated building has been rented or sold to the city's wealthier inhabitants, whose holdings will inevitably increase in value because of national and international awareness that our collective heritage, the great old city centers, will from now on and until the end of time be preserved from destruction.

Bologna, the testing ground, is no dead city, no greenhouse like old Bruges, no Venetian objet d'art to be displayed in a cabinet. It is the thriving capital of an industrial and, increasingly, commercial region, known for textiles, grains, wholesaling, but also for precision machinery. Its municipal population is 494,000 in a greater city (province) of 916,000, in a region (now the autonomous district of Emilia Romagna of which Bologna is the capital) of 3,827,000. Bologna's industrial growth rate has been among the country's highest, the ratio of working population has always been satisfactory, its farmers are among the most prosperous in Italy.

Bologna is near the center of a linear concentration of cities along the Via Emilia, the ancient Roman road from Piacenza to the coast. North to the Po Valley is an agricultural plain, south are the Apennine Mountains. Both plain and mountain areas have been losing population to the cities along the axis: Parma, Reggio Emilia, Modena, Imola, Forlì, Rimini, and Bologna, although after spectacular growth from 1951 to 1961 the latest decade has seen a stabilizing of Bologna's population. "We shouldn't try to be like Paris, with a concentration of activities; we should share responsibility with other urban centers," a Bologna official explains. While a similar land-use pattern is found all over Italy—rich cities draining population from depressed mountain and plain areas —the Bologna planners think restructuring is possible: industry in the plain, tourism in the mountains, to bolster the agricultural sector. Metropolitan planning should give way to regional planning, with new factories, public services and recreation zones set up not only in response to the requirements of a particular city, but of the region as a whole, encompassing both urban and rural territories.

Only a few years ago (1955), Bologna's municipal authorities had been planning for a future city of 1.2 million inhabitants. Later, in a modification (variante) of the general plan, they revised this estimate down to 600,000. Now they have decided to

hold the line at 500,000 and to grow not quantitatively but quali-
tatively. This means improving the physical surroundings of the
Bolognese who are crowded into deteriorated neighborhoods. But
Bologna happens to have one of Italy's best preserved historical
centers, the largest in Italy after Venice. Superb old monuments
are in use in the historical center, the *centro storico*, notably the
city hall. There are miles of arcaded streets unique in the Italian
and world townscape, spacious boulevards and squares. To save
the old city now, while the stones hold together and the original
occupants hold their house keys, will require all the effort and
expense that a city can afford.

Other Italian cities are acquiring population; does this mean
that Bologna's putting on the brakes is, as a Christian Democratic
prime minister suggested, selfish and reactionary? Bologna's Communist city administration replies that Milan and Turin grow at
the expense of Italy's south, that in fact 54 million Italians actually
dispose of 56 million rooms, an equation canceled out by Italy's
internal migration, which has created demands for 20 million new
dwelling rooms. And if Italy built these 20 million rooms, Bologna's planners say, perhaps they would solve the crisis, but at
what sacrifice? The houses would be ghettos isolated from the
real world of the city. Bologna's planners aren't opposed to new
housing, they only want it to be built where it is needed, in
metropolitan centers.

But is it realistic to clamp a lid on expansion when a city is
part of a region, a region part of a nation where citizens may
travel and settle when and where they wish? To this, Bologna's
comune replies: The growth of our city and other appealing
Emilian cities occurs at the expense of the rest of the region.
Under normal circumstances, Bologna acquires few migrants
because its industrial structure doesn't require it, while the
argicultural sector has already lost most of its surplus population.

Still, Bologna couldn't stop people from coming into the city
and demanding housing unless it first stopped the anarchic
development of industry. For new industry called for new crash
programs of urbanization, which would cost the city more than
it could possibly hope to receive in benefits from the new industry. It made sense to developers to develop, but the resulting
development required expensive services, and it created the spiral
effect of drawing new waves of immigrants to work in construction crews, one more drain on existing facilities. A city administration conscious of its responsibility to its citizens, with a level

of services and equipment unusual for Italy, was unwilling to accept uncontrolled expansion.

The Bologna bug may be contagious. Milan and other cities have begun to revise their own city plans in the direction of limiting growth. "We are ten years ahead of Milan," observes Pier Luigi Cervellati. "We have been preparing for zero growth for a decade."

How limit growth in a foolproof manner? A Bolognese city officer replies candidly: by refusing building permits, or better, by considering each request for a permit within the context of the Bologna plan and of the region's overall goals. The local association of industrialists protests vigorously against measures which reduce land available for factories (for 1,000 square meters of factory space the city requires that industry acquire 3,000 square meters of land). Such measures inhibit expansion, they say, while industry already established within city limits is not allowed to improve land already possessed.

And so Kenzo Tange's Bologna Nord, which would have drained resources while moving the Bolognese beyond their traditional borders, had to be abandoned. At the same time, a low-income public housing program in the periphery which when completed will provide homes for a population of 80,000—a progressive program which would do credit to any municipal administration —will be the last of its kind.

Bologna says no to suburbs which are popular with planners but hell for the populations of city centers, uprooted and condemned to long and tiring journeys to work. Yet since the end of World War II, Bologna has been a Red city. Today, 29 Communists and 4 Socialists dominate the city council, and 27 Communists form the majority of the regional assembly. The Communists could have rested on their laurels, showing off their attractive garden city developments such as Barca, Fossolo, Corticella, which were put up on expropriated lots by building cooperatives to provide modern living at less than $200 the square meter. Instead, Bologna began to trouble the little people by talking about expropriation of their decaying downtown properties. It has upset rank-and-file Communist voters, many of whom are small property owners themselves. It has even caused Italian Communists on the national level to worry that the Bologna experience will give them a reputation as a party of expropriators.

Paradoxes abound in Bologna. Shopkeepers have revolted at disruption of motor traffic following the city's closing of Piazza Maggiore, the central square in front of the basilica dedicated to

Bologna's patron saint, and the closing and pedestrianization of that extraordinary complex of sacred buildings at Piazza San Stefano, as if Communists and not shopkeepers dare to be the best defenders of the religious heritage and its environment.

Bologna's revolutionary housing plan is predicated on the fact that city centers are good to live in. The very wealthy demand the *centro città;* why shouldn't everybody else? An amusing yet deadly serious sociological survey by Dominique Schnapper indicates the importance to the upper classes, but to social and cultural institutions as well, of a site as close as possible to the heart of the city (its author measured precisely, in meters). Far from usual tourist itineraries, Bologna has always reserved its charms for its citizens and visiting scholars. Its sprawling university, the oldest in Europe (60,000 students, a tenth of them foreign), utilizes as its campus the city itself, with its 20 miles of arcaded streets, façades all in pastel colors, tinted ochre and pink. Half the Bolognese polled in a survey declared that a city without aracades didn't seem a city at all.

And Bologna's planners are unashamedly pro-city center. Tearing down buildings for parks doesn't seem to interest them: Bologna has its nearby hills for fresh air and sports facilities. Renovated old neighborhoods are to contain more population than they do now.

As drawn up by architect Pier Luigi Cervellati, the city's commissioner for public housing, and a team of young urbanists, the unprecedented Bologna plan includes the following procedures:

(1) The historic center is divided into thirteen districts, each of which has been subjected to intense investigation, architectural, sociological, economic. Five zones are earmarked for the opening round of Bologna's renewal program.

(2) New housing will be built on vacant lots in the immediate neighborhood of deteriorated groups of houses. Three of the five zones in the first renewal program happen to include lots left undeveloped after war damage had rendered them uninhabitable. The present occupants of buildings designated for rehabilitation will be housed temporarily and by rotation in these new buildings and in the many empty dwelling units found to be available in all five renovation zones.

(3) Although the original plan, released in October 1972, was based on expropriation of property in the five zones, the procedure was revised after public and private discussion (including discussion within the Communist Party). After arduous debate,

the definitive version of the program was approved by the city council of Bologna on March 7, 1973, with the abstention of the Christian Democrats, Liberals, Social Democrats, and Republicans, and a negative vote of the MSI (neo-Fascist) representative. Expropriation remains the procedure for vacant property and buildings in peril, while for dwelling units in normal use it will be necessary to attempt to come to terms with the owner. He remains in his home or agrees to allow his tenants to remain for twenty-five years at a rental based on the tenant's income and set by the city. The city guarantees loans for rehabilitation on a sliding scale in inverse proportion to the owner's resources and the size of his holdings. If the owner himself lacks resources, renovation can be 100% city-financed for the space he actually occupies. If a private enterprise wishes to finance a rehabilitation without a subsidy, this too will be considered: a concession to minority opinion which increases the range of possibilities available to city and citizen.

The rule stands: "An absolute guarantee that the present inhabitants, tenants or owners, remain in the same rehabilitated neighborhoods and in the same buildings that they now occupy." And whatever the formula chosen for rehabilitation, tenants are assured that rent will be based on income. In a dramatic televised session of the city council in January 1973, the small property owners were promised that the city would not interpret the new law in a "Marxist" spirit. Despite the opposition press campaign which put the spotlight on the fate of low-income home owners, it turned out that 85% of the inhabitants of the five zones were rent-payers.

(4) Although not covered by guaranteed low-rent provisions, small shopkeepers and artisans will be encouraged to stay put; they too will pay rent according to income.

(5) If a property owner desires to sell, the city can buy at a price calculated as a capitalization of the rent then being paid to him. If a tenant desires to move, the city reserves the right to replace him by someone else qualifying for subsidized housing.

(6) The intention is to share management of the renovated neighborhoods with inhabitants, while relations between owners and the city are hammered out in sessions of a commission in which all political groups will be represented. Only in the case of noncompliance with the law will expropriation take place—as a "last resort," promises the mayor.

The first contingent of tenants has already been moved into new houses in the San Leonardo sector; tenants will return to their original dwelling units once renovations are completed. San Leonardo had been chosen because of the availability of vacant lots left over from wartime destruction, no one having considered this depressed sector worthy of renewal until now.

Soon, indeed, the new houses will be unrecognizable as new. They conform to the style prevalent in the neighborhood, so that only the patina is lacking. Plans of houses originally existing in the street were found in the city property office.

But inside the houses there is a difference. Units are designed for families of varying sizes, but also for students and the aged. For the latter there are ground floor dwellings opening on tiny gardens. A roving medical team provides assistance to old people, who will be watched. They will also find specially designed bathing facilities in their units.

"I'm 80 years old," a woman standing outside her dilapidated quarters on Via San Leonardo informed a visitor to the rehabilitation project. "Every stone in this house had a meaning in my life. I cried when I heard that they were going to move me. But I go down the street each day to see the new building going up. The workers show me what they are doing. They call me *bella signora!*"

"What she means," city architect Carlo de Angelis explained, "is that if she had been sent out to the periphery, even to a new apartment there, she'd soon be dead. She's going to stay near her friends."

He turned to the *bella signora*. "Now you go every day to see the new house going up. And when you are in the new house you'll be able to walk back here to see the progress on the restoration of your old house."

"When I'm 81 I'll have running water for the first time," she said.

When the reader sees this page, if the *bella signora* is still alive, she *will* have running water in her apartment.

For the first sector, bids were solicited. A local building cooperative won with a lower bid than the estimate set by the city. Each sector will require a new invitation for bids. Bologna's first five zones contain 6,500 residents, and work is now underway in each. The program will be pursued in the other eight sectors, containing 32,000 inhabitants, for completion in 1980. And then the program will be extended beyond the *centro storico* to other areas on the periphery, including housing projects of the 1950s which have not withstood the test of time (suburban renewal, it might be called).

To accompany the rehabilitated sectors, Bologna has earmarked nearly a dozen old palaces and monasteries for transformation into neighborhood social and welfare centers, containing such features as elementary schools, student centers, an art gallery or craft museum, and social welfare services. The first project to be completed was an ancient orphanage called the Baracano, serving the San Stefano neighborhood.

As for costs, they were originally estimated at $50 million, of which $8.9 million had been raised, but in fact it is difficult to estimate costs because it is not known how many property owners will agree to a convention, how many will have to be expropriated. The city intends to use public funds available under employer housing plans such as Gescal (Gestione Case Lavoratori) and the national housing law (Legge sulla Casa 865). Indeed, the list of hoped-for sources of financing is a long one. The least likely source of help is the local business community. "The city is already in deficit," a representative of the industrial association remarked. "Marxist," "collectivist" are typical terms employed in the local press to describe the program. At present, only 2% to 3% of building in Italy is government-sponsored. Government funds, such as they are, are meant to be used for construction; why not for rehabilitation? Bologna's planners also hoped that public money could be used to compensate owners of expropriated property, but this was evidently asking too much.

The national housing program is known as PEEP, for Piano Edilizia Economico Popolare. It is not unique to Bologna; it is only that Bologna has known what to do with it. In fact, the law is a national one (number 167 of April 1962, modified by the aforementioned 865 of October 1971). The moment it was passed, Bologna decided to use it to contain real estate speculation and redirect urban renewal into a social context. The law also seemed to allow public authorities to choose between "conservative" and "progressive" applications. After seven years of operation under PEEP, during which the city produced 64,000 dwelling rooms, 38% of them financed with public funds such as Gescal, 47% by cooperatives, 15% by private builders, Bologna's decision is that the truly progressive option is urban rehabilitation, since the alternative use of public funds to expand suburbs perpetuates the "ghettos of misery" of the major cities. "In the end," says Bologna's mayor Renato Zangheri, "we understood that this procedure was not economical. To urbanize a suburb is expensive. And if the urbanization is only half-finished, as usually happens, the costs are not only financial, but social."

Bologna's plans for central-city PEEP are well worth looking at. They are a work of art as well as an obvious labor of love. The preparations for renovating Bologna's slums included painstaking research into old books and records; the resulting reports are an anthology of fine prints as well as a tool for planners. Of all Italian cities, Milan is the only other one now considering use of the PEEP program to rehabilitate an old neighborhood. The Bologna experience was one of those highlighted by the Council of Europe's European Architectural Heritage Year in 1975.

If one man can be said to be responsible for the Bologna plan, he is Pier Luigi Cervellati, member of the city council, commissioner responsible for building and preservation since 1965. The opposition press refers to the renewal program as the "Cervellati plan." In his demeanor Cervellati is more humanist than technician; friends see him as a benevolent pope. Cervellati himself insists that Bologna's planning comes from below.

The city is divided into districts, *quartiere*, 18 in all, each with a council of 20 members presided over by a deputy mayor. These grass roots councils discuss the city budget, zoning problems, and similar matters before they go to the municipal council. They also control certain social welfare and administrative functions on the local level. While the *consiglio di quartiere* is a Bolognese innovation (1964), today Rome, Milan, Turin, and Venice have begun to imitate Bologna. It is Pier Luigi Cervellati's contention that the plan to save Bologna's *centro storico* for its inhabitants came from the grass roots and not from exterior philosophical or urban planning influences. It was the councils, for example, which ratified the decision to use vacant lots left by war destruction for housing and not for parks. In the same way that the local council knows its problems better than city hall ever can, provincial governments can do a better job on regional problems than can the national government. Yet the regions must wait for a "framework law," *legge cornice*, from Rome before they can pursue their own urban planning.

"Bologna is the largest Communist city in the West," Cervellati told me, "and there are many eyes on it. In order to carry out a controversial program such as pedestrian zones in the downtown shopping area, public participation is necessary. We are not a Red island, not San Marino. Bologna is in Italy; we must adapt and make concessions."

"The city doesn't want to destroy the interests of small property owners," he argued on another occasion. "It wishes to offer a real alternative to the predominance of real estate speculation, so that speculation does not again exploit the situation of those most in need. This is why the plan has as its fundamental objective to keep the present occupants in their homes, to be guaranteed by low rentals and integration with other components of our society such as students, craftsmen, persons on old-age pensions, and small shopkeepers." Still, small owners were alarmed. Their property, seen as a defense against inflation, was to be taken from them, or so they told interviewers from the press. "In Bologna the wealthy will not have the heart of the city," read a headline in daily *Il Giorno*. The opinion at city hall was that thanks to the excitement created by Bologna's plan, Venice might also be saved from becoming another Monte Carlo for tourists; workers might at last win the right to stay in their homes in Naples, Turin, Palermo, Genoa, Bari, and Florence.

Never had an urban proposal been talked and written about more. The city put together a press album containing the attacks and false interpretations as well as the applause. A visit to the local industrialists association during that feverish period produced a clearly stated dissent: The city's plan paralyzes the building industry, slows down the economy. No one will want to invest in property after hearing that rents are going to be lowered. "The city is unrealistic in thinking that it can build all that cheap housing, considering the rising costs of materials and labor." Ruling out park and recreation areas in the center of town to put them on the nearby hills seemed "ridiculous, because mothers can't take their *bambini* that far." (The city could reply that within space limitations small parks were to be included in renovated neighborhoods, along with nurseries and kindergartens, heating plants and other amenities.)

If Bologna intends to limit growth, there would seem to be no limits to its planners' imaginations. Prior to launching their radical program of inner city rehabilitation, they had undertaken a "visual" survey of the old city, district by district, street by street, seen from the point of view of the citizen on foot. Participation of citizens in planning through the district councils has contributed to the development of an "urban consciousness" which the city feels is not the smallest accomplishment of these years of struggle.

After a major program of pedestrian zones, a new plan attacks a more essential element of urban existence: public transportation. Bologna has already done what many other cities have on the drawing boards, which some would like to try but don't dare. Public transportation is free to users for part of the time and part of the public now (from 5 to 9:30 a.m., from 12 noon to 4 p.m., then from 6 to 8 p.m.). When more buses are available, free transport will be extended to all hours and all categories of the population at an estimated increase of only 3% to 4% in the deficit of the operating authority. As is true in many large centers, it costs more to collect fares than the revenue gained from them; Bologna feels that the employees who collect them are needed elsewhere (in the schools).

A system of priority lanes for public buses has also been put into effect. At the same time, the original center-city pedestrian zone has been duplicated elsewhere. The city promises additional pedestrian zones not only in the center but in the peripheral districts. Comments a representative of Bologna's retail merchants association: "We'd favor pedestrian islands if parking were possible nearby. But the city is doing the opposite, making it more difficult to park. The city is interested in traffic flow, not in parking."

The original pedestrian zone on commercial Via d'Azeglio described in a previous chapter is still being called—by the retailers association—an "authentic tragedy." "The city could solve its problems if it allowed private enterprise to build parking lots," a representative of the manufacturers association told the author. "To close streets to automobiles only means more traffic on other streets." Bologna's conservative newspaper, *Il Resto di Carlino,* a regular critic of city initiatives, gives frequent airing to complaints about increasingly difficult traffic movements caused by the municipality's efforts to discourage automobiles from using the center. The position of the press has been termed "provocative" by the city's tramway employees.

The response of the city has been a monumental survey (in eight volumes) prepared by the traffic commissioner which demonstrates the energy that has been going into study of existing traffic and possible ways to reduce its harmful effects. One thing is certain: City hall believes that it is "absolutely" impossible to put parking lots or garages into the *centro storico.* Downtown parking is reserved for "operational" traffic, to cut down on random stopping of cars. An earlier priority whose successful accomplishment is now a matter of history is the road network around the city: Twelve miles of ring roads ward off the effects of the four *autostrade,* eight national and two provincial highways which feed into this turntable of Italy's north-central traffic network. Bologna has counted, for its half-million citizens, 200,000 motor vehicles, among them 450 buses, 60 trolleys, and 500 taxis.

As the West's number-one Communist outpost, Bologna has evolved a program which is remarkably conservationist. Its plan can be compared to that of the cities of the Socialist bloc, which are also proud of their center-city conservation. As for the brave new architecture of the future: Bologna will have a sample of it all the same. Kenzo Tange, architect of the reconstruction of Skoplje in Yugoslavia, of the Tokyo Olympics facilities and a convention hall in San Francisco, will be represented in Bologna by an administrative and trade center in the industrial fairgrounds area, sponsored by private capital. There will be high-rise apartment buildings, to avoid another downtown which dies at nightfall; offices of public and private agencies; shops, restaurants, hotels.

Is it pleasant to live in Bologna? Italians from other cities have thought so for a long time, as have foreigners fortunate enough to have spent time there. In a not-too-distant future, Bologna should be irresistible.

16. Living with Density: Holland's Ring of Cities

"Even if the great cities were not an economic necessity," a United Nations population study warns, "they would be a spatial necessity. Since the present population of the world is large and increasing, the reduction of per capita space available makes some degree of population concentration inevitable." It has been demonstrated that if West European nations such as Belgium, France, the Netherlands, or the United Kingdom dispersed their populations into smaller towns, there would be little if any agricultural space remaining. In the words of Jean Gottmann:

> The rural areas left between the urbanized districts would just be narrow strips in which the need for intensive agricultural production would probably preclude the undue wanderings of city dwellers. Such a solution applied to the Netherlands, Belgium and Britain, with their much higher average densities, would mean covering their territories with a kind of dispersed city network, within which the specialization of each would cause an incredibly dense traffic between all of them. Thus the generalized "small-town" solution, even on a modern scale, is bound to produce more congestion and more frustration than ever.

If there is going to be any antidote at all to the ravages of urban blight, the cancer-growth of suburban sprawl, the Dutch may discover it. They'll have to, if that country with its record population density is to survive. The Dutch can't afford to waste vital space in city centers, can't allow the house-and-garden syndrome to preempt undeveloped land in the immediate periphery of their cities, above all can't sit by while the last green fields disappear under cement.

The population density figures (per square mile) explain why: U.S. northeastern seaboard, 700; New Jersey, 800; Netherlands, 1,007.5; Randstad (western) Holland, 6,638.

The easy way, in most of the world, is to allow the laws of the

213

market to work themselves out, with land use determined by the immediate or the imagined needs of various sectors of the economy. The Dutch, who have already said "no" to the sea, to the winds and tides, to the topography they and their fathers were born to, seem to be ready to say "no" to the ineluctable determination of laissez-faire economics. It costs more that way, but it means buying a chance for survival.

Fly over Holland en route to Amsterdam's Schiphol Airport. From the plane window you can see how planned this country is. No acre of cultivated land seems to have been conquered from natural forest; it was all put there, as if pasted on. Houses, towns are in clusters. Cities start and end abruptly, giving way to green patches—neat quadrangles bordered by drainage or transportation canals.

Or take the train to Amsterdam from Paris and Brussels. Even the rapid Trans Europe Express makes frequent stops; each stop turns out to be the central station of another city. And these cities follow each other with astonishing rapidity, like stops on a commuter line:

> 11:28 a.m.　Rotterdam
> 11:46 a.m.　The Hague
> 12:28 p.m.　Amsterdam

On a map they seem to be strung out along a curve, often described as a horseshoe. This is Holland's Randstad, "ring of cities." It runs, moving north, from Dordrecht to Rotterdam, Delft, The Hague, Leiden, and Haarlem to Amsterdam, down and around again to Utrecht. The diameter of this horseshoe is about 35 miles, wide enough to encircle Greater London or the Paris Region. Nearly half of the population of the Netherlands is here, crowded into a fifth of the tiny nation's land surface. It is also a thriving industrial region, for heavy and light manufacturing, the whole range of services, major continental seaports. In all, close to six million people live and work in Randstad Holland. They increase in number at a higher annual rate than any other major industrial nation.

The 70-odd towns grouped in the Randstad may be said to form a single metropolis with a division of functions:

Amsterdam	1,036,000	population *	financial and cultural
Haarlem	239,000		residential, industrial
The Hague	710,500		government
Rotterdam	1,066,000		industry, trade
Utrecht	459,500		university, industry

* City and suburbs, 1971 figures

Indeed, metropolis becomes megalopolis when the nearby Belgian cities, joined to the Randstad in virtually an unbroken belt, are added:

Antwerp   672,700 population
Brussels 1,074,700

A similar division and sharing of functions exists in the northeastern United States, the region called Megalopolis by Jean Gottmann in his ground-breaking survey: Boston and New York, Newark, Trenton, and Philadelphia, Baltimore and Washington, and all points in between.

Indeed, my curiosity about the Netherlands and its proposed solutions to our common problems of city survival, and our survival in cities, originated in a conversation with Professor Gottmann at Oxford. My walk through that tranquil town, then my comfortable armchair in his scholar's study whose windows open to leafy trees, made it difficult for me to remember that we were going to talk about the problems of metropolitan centers. When we got around to the subject, Professor Gottmann urged me to take a closer look at the Netherlands. The Dutch were very good at planning; they believed in the efficacy of zoning; their laws had teeth. You can't do what you want with your own land. This was true in Britain, too, Professor Gottmann pointed out; Oxford with its leafy trees was itself an example of this planning of restraint. In the Netherlands the discipline and the constraint were, if anything, stronger. The Dutch also have a tradition of independent local governments, which evolved from the need to defend their towns from flooding. It helps them work together to fight other kinds of flooding, that of population in the cities.

What the Dutch had done is a subject of universal legend. Every plot of ground that counts for something today was literally conquered from the waters, reclaimed from marshes in a public works program that has been going on for nine centuries. Cities came into being only after construction of seawalls; Amsterdam itself could be developed only after dikes were erected along the shores of the old Zuyder Zee. Cities expanded as their canal systems, with locks and dikes, spread outward. More recently, of course, the Zuyder Zee was closed by a dike topped by a highway, and gradually it is being pumped dry to increase the land area of the country. In the 1960s and 1970s, the Delta project in the south has closed off southern Holland from the sea, adding bridges and roads for development. Eventually, the soil will be cleared of salt water, providing new land for agriculture and industry. The energy which the people of the Netherlands now apply to such planning is reflected in the abundant literature published (even in the English language) by the Ministry of Housing and Physical Planning in The Hague, and by individual cities.

The growth of cities produced a new challenge. Like other humans, the Dutch prefer individual houses, a garden in front or in back (preferably both). But there would eventually be enough Dutchmen to cover all the available land in and between the metropolitan areas of the country, should all elect to live the suburban life. National emergencies come easy to these people; they set to work early to deal with this one. From the Housing Act of 1901 on, all cities in the nation have had to produce expansion plans. In a 1963 measure, means were spelled out for planning in the "ring of cities." On the national level, general principles are set forth: protection of farm lands, zoning, conservation of historic city centers. Land use is controlled on the provincial level.

But in a nation with a strong tradition of self-government, it was on the township and the municipal levels that planning acquired legal force. At once a tribute to Dutch democracy and a concession to local power and interests, the fact that each municipality makes its own vital decisions, even within the Randstad, has led to wide disparities in land-use philosophy. If one city stanches the dike of suburbia, another allows its buildings to spill over onto what had been green fields. A very few years ago a British town planner called the agricultural land within West Holland's ring of cities "Greenheart Metropolis." Although a government report in 1958 set down guidelines for maintaining the green heart, recent land surveys show that it is diminishing in surface. Every Dutch planner knows what the problem is, which are the offending villages and towns.

So that even in the Netherlands the solution becomes one for local authorities. Coping with fast-increasing population, with the growing needs of a citizenry getting richer and demanding more living room, more ground for leisure-time gardening and sports, is the job of the city. And the city that seems to be doing most, demanding most from its inhabitants, is also one of the two largest in that nation. In Amsterdam we find not only a recipe for coping with Dutch problems, but a number of schemes that could point the way to dealing with our own.

In the office of Dr. C. Wegener Sleeswijk, in Amsterdam's city planning department, I was shown a large map of the city. On a white background, most of the map was colored yellow, to the very boundaries of the city. There was a scattering of squares and quadrangles colored red. At the bottom of the map was a legend:

Yellow — Land owned by the city of Amsterdam
Red   — Land under the leasehold system

Looking again, I found very little of the surface that was neither yellow nor red, except in the central area crossed by the famous semicircular canal belts: the Prinsengracht, Keizersgracht, Herengracht, and Singel. Everything outside the city existing before 1900, then, is publicly owned or controlled. Since the early part of the century, nearly half of Amsterdam's housing has been built with governmental subsidies. Since 1945, up to 90% of dwelling units were built under this system. Amsterdam's growth has been a creature of planning for over half a century. What was done, or not done, could be attributed to people who were supposed to know, and who were supposed to be concerned with the public interest as their number-one priority.

While all cities in the Netherlands have been able to acquire the land necessary for their development since early in our century —by negotiation if possible, by compulsory purchase if not—Amsterdam has been applying the rules more strictly than other municipalities. In a land acquisition policy similar to Stockholm's, all newly developed land stays in public hands, which guarantees that the designated use of the land will be respected. And yet in this eminently capitalistic economy—not the least of the Netherlands' paradoxes—the users of this land can build factories, own their businesses, reap profit. Indeed, the Dutch have some natural advantages which the Swedes do not have: "New" Dutch land can hardly be said to exist until another bit of the sea is dried, filled in, by public authorities. The Dutch must create their land before leasing it out for use.

Amsterdam's city council made the decision to apply leasehold in 1896. The feeling was that increased value of land in an expanding city should accrue to the community, not to individuals. While nearly everywhere else in our world speculators have controlled urban extensions at the periphery of cities, in Amsterdam a policy worked out in a quieter time has had ever-growing significance. If the land under city control increases in value, the ground rent charged to the city's tenants is raised. In this way, the city obtains revenue to finance increased responsibilities. If zoning sometimes proves inadequate, the city can build the restrictions it desires into its leasehold contracts. As city officials point out, leasehold has clear advantages for business, too: Industry doesn't have to invest in land, can thereby use more of its capital for operations. Industry is protected just as ordinary citizens are: There is no likelihood that a sand lot would be authorized next door to a factory manufacturing precision instruments. And since 1966, companies can also benefit from a system of perpetual leasehold. Ground rents are raised (or, if appropriate, lowered) every five years depending on the cost of living and the value of money.

Of course, Amsterdam feels that in an era of growing cities, new land being demanded for residences, schools, parks, and recreation areas—not to speak of factory sites and even parking lots—a policy of leasehold is the way to guarantee orderly growth while avoiding the abuses of speculation and unchecked expansion. In practice, when an as-yet-untouched area is earmarked to become part of the city, no private real estate dealer but the city itself moves in, buys it with the consent of the owner, seizes it with just compensation otherwise.

Among other restrictions, a leaseholder is not permitted to change the use of land or the buildings on it without city permission, to use it in a way that would lead to "danger, harm or nuisance"—to impair the quality of the environment, in other words. Neither can he divide the land or transfer his right to any part of it without authorization. There is a plethora of such restrictions, but none of them prevents a business from doing business, a farmer from farming, a resident from enjoying his place in the sun. The Netherlands is famous for its capitalism, and for its individualists.

When subsidized housing is put up on public land—though under recent conservative governments the nature of grants has been changing from "object" to "subject" subsidy, from the building itself to the tenant's rent based on income—it is evident that buildings will go where the city feels they should go. If little is being done in the city center—which is still subject to private ownership, although many of these owners are not in a position to renovate buildings and maintain low rentals even if they desire to—Amsterdam has been looking to its periphery for its growing ill-housed population. Meanwhile, in the center, there is vigorous protection of historical buildings—perhaps more systematic than in any other city of its size. Amsterdam contains 7,000 landmark buildings in the inner city. The municipality is justifiably proud of what it has invested in their preservation. So far, 1,636 buildings have been restored under a program financed by the city, province, and Ministry of Culture together with property owners. In 1971 alone,

179 buildings were restored at a cost of 31.5 million guilders; total 1972 funding was 41 million.*

But renovation of outdated buildings is possible only if the majority of tenants agree with the proposed improvements and future rental scale. "No deportations" has become a political slogan, which is why block renovation usually takes a long time in Amsterdam, and why the improvements often remain modest. At the same time, it has kept some Amsterdamers where they wish to be: in their old neighborhoods, in their old homes.

It is possible to work out a program of compulsory purchase of buildings in private hands, but the process can take years. Property owners can appeal all the way up to the Crown. Alternatively, an owner can be required to rehabilitate his property, but what does one do if the owner can't afford to? Occasionally, the city buys the property from him. Amsterdam is also experimenting with finding developers for blocks to be renovated, and after years of campaigning by concerned citizens against the destruction of the 150-acre Jordaan quarter, a detailed program of conservation and rehabilitation is now in progress. The city estimated that 13,000 home units would have been vacated in the period 1971–75 and that, as a result, 10,600 relocation cases would require assistance.

Amsterdam's city planning unit was set up in 1928. At that time, it predicted a population growth from 750,000 to one million by the end of our century, which it felt could nevertheless be housed within city limits. Some of the new quarters were newly created garden suburbs: Amsterdam-West, Buitenveldert, most recently the controversial Bijlmermeer. Meanwhile, as a result of the loss of population in older areas, as lack of space reduces the number of inhabitants per dwelling unit, the city has been losing population steadily over the past dozen years. The population moves farther and farther out, beyond the Amsterdam agglomeration (which is also losing population) to the Amsterdam "region," which includes all the territory from the sea to Hilversum, up to Alkmaar and Hoorn down to the provinces of Utrecht and South Holland. This region has increased its population from about 2 to 2.5 million.

Here is where Randstad Holland stands or falls as an example. To preserve woodland areas, for example, the Dutch need to keep suburban sprawl within bounds. The solution seems to be to group dwellings, if possible in strictly demarcated new or satellite towns.

---

* $12.5 million and $15.96 million, respectively, at the time of this writing.

The ideal population of such a town is 100,000 to 200,000. One way to restrict the area of these new settlements may be the Le Corbusier way: tall buildings. The 1966 government report on physical planning calls this "concentrated decentralization." It allows some additional accumulation of population in the major centers, but spread through the city region, in the hope of alleviating the pressures on undeveloped land. It could also keep people in West Holland and save the nation's real lungs, the eastern half of the country now shown as green on maps.

Meanwhile, it still seems easy for a town to grant exceptions to zoning laws protecting undeveloped property. Small villages won't be stopped from growing. On land just south of Amsterdam, for example, in an attractive green area between two outstretched fingers of urban development, a charming village has a mayor who has been allowing a certain amount of growth at the expense of the green belt. This sort of problem should be kept in manageable bounds by a new Greater Amsterdam Council bringing together 29 municipalities. A rapid-transit network, to run underground in the city, would be another way to assure some coordination between outlying satellite towns and urban centers. The first line is to go from Amsterdam's Central Station to Bijlmermeer.

The latter is a testing ground for "concentrated decentralization." Bijlmermeer is within the city limits of Amsterdam; if Amsterdam does not succeed with Bijlmermeer, a regional network of Bijlmermeers certainly won't. Rather than string people out from the edge of the downtown all the way to the next city, which is the American sprawling-suburb answer to population increase, the planners of Amsterdam are attempting to put a lot of people together in a controversial development removed from the city center, bridging the distance with a subway line. A number of modern concepts have been utilized here: separate streets for pedestrians, who have the ground level to themselves (with bicycle traffic), vehicular traffic routed on a system of elevated roads. Garages connect to sheltered interior streets leading to elevators and stairs at 50-yard intervals for access to apartment units. In the Le Corbusier manner, the interior streets are the scene of social contacts, with windows along one side facing the garden area. They are equipped with hobby rooms, playrooms, nurseries, buffets and meeting halls, study and music rooms, even guest rooms. Electric carts are able to circulate along them to deliver milk and mail, or to collect garbage. The apartments themselves include all comforts. The average rent of a four-room unit in 1970 was 350 guilders including heating and services, with about 1,080 square feet of living space, a full-length balcony, radio and television outlets, and garbage disposal shafts.

The density of these high-rise buildings equals that of the garden suburbs of a previous generation of public housing, the difference being that space is saved here for vast parks. When it is completed in 1980, Bijlmermeer will contain some 40,000 apartment units, part of a master plan for relocating 100,000 Amsterdamers in the southeast of the city, with 1,125 acres designated for recreation and as much again for factories, office buildings, and cultural facilities. "It is the most criticized project in the Netherlands," Dr. Sleeswijk remarked with a trace of pride, because he believes that the experiment is worth discussing. Thanks to the subsidized rents of Bijlmermeer, lower-income families from older neighborhoods found housing better than they had left. (But it is likely that we shall have to wait a while before being convinced by the Bijlmermeer experience, for at the time of writing the new project is being used to house large numbers of recent immigrants from the former Dutch colony of Surinam and so is not available to house the overspill from Amsterdam itself.)

Bijlmermeer's preoccupation with pedestrians is an old Amsterdam tradition. As far back as 1842, a one-way traffic plan was introduced on narrow Kalverstraat. It was tightened in 1932 to make it impossible to use it as a through street. In the early 1960s, a complete ban on motor traffic was established on Kalverstraat and its neighbor across the Dam square, Nieuwendijk, with a provision for delivery vehicles at specified hours. The busy Leidsestraat and Leidseplein were closed to all but trams in 1971; other streets have been added since, totaling nearly 3 kilometers of pedestrian zone, under a commitment to discourage use of automobiles in downtown Amsterdam gradually as the underground transit system is extended.

In a sense, Bijlmermeer was built around the transportation solution. Amsterdam's planners hope to transfer 60% of journeys-to-work traffic to public transportation. At Bijlmermeer, the high-rise buildings are placed within 1,800 feet of the subway station, and the plan is that, all along the line, 80% of apartment dwellers will be no farther from a station, where shopping centers will also be placed. Apartments in the project are arranged to be within 1,300 feet of the tenant's parking space, but that is another story. The hope, or the dream, is that when the subway reaches Bijlmermeer in 1976 most residents will prefer it to the increasingly (purposely) difficult drive into downtown Amsterdam.

But another consideration in rehabilitation, in preference to new construction, must be cost. An official city document dating back to 1967 compares the satellite town of Bijlmermeer with new construction and rehabilitation of deteriorated housing in the central city:

	BIJLMER-MEER	NEW CON-STRUCTION	REHABILI-TATION * IN CENTRAL CITY
Living space in square meters (1 sq. meter = 10.76 sq. feet)	80	80	72
Number of dwellings per hectare (1 hectare = 2.471 acres)	40	80	80
Parking places per dwelling	1.35	1.2	1
Land acquisition cost per dwelling (in guilders)	15,000	20,000-50,000	15,000
Building cost per dwelling	50,000	50,000	30,000
Project cost per dwelling (including parking)	75,000	80,000-115,000	55,000

* Of deteriorated dwellings but *not* historical landmarks

One must conclude—putting aside such considerations as convenience, individual preference, the comparative life-enhancing qualities of a building in a park and an old city neighborhood—that it is cheaper to rehabilitate an old building than build a satellite-suburban one, even if the tenant has to make do with somewhat less space for himself and his automobile. Urban renewal through rehabilitation is now a declared goal of Amsterdam's city government; in the face of criticism that it is not the most economical solution, the city replies that economic development requires comfortable housing for all.

The final question, of course, is what people want to do. Almost everywhere, in democratic or in totalitarian states, people can find ways to violate, or to win exceptions from, undesired regulations. Will the Dutch agree to limit growth in and around the Randstad, to keep within the boundaries of the new towns? Will they, for the greater good, make the sacrifice of their freedom to have a garden of their own next to a house of their own?

So far, as we have seen, the figures show a thinning out of the older sections of cities. Townspeople are abandoning inadequate housing to find more room and daylight in a suburb, even if the suburbs are not ready for them. The Dutch call this an "Americanizing" trend. It is expected that the polders (land reclaimed from the old Zuyder Zee) will be able to take 500,000 inhabitants, perhaps half of them overspill from the Amsterdam region. Meanwhile, city growth is encouraged not only by internal logic but by the fact that national subsidies are given to local planners on the basis of the number of inhabitants in their municipalities. For the final truth is that the means to channel urban and suburban growth are already in the hands of local governments, thanks to leasehold, thanks to zoning and to centuries of Dutch tradition. It's the quality of constraint, self-discipline, that is at stake here. But if the planners of Amsterdam, Rotterdam, and The Hague accept limitations on growth, the small villages in the green heart are more reluctant to do the same. Is it possible to ask individual citizens to forego their search for individual green pastures? The four largest cities of Randstad Holland, in any case, have banded together to bring this matter of untidy planning to the Ministry of Housing and Physical Planning.

For the moment, the answer to the problem of cities, the Dutch way, seems to be: more cities. Should you freeze their orderly growth, or discourage people from finding happiness and convenience within them, you send them out to new suburbs; you destroy the green heart. Amsterdam, at any rate, has no fear of over-urbanization. Plan cities for growth, even plan the Randstad as a single metropolis, and save the rest of the country.

And if the Dutch way has anything to communicate to us, it is precisely this. We are ashamed of our cities, but we cannot live without them. A program aimed at revitalizing the centers, tied to a re-examination of suburban sprawl, would seem to follow naturally.

17. Culture in the City: Grenoble

Because Grenoble has one of the few Houses of Culture functioning in France, and not badly, the "culture" label has stuck to this city. Indeed, this Alpine capital of 170,000 inhabitants has been considered a prototype. In less than five years, a young team of city elders, consciously pursuing a two-pronged offensive, has changed the exterior environment, force-feeding works of art into the topography and daily life of the city, and then through the unusual device of a Maison de la Culture has begun to reach the minds and perhaps even the emotions of the citizenry.

Grenoble spends 13% of its budget on culture. Such a statistic might not evoke surprise in a decaying, artificial, or museum city, say Venice or Williamsburg. It is momentous when attached to a rapidly expanding industrial center in the top rank of the nation with respect to its growth rate, a pilot region in planning for the year 2000. Observers from inside and outside the city agree that Grenoble has been transformed. The question is, would a similar effort elsewhere bring similar results? Alas, not often do these particular conditions apply: an unusually dynamic population with a higher than average percentage of technicians, young people, people who want to change things, at least for themselves (many migrated to Grenoble to do so). True, the group in charge of Grenoble's city hall was an exceptional one, of which any community might be proud. But, then, didn't the people of Grenoble elect them to office?

Grenoble's modern growth began with the development of hydroelectric power, leading to a concentration of mechanical and metal industries. With a large working population and a smaller than average nonproductive group, Grenoble had the highest immigration rate in France in the last decade. Between 1954 and 1962, the population increased by 44.5%, and it shared with the Riviera the distinction of receiving more people from Paris than it sent. There was also an above-average proportion of skilled workers, researchers, and technicians, encouraged by and encouraging a good university. Engineers represent 11% of the active population (compare the national average of 5%), technicians and middle-level management 19% (11%), foremen and skilled workers 52% (46%). Grenoble provided an early example of Western middle-class civilization (the temptation is to say "suburban, split-level," but it isn't). Its combination of research talent and quality production led to what observers classify as "American" behavior. (But someone else called it an "Israel": In the middle of an undeveloped region, Grenoble is rich, hard-working, a bit parvenu, insisting on being recognized.) Pierre Mendès-France referred to "the myth of Grenoble," and most agree that it is in part myth. A lot needs to be done before Grenoble will become an ideal city, as those who suffer from its inadequate housing (for example) know.

The healthy economy and the citizens who made it function brought about a phenomenon relatively rare in France: concern by the average townsman for his environment and a belief that he could do something about it. Grenoble was one of the first French cities to engender neighborhood associations, called here *unions de quartier* and covering every part of the city, in which the managerial and technical class and the university people joined with local labor leaders to take civic affairs into their own hands. Out of these unions grew GAM, the Groupe d'Action Municipale, a coalition of left Catholics, left Socialists, labor leaders, university and technical cadres. GAM was headed by an engineer in Grenoble's Center for Nuclear Studies, Hubert Dubedout, who had become involved in community issues when a lack of water pressure dried up the faucets in his bathroom.

Though the neighborhood unions were essentially apolitical and GAM was "technocratic" (at least as viewed by the Communist Party), Dubedout ran for mayor in March 1965, and when he succeeded he brought the young technocrats with him into city hall. The neighborhood associations and GAM had captured the municipal government. Their advent resembled that of the Kennedys to Washington a few years earlier, at least in their austere dedication to public service—for the charisma of the Kennedys did not obtain here. In 1966, an Agence d'Urbanisme was set up with the participation of P. A. Emery, a disciple of Le Corbusier. The university men who worked in it embraced all the appropriate disciplines, thinking in terms of region as well as city. The new

mayor held town meetings to explain his budget. He was determined to pursue Grenoble's industrial development. Attracted
by the new men in city hall, Pierre Mendès-France, the country's
most consistent outsider, stood for parliament there in 1967. He
won with Dubedout's support, but a year later when the student
revolt of May 1968 forced De Gaulle to call for a vote of confidence
he was defeated by a Gaullist cabinet minister.

Still, Dubedout was able to count on the help of the national
government. The decision to hold the 1968 Winter Olympics in his
city was taken a year before his election, just as the tactic of using
the Games as a lever to bring about a renewal of Grenoble's
infrastructure was initiated by Dubedout's predecessor in city hall.
French cities are financed in part by grants from the central government, in part by public administrations, and then by local taxes.
Out of the Olympic Games Grenoble got a new and striking city
hall, a new railroad station, post office, police headquarters, hospital annex, museums, a press center and Olympic Village (which
would become residential developments of 630 and 1,800 units
respectively), and the Maison de la Culture.

There were stadiums, too, of course. But it is estimated that
sports-connected investments represented 15% of the facilities acquired by Grenoble; highways, access roads, air and railroad facilities, 40%; new constructions, 45%. Some felt it scandalous that it
took the Olympics to build these essential buildings. But André
Wogenscky, architect of the Maison de la Culture, reminded me
that the Olympics not only brought funds, but simplified formal-
ities. The city had to be ready to receive the outside world at a
specific date; red tape could not be allowed to hold up planning
or construction. Wogenscky designed the House of Culture and
built it in a year, half as long as it would have taken in normal
circumstances.

There were aftereffects. The central government seems still not
to have recovered from the financial strain. A July 1970 post-
mortem of the budget laments the billion-franc Olympic investment
and expresses concern at how Grenoble and adjacent communities
will use the leftover sports equipment. Grenoble's ice palace is
something of a white elephant (a cabinet minister is quoted as
calling it "the finest ruin of the 21st century"). City taxes continue
to rise unattractively, though Grenoble was always an expensive
city to run.

Not that Grenoble was utterly lacking in taste before Mayor
Dubedout and the Olympic Games. But its provincialism was a
matter of public record; Stendhal was born there but left early.

Gabriel Chevallier, who documented small-town feuding in *Cloche-merle,* describes Grenoble's in-grown bourgeois society in *Les héritiers Euffe* (1945). On one hand, the progressive Peuple et Culture organization got its start in this city; on the other, the incurious Grenoblois had driven progressive Jean Dasté's theater group from its territory, Dasté going on to St. Etienne to create France's first successful regional theater. We are told by Dominique Dubreuil in a 1968 study, *Grenoble Ville-Test,* that there are three kinds of Grenoblois: the original residents, the newcomers, the workers. The first are in the liberal professions, prudent and reserved. The second are young managers and engineers. Workers count in elections and in the *unions de quartier.* Obviously the Dubedout forces leaned heavily on the new Grenoblois, though some of the technocrats seem to prefer skiing on nearby slopes to culture in the city.

In fact, there had been enough troops to man a cultural crusade even in the teeth of an unsympathetic mayor (Dubedout's predecessor). As early as 1958, an Association Culturelle pour le Théâtre et les Arts, ACTA, was established. The Comédie des Alpes was a small but lively theatrical troupe. There were neighborhood *maisons des jeunes et de la culture.* These organisms and an unlikely alliance of the leftist Peuple et Culture and young businessmen met from time to time to discuss the city's needs. Were I writing for the French reader, I should linger over the details of this voluntary organizational activity, so seldom do the French get together to work out their common problems when they aren't prodded to do so by some official body. I have seen the program of the Jeune Chambre Economique, *Pour une Maison de la Culture à Grenoble,* in which the young business leaders pointed out that Grenoble had all the prerequisites for a proper House of Culture: It was then the center of an agglomeration of 250,000 persons, with the highest growth rate among French cities, the highest percentage of young people (49% of the population under 30, against 45% for all France) and technicians, plus 12,000 university students and the cultural and neighborhood associations already mentioned.

Under André Malraux, the Ministry of Culture had sent a man to Grenoble to explain what a Maison de la Culture could be. Hubert Dubedout promised to build one if elected, and the 2,000-member Association for a House of Culture gave him its support. Later this group would be transformed into a general assembly of members of the House of Culture, joining in its management with representatives of government, but the nonofficial forces hold a 15-11 majority. Some 460 groups are on the sponsoring committee, and it is estimated that the assembly represents 80% of users of the House. Such a thing might seem normal and democratic; it had never been so in France.

One would like the reader to have in front of him, in default of the Maison de la Culture itself, a set of photographs and diagrams, a list of its facilities. The Maison published an attractive brochure giving its vital statistics: three theaters, an exhibition gallery, a library, discothèque, television room. There is a service through which visitors can select original works of art to take home for a modest rental covering insurance charges. Finally, there are a children's playroom, a cafeteria, attractive reception lobbies. The organization of the interior space allows easy communication, facilitating the transition from one activity to the next, allowing for those who care for a true marriage of the arts. In a statement of intentions, architect André Wogenscky said that he wished the Maison to become a center of gravity, rallying the city's creative forces, intensifying their energy, and dispersing it again throughout the city.

Wogenscky explained to me that as a lover of the theater—he had hesitated between a career in theater and in architecture—he wanted to emphasize audience participation, allowing the actors to "envelop" the spectators. For this he devised a 538-seat *théâtre mobile* where the seated audience rotates, the surrounding stage ring rotates, together, separately, in the same or opposite directions, at varying speeds, while an elliptical and stationery stage exists to ground our orientation all the same. The inspiration was the total theater for Erwin Piscator advocated by Walter Gropius at the Bauhaus. In action, such a theater should shake up normal perceptions of space and time in the spirit of the theory of relativity, or so the architect felt. The new stage worked successfully for the inaugural ballet, the architect collaborating with choreographer Maurice Béjart. Members of the audience rose from their seats, frightened; normal perceptions were indeed shaken up.

For the Maison de la Culture Monsieur Wogenscky also designed a larger auditorium for 1,253 spectators, and a smaller 323-seat hall, this for cinema, concerts, and lectures. The exterior of the Maison is functional, but it is more inviting than, say, the Philharmonic Hall in West Berlin (absolutely magnificent inside, a disorderly heap of crates outside). When it was inaugurated on February 5, 1968, just in time for the Winter Olympics, André Malraux had the opportunity to deliver a brilliant dissertation on Houses of Culture, which elsewhere he had referred to as the cathedrals of our era. He argued that "everything which calls for participation of the public is good."

"Ladies and gentlemen," he declared, "the first reason for being of this House of Culture is that everything essential that happens in Paris should also happen in Grenoble." The Maison would aid in "the great intellectual combat of our century." He admitted that Stendhal would be "stupefied" at what Grenoble had done.

Malraux has gone, but the Maison pursues its work. Of some 30,000 members, half are Grenoblois, but 26% come from 16 neighboring communes, 20% from other areas of the *département*, though only 2% of them are in agriculture. Then 3% of the membership come from other *départements*. Of the total, 12% belong to the liberal professions, management, and engineers, another 12% teaching, 45% the university, and 3.1% are working class, in fact down some decimals from the earliest period. This last statistic was a constant source of regret to the Maison, which sent *animateurs* into the factories whenever it could, to neighborhood associations and youth houses, to workers' dormitories, to schools.

Those who have thought about the problem of the absence of a working-class audience blame factory conditions, but also the unions and the Communist Party, which participate in the operation of the Maison and publicly support it, while continuing to act as if the cultural locus of the worker is the factory floor. The result is that the Maison seems to be at the service of people who hardly live in Grenoble at all: students, first of all, who come from everywhere and live and work apart from the Grenoblois, technicians whose homes are outside the city, as are their factories.

Scanning a program chosen at random, one finds that the troupe called the Comédie des Alpes is presenting Corneille's *The Liar*. A chamber music group plays Beethoven trios; the Rhone-Alps Philharmonic Orchestra performs Samuel Barber, Leonard Bernstein, Aaron Copland, and Francis Poulenc. There are visits from the Tunisian National Peoples Arts troupe and the Casablanca Municipal Theater, a cinema festival, Sunday screenings of film classics, an exhibition of tapestries, weekly lectures on political issues, women's labor, protection of nature. All this, and the permanent library, discothèque, art lending service.

In his inaugural speech, Malraux had said: "Sooner or later, culture must be free, as education is." Certainly, many events at the Maison de la Culture are free. Theater tickets cost less than they do in commercial theaters (with a significant discount for members of the Maison). As might be expected, the major source

of revenue is the subsidy, that of the national government, of the
city and the *département*. Like the other Houses of Culture, Grenoble's was constructed with a 50-50 national-municipal grant. Sum-
marizing the heritage of André Malraux in the French daily *Le
Monde*, Jean Lacouture saw reasons for optimism in the record
of Grenoble's House of Culture. He noted that attendance at events
averaged 75% to 80% of capacity, while the Comédie des Alpes
visited 430 groups outside the Maison.

With respect to the topography of the city, Grenoble's House
of Culture stands between the old city and the area of expansion
to the south. There is adequate parking space for private vehicles,
and bus service from the town center. It is made easy for a Grenoblois to use his House. Once inside, he can visit an art show on the
way to the theater, browse through new books en route to the
cafeteria, look over the cinema program en route to an exhibition.
That may be the reason for being of a House of Culture, which
has been more successful in Grenoble than elsewhere, undoubtedly
because of reciprocal confidence between mayor and city council
on the one hand and the House's director on the other, not to
speak of the collaboration between Paris and local authorities.
Elsewhere, in Bourges, Caen, and St. Etienne, for example, conservative local forces have clashed with the crusading emissaries
from Paris and left-leaning theater directors who seemed to have
been parachuted in to change life. The result was destruction of
many of these Houses of Culture, to everybody's loss. Extreme
concern for local art and culture on the part of the national government of course has its other face: extreme interference, and a desire of each succeeding national regime to stamp its own mark
on the provinces.

Perhaps Grenoble was the ideal city, the House of Culture the
ideal size for it, and the timing right. Urbanist Emery points out
that if the House of Culture has had a clearly discernible influence,
this was well prepared for by the cultural policies pursued by the
municipality since 1965. While it lasts, and it may very well last,
Grenoble's House is the best of its kind. Obviously underemployed
at the moment, it can continue to serve a growing city for a long
time to come, eventually the new suburbs too, as a general headquarters supervising local branches.

Contemporary with the House of Culture, also products of the
Winter Olympics' jet thrust and the Dubedout administration, is
the striking architecture of the other official buildings (the city
hall already referred to; the university campus), the advanced
urbanism of the Olympic Village, archetype of the future with

separate levels for pedestrians and motor vehicles. In a park close to the city center, three bold skyscrapers astonish the visitor used to the make-do banality of contemporary French housing. France has a scarcity of music schools, and Grenoble's recently inaugurated Conservatory is another architectural attraction (there are plans for a regional symphony orchestra of 50 to 60 professional musicians). On the same day as the Conservatory, the regional Musée Dauphinois was opened in a restored 17th-century convent, the Stendhal Museum in 18th-century walls. A new art museum will be built, possibly atop Grenoble's Bastille, with a plunging view over the city. In its present quarters, the museum is already known for possessing one of France's best collections of contemporary art, and recently added a Dewasne mural running 150 yards around the walls of what had formerly been a lugubrious neo-Byzantine gallery.

Grenoble also possesses a downtown pedestrian mall.

Is it possible to live in Grenoble and not be exposed to art-in-the-city? Probably not, unless one has the perversity to trace an itinerary through the sunless alleyways of the old town, turning one's back on all that has happened in recent years, eschewing the city hall and the House of Culture. Undoubtedly there are Grenoblois who do something of the kind, at least in spirit, but they are not the majority.

One cultural innovation leads to another. "Inside the city hall you get the feeling of being in your time," a visitor remarked to me. Citizens who live in such surroundings may, for example, become receptive to closing streets and squares to traffic, allowing them to serve as outdoor salons, making city living more livable. Those who have friends in the Olympic Village may be less ready to accept the mediocre housing found almost everywhere else in France today.

They may, too, understand what Grenoble's mayor and his aides have planned for the future of their *ville pilote*. "A cultural budget is not a necessity," remarked Hubert Dubedout, "and we had to convince elected officials as well as the public. It seems that this effort is accepted now, which wasn't the case at the beginning, and I am hoping that this cultural activity will no longer be defined as a percentage of the budget but as an overall view of requirements." The mayor is assisted by a cultural deputy, a one-time factory worker and village schoolteacher, who made plans for the time when the nearly 350,000 inhabitants of greater Grenoble, twice that of the city-limited population, will become 600,000 (the estimate for 1985). At that time, it will be more than ever necessary to reach sectors of the population which the Maison de la Culture had not been able to reach until now.

The new town of Villeneuve-Echirolles, which I have referred to earlier, is at the center of this planning. Usually in France, culture has not been planned for, but represents an accretion. Such accretions can be quite successful—see the last ten centuries of the city of Paris—but is the same thing likely to happen without stimuli in new towns?

Among other things, it will be necessary to provide for some decentralization of the House of Culture, the art museum, and the music conservatory, with performances on a smaller scale and closer to the people, in the manner of the Open Theater and the Bread and Puppet Theater, two examples which are actually mentioned in the project of the Grenoble planners. There would be circulating art shows, neighborhood cultural festivals requiring audience participation, local closed circuit television. This cultural planning has been linked to other urban amenities, such as an extension of the area of streets and squares closed to traffic, which may permit art to come out into the street through outdoor cinema, or loudspeaker discothèques. "We are against the idea," said a Grenoble cultural warrior, "that culture in Grenoble can be found only in the House of Culture."

Let us not overstate Grenoble's achievement. Much of what exists is undoubtedly operative thanks to the impact of Grenoble's important university. (Where the new cultural policy has failed, the university has not been involved.) Yet it would be wrong to minimize the intentions. "Innovations such as these work best in a young city, a university city undergoing industrial expansion and an increase in population," an observer remarked to me. "The same qualities led to the election of that particular mayor and his council. Yet Mendès-France was eletced their deputy in 1967 and lost in 1968, showing that the public mood can change."

There also signs that a neighborhood may not always be able to support all the cultural infrastructure provided, at least when the impetus comes from outside. A visit to one renovated quarter of Grenoble showed that many commercial enterprises brought in when the area was renovated for the Olympic Games have since closed, or are up for sale, because the neighborhood is not quite viable. The questions, then, may be how to bridge the gap between the inaugural of a new city and its final or ideal stage, and who foots the bill during the trial period? Or: "The provinces are still the provinces," as a pessimistic Parisian put it to me.

A pilot city, the prototype of a community setting a high value (even a certain priority) on cultural matters, Grenoble is yet only one of the possible models for a city of our dreams. We may not appreciate the institutional character of French cultural life, the habit of national governmental involvement with almost everything, the overtones of creative monism which any House of Culture must carry with it. Still, unless we are building our ideal city in a wilderness, we shall not easily find a better model.

The hypothesis is that local powers can have a measurable effect on the practice of culture in their communities. The experiment is to inventory cultural activity and cultural infrastructure. The end result should be to encourage municipalities in the rationalization of cultural policies, on the basis of mutually agreed upon criteria.

And because it is a project of the Council of Europe, the experiment would be an international one. Launched in 1972, with a schedule of activities planned through 1975, the project initially concerned ten cities. The number eventually went up to 14: Akureyri (Iceland), Annecy (France), Apeldoorn (Netherlands), Bologna (Italy), Esbjerg (Denmark), Exeter (England), Krems (Austria), La Chaux-de-Fonds (Switzerland), Lüneburg (West Germany), Namur (French-speaking Belgium), Öbrero (Sweden), Stavanger (Norway), Tampere (Finland), Turnhout (Flemish-speaking Belgium). Several other towns have since indicated a desire to join the group or have made an effective contribution to its work: Montbéliard and Rennes in France, Asti and Turin in Italy.

As a first step, it was agreed that each locality would prepare a preliminary report setting forth the grand lines of its cultural policy; to facilitate comparisons, the same outline was utilized by each. At a meeting of experts for the purpose of implementing the project, it was noted that several participating cities were already planning their cultural policies ahead to the year 2000, without necessarily neglecting the five immediate years to come.

An elaborate guide proposed a nomenclature, sample charts, and index cards to help the test cities set up the instruments necessary for the experiment. Preliminary reports were submitted to the Council of Europe during 1972. They contained concise accounts of the socioeconomic characteristics of each locality, the cultural policies in effect until now, and a program for the future. The participating towns had few common denominators, except that all but two are cities of 50,000 to 100,000 inhabitants. In any case, this was not really to be a comparataive study, and true synthesis would never be possible.

Example: Namur, in Belgium, mobilized an already existing Socio-Cultural Research Center, which broadened the survey to the level of the agglomeration, including the communes of Jambes and Saint-Servais as well as Namur itself. The population of the province is 385,000, rural and tourist-oriented. Namur defined its cultural policy essentially as encouragement of private initiatives through subsidies and provision of infrastructure. At the time the report was submitted in April 1972, 25 to 30 cultural groups were being helped. The exception to this principle was the city's direct sponsorship of art and music education. For the purpose of the Council of Europe program, the three communes participating in the study formed a cultural council whose role would be consultative. Namur promised its European partners that it would ask for no funds from the Council of Europe, only assistance in coordination of the project and a recommendation to the Belgian government to help finance it.

In a progress report in 1973, Namur's research team indicated that the going wasn't easy. There were problems of nomenclature, but also of financing the research. To learn more about their constituency and to make its work known, the Namur investigators staged a "cultural fair" with 60 participating groups from sports, theater, poetry, cinema, photography, painting, music, and other fields.

And as the study proceeded in over a dozen separate nations, some local preoccupations, political or otherwise, were betrayed. From the beginning, Belgium had to offer two candidate cities rather than one, a representative of Flanders, another from rival Wallonia. We oppose commercial culture, warned the Communist-run city of Bologna. "Our intention is to protect the community from the laws of the cultural industry." Meanwhile Exeter said: "The objective of the town will be to satisfy needs as far as possible by dealing both with the public and private sectors." This was seconded by La Chaux de Fonds: "One of the objectives of local cultural policy," it reported, "will be to organize the demand for cultural 'products.' The commercial sector will thus be integrated into the general policy."

At a meeting of research teams in Strasbourg, it was agreed that the objective way to study the cultural policies of a city was through the utilization of anthropological procedures, encouraging and developing cultural activities peculiar to each social group in turn, with a view to enriching global culture. The real problem would come when it was time to evaluate results. This evaluation would have to be done on the basis of stated objectives and on the novelty, or noninstitutional character, of the experiment, yet without neglecting traditional activities and institutions.

An effort was to be made to include the world of the migrant laborer, to consider his insufficient participation in the benefits of economic and social progress, his marginal situation in society that prevented his active participation in the culture of the community. It was decided to consider this problem in the framework of minorities in general, women, older people, youth—including young delinquents.

Experts from each of the test cities congratulated themselves at having created "a kind of collective workshop of reflection and of action" in which some 30 persons were devoting all their time, in addition to the investigative teams. Officials and citizens of test cities were beginning to ask pertinent questions about their new role in promoting culture and about the very objectives of cultural activity. Among the sociological studies in progress: research on publics, on children's theater, on migrants, on cultural needs, cultural goals of each social group, decision making in the cultural field, analysis of specific groups. While it was recognized that the originality and value of the project will come to a great extent from the diversity of local experiences, it was also felt that in the interest of coordination, and in order to show certain converging lines of activity, the final report would follow guidelines agreed upon by all. The work was to proceed through 1975, when meetings in Bologna, Strasbourg, and Krems would close the "first phase" of the experiment.

This first phase may well provide hard information for city planners concerned with culture. In order to qualify for their jobs as administrators of culture, they have already answered (at least to their own satisfaction) such questions as: Is culture only an increment, an accident of development and of local history, or can it be planned? If not actually planned, can it be recorded, arranged in intelligible order by and for planners? The first round of reports had shown that with only two exceptions the cities under observation had not drawn up any cultural policies at all until the 1960s. Culture had been a private affair, linked to existing economic structures. The question of state intervention, local or national, was usually new, its advantages occasionally questioned.

But culture, what remains when all else is forgotten, is henceforth being considered one of the measurable assets of the community, to be included on the positive side of the balance sheet with a good road system and efficient distribution of goods and services; eventually it may be invoked to draw new settlers and industries and to raise the tax base. One would not be surprised to learn that its cultural attitudes not less than its good and intelligent governing class have already brought desirable immigrants to Grenoble.

18. The City and the World

Our generation's breakthrough in town planning may come about when town planning leaves town, to be conceived on a broader geographical basis: the metropolitan area, its province or district, the region or state, or better a group of states with similar geographical and economic problems; eventually an entire country (the United States) or continent (Europe). A report of the U.S. Urban Growth Policy Study Group, published by the Department of Housing and Urban Development, laments the failure of the United States to establish a national growth policy of the kind already under way in Europe. Nothing on the United States' metropolitan scene compares to the Greater London Council (1966), the District de la Région Parisienne (1961), the Stockholm County Council (1966), or the Warsaw administrative region which alone grouped 3.8 million people in 29,851 square kilometers in 1969. Comprehending the symbiotic relationship of a city to its hinterland is the first step toward dealing with any of the elemental problems: growth or decline, urban blight and suburban sprawl.

Now another step has been taken. Town planning and environmental studies are being discussed, occasionally are being implemented, by groups of nations with a common orientation or strategy, by whole continents, and for some problems on a global basis. These things are happening while the United States continues to lack the means to coordinate urban development between cities in a single state, with the exception of the Appalachian Regional Development Program.

Undoubtedly, some of this new acitvity can be attributed to the dynamics of organizations—that is, they tend to look for things to do, devising programs to supply work for their bureaucracies.

Naturally there is some rivalry between organizations as to which is to have the responsibility for what program. But it is also evident that the needs are genuine, the subject matter of the international efforts is well founded, the work so far accomplished (or the studies undertaken, the recommendations formulated) is praiseworthy. Some of the international organizations involved in urban and environmental studies are producing first-rate comparative studies (for example, on the financing of new towns) or technical reports ready to be utilized by plant engineers.

The listing that follows is offered not as an exhaustive census but rather as a table of contents, suggesting where further information can be found.

United Nations

Perhaps there are too many contradictions prevailing in the UN structure to allow it to mobilize international force for a specific goal, and this has even been true in the relatively benign area of urban and environmental studies, where the naive might think that consensus is easiest to obtain, as well as on major political issues, where a majority of countries has often been found, for example, to condemn an attacked nation rather than the aggressor.

An ambitious undertaking, of course, was the first United Nations Conference on the Environment held in Stockholm in June 1972. Obviously, the stakes were high. The crisis in our life-supports is worldwide; the seven billion people promised for 1999 will spread over every country, every city. If more of them will have to live in New Delhi, Lagos, and Rio de Janeiro than in Paris or Washington, the latter capitals will feel their effects, as we have been learning from our experience of the third quarter of this century. It was only to be expected that the humanist bureaucrats who plan the programs of the United Nations would want to call attention to the findings of futurologists and the computer predictions of the Club of Rome: Our world is running, not walking, to disaster.

But the countries of the world, in the present state of our civilization, are not ready for planning across continents. Before Stockholm, experts from African countries meeting in Dakar had already decided that environmental rules "imposed from outside" could not be applied to developing nations. They did not say it, but implied that their economies required the crash programs of industrialization which had wrecked the environment of Northern

Europe one hundred years earlier. Paper mills and refineries took priority over pure water and air; environmental concerns were for the moment rich men's whims. "One earth" was the slogan of the UN meeting, but did anyone believe it? The Chinese, then new to the United Nations system, used the Environment Conference as a political forum. Countries of the Third World predictably refused to pay their share of the program against pollution. Mrs. Indira Gandhi suggested that they would have to raise their living standards before joining the fight. "How can you preach protection of animals to those who are hungry, speak to them of pure air and clean oceans while they live in filth?" she asked.

At the close of the 114-nation meeting it was decided to set up a special Environment Fund of $100 million and a United Nations Environmental Council. The representative of the most heavily populated nation of all, China, abstained from the vote on the final declaration because it contained an implied appeal against further nuclear tests, considered by many to be the supreme pollution. The concern of the Third World was reflected in the language of Principle 11 which proclaimed that "the environmental policies of all states should enhance and not adversely affect the present or future development potential of developing countries, nor should they hamper the attainment of better living conditions for all." In less ambiguous words: one law, restrictive, for the rich, another, permissive, for the poor. The assembled nations were not even able to agree to the principle obliging all nations to inform their neighbors of development plans which might affect the environment of other nations. This was perhaps the best proof that a single program or organization for our diverse continents could not yet function, despite the many programs approved in Stockholm in June 1972. It provided a foretaste of what the United Nations Conference on Population was to become in 1974, when developing nations allied with the Communist nations rewrote the experts' draft plan for population control to remove the control factor, in effect demolishing the reason-for-being of that meeting.

The United Nations has nevertheless created the council just mentioned to promote international cooperation in environmental protection, to be based in Nairobi. And a second Environment Conference, in Vancouver (1976), devoted to urban problems, represents another opportunity for the world community; perhaps there will be more community and less conflict in this attempt to study the whole range of problems connected with the improvement of human settlements.

UNESCO

Although its charter limits its range of activity, UNESCO (with a global constituency of 136 member nations) has been able to undertake limited activities of international scope and utility. The General Conference of UNESCO has adopted a Convention concerning the protection of the world's cultural and natural heritage (November 1972), and at the time of writing was deliberating on the need for an international instrument setting forth guidelines for the protection of historic towns, quarters, and sites "and their integration into a modern environment," either taking the form of another international convention or as recommendations to member states. Previous "recommendations" put forth by UNESCO concerned the safeguarding of the beauty and character of landscapes and sites (1962) and the preservation of cultural property endangered by public or private works (1968).

On a more tangible level, UNESCO has published technical manuals on the protection of monuments and cultural property, while engaging in international campaigns to save the monuments of the Nile Valley, of Borobudur (Indonesia) and Mohenjo-Daro (Pakistan), Isfahan (Iran), and elsewhere; the uphill struggle for Venice was described in a previous chapter. UNESCO's Department for Cultural Heritage is involved or in touch with similar preservation projects in many areas. An international fund for protection of cultural monuments was created in 1972, and UNESCO experts have been sent all over the world to explore or advise on the saving of our cultural heritage, which is more commonly accepted as being universal than the air we breathe (see the results of the UN Conference on the Environment).

OECD

The next largest entity may be the Organization for Economic Cooperation and Development, whose 23 member-states produce more than 60% of the wealth of the world. The membership of OECD includes the United States and Canada, as well as Japan and the leading West European nations. OECD has set up an Environment Committee consisting of officials responsible in their own countries for environmental policies and programs. Under the Committee there are sectors on air and water management, chemical pollution, and urban environment.

This Environment Committee prides itself on its integrated approach to problems, as part of overall economic and social policy, so that its investigations and recommendations benefit from the support of OECD committees on agriculture, industry, education and science, even manpower and social policy. Because the members of OECD have demonstrable points in common, such as standard of living and level of industrialization, their findings can be meaningful.

Set up in the spring of 1971, the Urban Environment Sector Group of OECD is engaged in studies on the environmental impact of urban growth, the effectiveness of existing urban policies and programs, expenditures on urban growth and environmental improvement, innovations in planning and managing the urban environment. A series of studies on the financing of planned communities (new towns), published as working documents, together form a volume that will be of use to town planners for years to come. OECD work in the field of urban and social indicators is discussed in a previous chapter on the quality of city life.

One of this organization's ad hoc groups, treating the impact of motor vehicles on the environment, received international attention in October 1972 when it issued a report on automotive air pollution and noise based on a full year of analyses, consultations, exchanges of experience on an international level. In fact, the investigators saw their task primarily as one of identifying alternative control strategies and policy instruments; they concluded that uniform emission testing was desirable and raised questions concerning legislation to govern the content of lead in motor fuel. This was international thinking on a practical level.

A year later, several reports on road research were published, one of which, "Effects of Traffic and Roads on the Environment in Urban Areas," relates improvement of present conditions to their cost implications and concludes with a plea for international coordination of research on low noise and pollution-level vehicles and on highway problems. Another study, "Techniques of Improving Urban Conditions by Restraint of Road Traffic," is in fact the report of a symposium organized in the context of the OECD road research program. It shows how city planners are dealing with traffic bottlenecks and the protection of pedestrians.

EEC

The European Economic Community now groups nine advanced nations with clearly demonstrable covergence of interests in many areas. Their status as advanced nations would suggest that con-

crete matters such as the physical environment could be discussed
on a day-to-day basis with the strong possibility of a meeting of
minds. The 1958 Treaty of Rome which defines the Community
included among its objectives improvement of living conditions.

And indeed there is a Community program for environment,
encompassing the same subjects that are of interest to OECD (see
above) and to the Council of Europe (see below): pollution and
nuisances. There is also a group to study town planning and land
development. Still, to date nothing has been announced of the
progress of any of these programs; nothing has been published.
The Byzantine atmosphere of the Brussels headquarters of EEC
is undoubtedly a reflection of the relations among leading members of the organization.

Council of Europe

Paradoxically it is on this level—17 states whose interests are less
closely intertwined than one has been led to believe is true of
the European Economic Community—that concrete activity is being carried out. Or is it because EEC is preoccupied with matters
of commerce and trade and shopkeepers don't have time for higher
things?

In Strasbourg, headquarters of the Council of Europe, the organization held a European Conservation Conference in 1970,
which heard papers on air pollution (later published) and proved
the case for close and permanent cooperation between the public
and private sectors. The conference participants studied reports
on the problem of the automobile in the city center, so that the
most advanced thinking on the urban environment was available
to participants from countries, such as France, whose internal
policies until then suggested that they preferred not to worry about
the problem.

The Council sponsored another meeting, in Bonn, this time
consisting of cabinet ministers of member states responsible for
regional planning, in which the whole matter of dealing with
problems on a scale broader than metropolitan or even province
level was put on the table. Papers produced for this session include
a comparison of greater-than-city planning across the European
continent. It was recommended that planning strategies, at least
in some sectors, be undertaken on a continental basis. An earlier
Council study made a case for the creation of new towns as an
answer to some situations where urban growth cannot be contained in any other way.

The practice of making recommendations in a somewhat idealistic spirit cannot be separated from the fact that no supranational authority possesses real power. And so one must be content that an international body is publishing research and recommendations in fields where little is ever consciously done to affect the way things happen. The Council of Europe's Consultative Assembly has issued recommendations on housing policy, reduction of air pollution from motor vehicles, overall environmental policy—but it is only a Consultative Assembly.

In 1971, the Council launched a five-year plan for protection of European monuments and sites, focusing attention on the less-known ones, forgotten neighborhoods, isolated villages—not on Versailles or Notre Dame de Paris, Out of this came European Architectural Heritage Year in 1975, which was itself to lead to the adoption of a charter designed to serve as a basis for legislation in individual member states.

In 1973, a conference sponsored by the Council of Europe brought together 200 specialists from the 17 member countries for discussion on protection of the natural environment. Meanwhile, as I mentioned in the last chapter, member states are engaged in a pilot study (one city from each nation) on urban culture.

ECE

Less known to the public at large, the United Nations Economic Commission for Europe may take on increasing importance if environment continues to be seen as a global problem, for it is likely that UN decisions or recommendations will be passed on for implementation to the UN regional economic commissions, of which ECE is one. Already, member countries, which include states in both Eastern and Western Europe, the only European organization with such representation, appoint senior advisers to their governments on environmental problems. ECE has been active in research on the urban environment through its Committee on Housing, Building and Planning, working with the Center for Environmental Studies in London. The United States is a participating member of ECE.

NATO

Although it was founded as a defensive alliance, as a means of improving its image in a time of détente, the North Atlantic Treaty

Organization has been increasingly active in environmental studies. A NATO Committee on the Challenges of Modern Society has been dealing with air and sea pollution; in 1972, the United States suggested that the Committee investigate such diverse matters as the four-day work week and the creation of pedestrian zones, as well as conducting a pilot urban transportation project. In all, the Committee is engaged in eight separate pilot studies, offers fellowships for research, and is empowered to invite non-NATO members to its deliberations (for example, Japan, Sweden).

OAS

The Organization of American States has been providing technical assistance to projects within its member states in the Western Hemisphere for protecting and restoring historic neighborhoods and sites.

Nongovernmental organizations

If military alliances can discuss such subjects as priority bus lanes, then nonofficial citizens can surely get together to talk about their physical environment and their deteriorating cities. On the professional level, the International Federation for Housing and Planning in The Hague has for the past 60 years been a leading element in the exchange of information on city planning. Its congresses hear papers, which are later issued as monographs available from the Federation headquarters, on a variety of urban and environmental subjects.

Other groups active in these areas include the International Council of Monuments and Sites, Civitas Nostra, and Europa Nostra, and their national associations or affiliates; the International Union of Architects; the International Federation of Landscape Architects.

Ad hoc meetings

As an indication of the variety and levels of bodies involved in problems of our cities and regions, I have noted the following in the press in one six-month period:

April 1972: An international conference on sea pollution was held in Reykjavik, Iceland, to draft a program banning the disposal of mercury, DDT, and industrial wastes in the sea.

April 1972: Members of parliament from France, Italy, and Monaco took part in a conference on pollution of the Tyrrhenian Sea.

April 1972: Italy and Switzerland signed a convention for preservation of Lakes Maggiore and Lugano from pollution.

May 1972: The United States and the Soviet Union signed an agreement on environmental protection providing for joint research and mutual cooperation in 11 separate areas, including the consequences of unchecked urban growth, enhancement of the urban environment, air and water pollution, the influence of environmental change on climate.

September 1972: The newly formed joint US-USSR Committee on Cooperation in the Field of Environmental Protection, meeting in Moscow, approved 30 separate projects for cities, farms, rivers, lakes, the air. The two countries will carry out joint studies of urban environmental problems, comparing San Francisco and Atlanta with Leningrad and another Soviet city.

Planning in one country

Southeast England, the Paris Basin etxending to the mouth of the Seine, the Randstad (the southwest of the Netherlands), Italy's depressed Mezzogiorno are well-known examples of regional planning. In France, there are many other examples: the Marseilles metropolitan area, the three-headed Lyons-St. Etienne-Grenoble metropolis, or the Lille-Roubaix-Tourcoing urban community. Indeed, one has become used to triangular planning: Rouen-Caen-Le Havre, Strasbourg-Colmar-Mulhouse. Planning for a region may take in neighboring territories regardless of frontiers. Thus the Organisation d'Étude, de Développement et d'Aménagement de la Région d'Alsace, founded in 1972 in Strasbourg, must deal with neighboring West Germany: both banks of the Rhine, an international (Franco-German) airport near Strasbourg, daily migration of workers across the border.

Conclusion

What we admire most in the countries that I visited in the course of preparing this book is the result of many centuries of civilization. The happiest people are not necessarily those who live in a planned environment. But to conserve an environment which is the accretion of these centuries, to build around it, to duplicate its amenities in a new district, seem to require a certain degree of planned activity and collective responsibility. Sometimes planning fails, for planners are not gods and some of them are not realistic.

The areas with the worst problems would seem to be those, in the old world or the new, where no other consideration than speculation goes into the creation of city life. Whatever motivations of greed were responsible for the palaces of Venice or the towers of San Gimignano, the same instinct today is making Italian cities such as Rome increasingly unlivable, violating the basic human right to minimum standards. Real estate fever, the failure to take land use controls more seriously than parking violations, have brought about these crimes against Italy's citizens. Bulldozers have run wild in American cities, and usually it is with the consent of the planners that old and still viable neighborhoods, or neighborhoods with a potential for rehabilitation, have been replaced by new and unlivable ones.

When a desirable human environment is the product of human intentions, it is usually a matter of a collective design to accept constraint in the interests of all. I do not know how often, as in the Netherlands, this collective decision is a conscious and verbalized dedication, or how often it is merely observable in the practice or the results. When we see a great cathedral we know that it is almost never an accidental or a naive creation; when we see a beautiful city, or an eminently livable one, we cannot be so sure.

246

Concern for one's environment, constraint in its utilization; I was prepared to add a third C, for compactness. For the cities we consider remarkable are those that have learned to handle high densities. The test of a viable city may well be this ability to house large numbers of people, and the very highest densities seem not to be inconsistent with the greatest share of amenities, either in Manhattan or in Venice.

But I do not wish to insist on three C's; I fear a facility which may suggest to the reader that there is, or that I think there is, an easy answer to any or all of our urban problems. I should prefer to suggest that the answer in one place may be limiting growth, to make better use of what already exists, as in Bologna, while in another it may be expansion, or using the existing city as the point of departure for expansion, as in Randstad Holland or in Fos-sur-Mer, not so much to relieve pressure as to direct growth, saving the rest of the region or the nation from suburban sprawl. Is a skyscraper better than a suburb? I suggest that it may sometimes be better, without repudiating the demands for limits on height, or on new construction generally, in certain old neighborhoods and city centers. What has been happening to the world's energy resources in the present decade makes this drive for more compact cities, as Jean Gottmann suggests, a means to avoid the waste of matter as well as of space that we have accepted until now.

Building statistics in the United States reflect a return to urban living, with an increase in rehabilitated dwellings and a corresponding decline in new single-family housing starts (apart from the options determined by recession or tight money). If we attempted to give even the present population of the world a Los Angeles way of life, we would exhaust vital resources (some countries would, as I have shown, exhaust available land). Even in Egypt the expectation is that Cairo will become a city of skyscrapers in order to save precious land along the Nile.

National survival everywhere may depend on keeping people closer together. The question then becomes, What kind of life can we provide for the new urbanites? It will be important to remind professionals as well as laymen that high density does not have to be an evil; downtown living can be the best kind.

One reproach that will be made by critical readers is my seeming ignorance of scale. I am offering the examples of towns and small cities to planners and populations of the very large ones. But I have done so consciously, because I am not selling a master plan, but rather a set of options. If a medium-sized town such as

Oxford is growing harmoniously because of strict discipline in zoning, I am offering the reader the lesson of this discipline, not Oxford's size. A parking rule can be applied to a Cadillac or a Volkswagen, and we can use the operation of land use laws in Stuttgart to understand how they might have worked in Rome or Tokyo. I am aware that the good city planning of Switzerland cannot be applied to American cities, or even to British cities; it is the constraint which has governed the thinking of Switzerland's planners in recent decades that has something to say to us. We should certainly ask ourselves what led the minister of territorial planning in the capitalistic nation of France to say (1970): "The major enemy of city planning is private ownership of land. We must achieve progressive collectivization of land without pronouncing the word." The minister was undoubtedly motivated by the same drive to do a difficult job logically that Haussmann experienced in remaking Paris in the image of Napoleon III. Haussmann had a strong government and did not have to nationalize property. More democratic societies such as the Netherlands and Sweden have been buying it up gradually but inexorably. "Laissez-faire in real estate, contrary to what happens in theory in the industrial sector, doesn't necessarily lead to optimal situations or even coherent ones," concluded the group of French planners responsible for drawing up France's sixth five-year plan.

Can we learn from others, even from their failures? Cooperative urbanism has become a tool of official planners. An Urban Growth Policy Study Group under the chairmanship of an American congressman which visited six European nations in 1972 discovered "the applicability of European experience to the United States" in a number of domains: size and growth, suburbanization, transportation, city centers, housing, land use and new towns, financing public services, planning and development. Grants are taking the planners responsible for some of America's largest cities to the most successful of their European counterparts. Delegations are watching the Europeans build houses; for example, an expert team under NAACP sponsorship investigated the possibility of adapting system building as operated in Europe to programs of the U.S. Department of Housing and Urban Development. The hope was to see if America's bulldozed cities could do what Europe's bombed-out cities have had to do.

In this book I have tried to point to further avenues of investigation, without trying to include every example that may have turned up in my own research. Because this is not an encyclopedia of urbanism, I have not dealt with all the manifestations of air and noise pollution, for example; in describing the London experience, I meant to show how public policy can deal with one major source of pollution. Similarly, I have attempted to call attention to some forms of citizen participation without attempting to provide a catalog of all such activities. References to neighborhood and district councils in my discussions of Bologna's *centro storico*, Munich's traffic, and Grenoble's culture should suggest that participation and good city planning are often found together. Because it belongs in another book, I have all but ignored the achievements of London's postwar planning in every area of urban life—expansion and growth, but also traffic and transportation—just as I have merely hinted at the existence of the wealth of planning material being produced by the Paris district planning institute IAURP.

There used to be a time, when I was a young man, when Americans found many forms of planning abhorrent, especially if the term was used—as if planning had not existed from earliest times in societies we admire: We now know that it was a well-organized procedure among the ancient Greeks, whose gridiron city models are still being repeated in cities of the future. Prejudice against city planning in the United States may explain the continued reluctance of most American states to share federal government concern for their own major cities. Of course, a plan, by its implication that urban renewal is about to happen, can spell the beginning of the end of a traditional cityscape, but it can also represent a decision not to allow destruction of an old town, not to put a factory next to a landmark, not to allow obliteration of the next landscape beyond the present town and suburban boundaries. New York's mini-plans are being taken as anti-master plans, which is also all right. A town can be "important," we learn from the Swiss experience, even if it is small: Small Geneva and Basel are important even on the world scene, as a French writer noted, while large Seoul is obviously not important.

In fact, planning is an old American tradition. Washington, we learned in school, is a planned city. In the 19th century, the planners called attention to the ugliness of American cities and put us on the road back toward the City Beautiful. If we have not yet gotten there, in many places we are trying, and who is to say that San Francisco or old New England would remain to us had it not been for hard-headed planners?

Yet in rereading myself, I find that I have not paid much attention to green areas in cities, seeming to go along with those convinced urbanites who feel that trees and grass belong in the country, at the gates of cities, but not *in* the city. Perhaps I am also influenced by the futility of attempting to fight pollution or to bring in pure air through small parks and gardens. In the same way, I resist the anti-urbanism of the romantic writers, for they certainly contributed to the devaluation of the inner cities which remain so vital to us.

American and Canadian readers—and, I hope, British readers, also—will forgive me, finally, for having focused attention on Europe and beyond. They may argue that not only good planning, but loving restorations and utopian new towns as well, can be found closer to home. I am of course aware of the fact that many good examples of problem solving in these areas are available in North America; conversely, as I have endeavored to demonstrate, many bad examples can be found in Europe, where slums and even ghettos were invented. But often we need to see an exemplary resolution of a problem in someone else's backyard in order to grasp all of its implications. I am betting that this is the case.

Index